GIANTS
AMONG
MEN

Giants Among Men

Y.A., L.T., Big Tuna,
& Other New York Giants Stories

Ira Berkow

TRIUMPH
BOOKS

Library of Congress Cataloging-in-Publication Data

Berkow, Ira.
    Giants among men : Y.A., L.T., Big Tuna, and other New York Giants stories / Ira Berkow.
        pages cm
    ISBN 978-1-62937-046-0
    1. New York Giants (Football team)—Anecdotes. 2. New York Giants (Football team) —History. I. Title.
    GV956.N4B48 2015
    796.332'64097471—dc23
                                            2014048205

This book is available in quantity at special discounts for your group or organization. For further information, contact:

Triumph Books LLC
814 North Franklin Street
Chicago, Illinois 60610
(312) 337-0747
www.triumphbooks.com

Printed in U.S.A.
ISBN: 978-1-62937-046-0
Design by Prologue Publishing Services, LLC
Page production by Patricia Frey

For Dolly

CONTENTS

INTRODUCTION

LITTLE DID I KNOW that I began, as it were, covering New York Giants football in Minneapolis even before I arrived in New York to write sports. I was a young sportswriter for the *Minneapolis Tribune* when I was hired by Newspaper Enterprise Association, a Scripps-Howard feature syndicate based in Manhattan, in the fall of 1967.

It was about the same time that Fran Tarkenton, Scrambler Nonpareil, sometimes called "Frantic Fran," was traded from the Minnesota Vikings to the Giants (for two first-round draft picks and two second-round picks). We had a few things in common. One, we were the same age, 27 in 1967, about the same height and weight, 6'0", 185 pounds, and he enjoyed talking to the press, and I enjoyed listening to him. He was bright, affable, and hugely talented. He was a remarkable sight on the football field. While virtually all quarterbacks from the beginning of time would drop back to pass "in the pocket," Tarkenton broke the mold by running around like, as he once said, "a lunatic." He seemed to leap from the movie screen of the Keystone Kops, flying from the grasp of would-be tacklers from one side of the field to the other, avoiding them as though he was larded with grease, and some of the behemoths seeming to collapse of exhaustion in their madcap pursuit.

In one of Tarkenton's last games for the Vikings, in late November 1966, against the Green Bay Packers, I began my sidebar story this way: "A teeth-chattering, wind-whipped crowd of 47,426 craned their necks and a curious, big-yellow moon stood tiptoe over the east stands in Met Stadium as the Vikings tried to razzle-dazzle a come-from-behind victory in the closing minutes."

Tarkenton led the charge, but this time, unlike so many other occasions, he didn't succeed, as his pass in the last seconds was incomplete. "Tarkenton is the hardest quarterback in the league for a defensive back," said the Packers' Herb Adderley after the game. "You don't know what he'll do next."

And the sheer spine-tingling pleasure he brought to fans—and the press, including me, to be sure—was transported to the Giants games, and many of those that I covered in Yankee Stadium (before the Giants moved to Giants Stadium in the Meadowlands in New Jersey in 1976). Tarkenton, with a backdrop of the rattling elevated 4 train nearby, and under the iconic roof façade—the scalloped white frieze that ran above the scoreboard and the billboards of legendary Yankee Stadium—would quarterback a team that had had a losing record to decent seasons. He would—in blizzardy snow, in rain-soaked mud under the Stadium lights, or under a blazing hot Indian summer sun—be in the process of breaking numerous passing and quarterback-rushing records as he went scampering along. He played five seasons for the Giants, until, in 1972, he was again traded back to the Vikings. He would lead Minnesota to three appearances in the Super Bowl without, oddly enough, winning any of them.

Curiously, in Tarkenton's second year with the Giants, NEA hired him to write a once-a-week football column. I was assigned to edit it. It worked this way: we would talk on a Sunday night for the Monday column (either I was at the Stadium or, if a road game, by phone). I would take notes and then type up the piece, and call him back and read it to him. He was nearly able to talk out the column from beginning to end! One of my favorites was his description of playing against the Los Angeles Rams, and putting the reader in his shoes—and most quarterbacks' cleats—on the field: "You look across the imaginary dividing space called the line of scrimmage and you see assembled on a four-man front more than half a ton of aggressive humanity—1,088 pounds to be exact. When you're squeezed to make 190 pounds, like I am, that's a problem to start with.

"But when the ball is snapped, that 1,088-pound barrier represents the defensive line of the Los Angeles Rams, called the Awesome Foursome or some such silly name—fellows like David Jones (better known as Deacon), Merlin Olsen, Roger Brown, and Lamar Lundy....They can destroy you psychologically as well as physically if you let them....My old coach Norm Van Brocklin used to say that I ran out of sheer terror....Against the Rams, you try to confuse them with different formations and backfield sets and occasional rollouts. Frankly, I run more against them than I do most teams because I'd just as soon see those big guys with their tongues hanging out."

(Tarkenton was the forerunner, so to speak, of such out-of-pocket operatives as Michael Vick, Robert Griffin III, Russell Wilson, and Johnny Manziel.)

The years would roll on, and it wasn't until the mid-1980s when Bill Parcells (known widely as "Big Tuna" for his outsize personality and build) became the Giants' head coach that they would become Super Bowl winners, on the arm of another terrific quarterback, Phil Simms. Parcells could be tough and he could be sweet. He could also be funny, particularly after a game in which the Giants won. I remember being in his office after a victory with other writers, including Frank Litsky, then the Giants' beat writer for *The New York Times*, with whom Parcells had a friendly relationship. Frank happened to be bald. When Litsky and the reporters entered the office, Parcells said to Litsky, "Frank, can I borrow your comb?" Everyone, including Litsky, laughed.

Parcells once told me that at first his parents weren't happy with his decision to be a football coach. Even when he was named head coach of the Giants in 1983 at age 41, his mother, Ida, asked him, "When are you going to get a real job like your brother Don, the banker?"

He would hold himself as well as his players accountable, and learned that lesson from his father, Charles. "Growing up, whenever I was around some trouble," Parcells told me, "I'd tell my father, 'It wasn't my fault.' He'd say, 'Yeah, it's never your fault, but you're always there.'"

The Giants would have their good days and their less than good days. They would win two Super Bowls under head coach Tom Coughlin, in 2008 and 2012. Quarterback Eli Manning, boyish looking, even-tempered, often battered with criticism from fans and journalists—and sometimes even coaches—as well as abiding the occasional mauling from a 300-pound defensive lineman, would emerge nonetheless, in 2008 and 2012, with the Most Valuable Player trophy in each of the Super Bowl wins.

While Tarkenton was criticized for scrambling—and upsetting the play as drawn up by the coach, as well as sometimes frustrating his receivers in their pass pattern—and Simms had been knocked for lack of leadership (he, too, was named a Most Valuable Player in the 1987 Super Bowl), so Manning, from the time he joined the Giants as a first-round draft choice out of the University of Mississippi in 2004, had been chastised for, among other supposed failings, bad-looking passes ("quack, quack" would be the comment from critics for his wobbly passes). Even his general manager, Jerry Reese, in a loss to the Vikings, called him "skittish"—that is, to flinch when hit by tacklers. At one point, in his fourth season, Manning was the piñata for Boomer Esiason, the former Jets quarterback, and now a talk-show host on WFAN. Esiason wondered if New York was the wrong place for the mild-mannered Manning: "Maybe he should be in Jacksonville. Maybe he should be in New Orleans. New York is going to chew him up right now."

But Manning stayed with it, and the coaches continued to show confidence in him. Charles Costello, writing for Yahoo in 2012, said, "Eli Manning...may not be his brother Peyton, who has won one Super Bowl to Eli's two....he may not be Tom Brady, who's won three Super Bowls.... but he's been a very good quarterback....It seems Eli will never get the credit that he deserves."

For me, I was sold on Manning in the NFC Championship Game against the Packers on a miserable, frost-bitten January afternoon in 2008 in Lambeau Field in Green Bay. His opposing quarterback was the future Hall of Famer Brett Favre. Here was Manning, who played college ball in warm weather at Mississippi, who grew up in warm New Orleans, now battling the fearsome Packers in sub-zero temperature (minus-3 below at game time, with a wind-chill factor of minus-24)—the third-coldest championship game ever, and the most frigid of Manning's career—and, outplaying Favre, taking the Giants to an overtime 23–20 upset win, and entry into the Super Bowl. But what Manning said about the cold after the game gave an insight into his focus and intensity. "I didn't feel any cold," he said, and seemed to mean it.

Manning, at 33 in 2014, was returning for his 11th year with the Giants, after a very disappointing season in which the Giants finished with a 7–9 record, in which he said he should have played better—without saying that the rest of the team, especially the offensive line which was supposed to help protect him, wasn't so hot, either. After the season, Manning underwent ankle surgery. He returned to New York in April, wearing a protective walking boot, and saying that "We have a lot of work to do." The offensive coordinator that Manning had played for his entire career with the Giants, Kevin Gilbride—and with whom he had a lot of respect for— had been replaced by Ben McAdoo. "For me," said Manning, "it's getting healthy, meeting new teammates, and learning a new playbook. But I'm enjoying the competition of it all, the urgency we're having right now."

Despite the emergence of the sensational pass-catching rookie Odell Beckham Jr., and despite Manning having a standout season, the Giants fell to 6–10. While the Giants were among the NFL leaders in passes dropped by receivers, Manning still set new personal highs for completions in a season (379) and highest completion percentage (63.1), along with second-most touchdowns thrown in a season (30), second-fewest interception ratio per game (2.3), and, for the fourth time, over 4,000 yards passing (4,410) in a season. It didn't help that Victor Cruz, another sensational pass-catcher, was injured early in the season and never returned to the lineup. And it didn't help that the running game faltered, as did the offensive line.

Terry Bradshaw, commenting on the Giants' final game of the 2014 season, a narrow 34–26 loss to the Philadelphia Eagles, said of Manning, "He's played big when he's had a supporting group around him." In other words, the supporting group was not so supporting.

And I like what Mike Lupica, the highly respected sports columnist for the *New York Daily News*, wrote in September 2014: "No matter what he does the rest of the way, Eli Manning will go in with the great winners in the history of his franchise. In the most important moments of his career, he has been as much of a money player as any New York team has ever had in any sports.... [And] in this time of well-publicized bad behavior in sports, all over the map, he has been a gentleman, taken on all the responsibilities of being a star for a New York team."

Manning, the durable Manning, has started in 167 consecutive games, over a period of 11 seasons. He plans to add to that record in 2015. After the loss to the Eagles, in which he took responsibility for a "poor throw" that wound up a late fourth-quarter interception and ended the Giants' chance for a comeback, he looked forward to the next season. "We made strides this year," he said, "and I'm sure we're going to play at a higher level next season."

Just as it was a delight to watch Tarkenton—and Simms—so it is for me to have seen the growth and determination and success that Manning has achieved (and may yet continue to achieve—I've learned, as have many others, never to underestimate him). As a sports columnist and feature writer for NEA for nearly 10 years, and *The New York Times* for 26 years (retiring from the paper in 2007)—and with a few years in-between and after as a freelance journalist—I wrote on a variety of sports and sports figures. What you will discover in this book are a number of the pieces that I did on football over a period of more than 40 years. While they center on the Giants, they also include many who played against the Giants, or who made their mark in the game. While I write about games, I also sought out people in the gridiron world, sometimes in an idiosyncratic fashion, who simply interested me, from Red Grange to Refrigerator Perry to Henry David Thoreau (you'll have to look it up, in the last section of the book).

It was always a challenge to get the story, to have a cogent opinion on a column—sometimes on deadline—to write as well as I could, as accurately as possible—and spelling the names right!—and often to, it was hoped, give the reader the sense of "being there." Also, in the best of all possible worlds, perhaps understanding the people who play the game, and who it is we are rooting for, or against, and why.

I.

GIANT QBs,
POCKET-SIZE AND
OTHERWISE

Y.A. TITTLE: AT HOME AND ABROAD

December 29, 1984

Y.A. TITTLE WAS RECENTLY in New Caledonia, a beautiful South Pacific island, to start a vacation and visit a festival featuring folk art, of which his wife, Minnett, is a devoted collector. Tittle and Minnett were there only a short time when he decided that he wanted very much to leave.

For one thing, he couldn't get the results of the Giants' last regular-season game, against New Orleans. And had they made the playoffs? There was no such news coming in from the outside world. It seems the citizenry was preoccupied with other matters.

"A semirevolution was going on," Tittle would recall.

He learned that 13 people had been killed outside the capital city shortly before he arrived. And, from his hotel room, he could hear sporadic gunfire ringing through the hills.

For those two reasons, and not necessarily in that order, Yelberton Abraham Tittle Jr., star quarterback for the Giants in their glory days of the early 1960s, was not unhappy to learn that the folk-art festival had been canceled. The Tittles were able to hop a plane to Auckland, New Zealand. There the surrounding countryside was quieter, and Tittle didn't need earplugs to sleep. He could also get the football scores.

He got them at the American Embassy. ("I couldn't find any newspapers that had the information," he said.) But he didn't know until last week, when he returned to the United States, that the Giants were in the playoffs.

"I'm a great follower of the Giants, been pullin' for 'em strongly," said the Texas-born Tittle. He has been pulling, too, for the 49ers, whom he also played for, and the two teams meet today in a divisional playoff game at San Francisco.

"I got real mixed emotions about this game," Tittle said by telephone from his office in Palo Alto, where he is the executive vice president for northern California of the Rollins Burdick Hunter Insurance Company. "I was sorry to see that long drought the Giants had, and I still am close to Well Mara. But I also played for the 49ers for 10 years, and I still have friends with the organization." Among them is Bill Walsh, the 49ers coach, who is a tennis pal of Tittle.

"I was in New York for their game in October," Tittle said, "and I sat on the 49er side the first half and then joined my wife, who was sitting with the Maras, for the second half."

The 49ers won that game, 31–10. "They blew the Giants out with a 21–0 lead in the first quarter," he said. "I think that was the Giants' worst game of the season, and one of the 49ers' hottest."

He expects a much closer game today. "The Giants are a good team now," he said, "but the 49ers are the best team in pro football, even better than Miami. And yet the Giants could win. That's because they've changed the rules to make the game wide open for forward passing. You're allowed to use your hands in pass blocking and not keep them six inches from your chest, like it used to be. And you can't bump pass receivers beyond five yards. Makes it easier for 'em to get clear. The players are better today than in my day. But in some ways the game is easier, because of these rules. It's like goin' fishin' and catchin' fish every time you cast."

He has praise, though, for the teams' quarterbacks. Phil Simms of the Giants, he says, "has a good, strong arm," and Joe Montana of the 49ers "is probably the best quarterback in football."

"He knows Walsh's offensive system so well," Tittle added, "and he has great timing. He mostly throws short—dinks, dunks, here and there, and underneath the defense. Very effective. And he might have a better cast of characters to go with him than Simms does."

Tittle played for the 49ers from 1951 through 1960, or until the 49ers believed that, at age 34, he was washed up.

In a now-famous trade, San Francisco sent him to the Giants for a young guard named Lou Cordileone. The young guard was little heard from again. Meanwhile, Tittle, with sellout crowds roaring at Yankee Stadium, led an exciting offense for the Giants, who, behind his strong passing and slippery bootleg plays, won three straight Eastern Conference championships.

Early in the 1964 season, in a game against Pittsburgh, Tittle was hit by the Steelers' John Baker just as he was throwing a screen pass, and was slammed to the ground. A dramatic photograph, now widely known in the sports world, captured that moment. Tittle is seen on his knees, his helmet off and his head bald, and blood is streaming down his face.

"It looked like my head was hurting," he recalls, "but it was actually my rib cage. I pulled cartilage there. My head was bleeding because my helmet cut it when I hit the ground."

Nonetheless, the picture might have been titled, "End of the Road." Tittle would never be the same after that; nor would the Giants. They finished last in the conference that season, and Tittle retired, at age 38. That was two decades ago, and this is only the second time since then that the Giants have been in the playoffs.

And whom will he be rooting for while he sits in the Candlestick Park stands this afternoon? "Whichever team wins, I win," he said. And what about the team that loses? "I'll lose a little, too."

He will, of course, remain recognizable. The man who was known as the Bald Eagle said that he hadn't discovered any cure for his smooth pate.

"I've been old and bald-headed and ugly since I've been 28," he said. "I've always looked 58, and, now that I am, I feel I'm just reachin' my prime."

WHEN SIMMS SAW RED

January 28, 1987

SOMETIMES YOU CAN'T EVEN trust a good cliché. There is the belief, for example, that bulls get mad when they see red. There are those, however, who contend that this is false, that bulls don't get mad when they see red. They say cows get mad when they see red, but bulls get mad when people mistake them for cows.

Whatever the cause, it's the effect that counts. And Sunday in the Super Bowl in the Rose Bowl, Phil Simms saw red.

"When you think of the Broncos, you think of Elway," Simms said after the game. "When you think of the Giants, you don't think about Simms. That doesn't bother me. What bothered me was that no one was even talking about our passing game."

To some, that thought might be vaguely reminiscent of the bulls and the cows argument, but no matter. People are now talking about the Giants' passing game, and will be for some time.

Simms, who has been called many names in his eight years with the Giants—not all of them fit for a scrapbook—turned every negative remark about him on its head.

He had been compared unfavorably to such Giants ghosts and former quarterbacks as Conerly and Tittle and Tarkenton.

But now Simms is no longer a loser, he is no longer one who can't win the big game, he is no longer one who used poor judgment and threw into double coverage and flooded zones, he is no longer one who would take a winning first half and invariably in the second half turn in a natural disaster.

But on Sunday, in the biggest game of his life, he rewrote the record book. No one ever had a better completion record in any National Football League playoff game. No one ever completed 10 straight passes in the Super Bowl.

Simms was 10 for 10 in the second half, finishing the game with 22 for 25 for 268 yards and three touchdowns and was named the Most Valuable Player in the Giants' convincing 39–20 triumph.

"After all the guff I've taken over the years," said Simms, "this makes everything worth it." And so we have a Cinderella story of sorts, of the sweet, blond-haired kid from Nowheresville—as many saw Morehead State—who comes to the big city seeking fame and fortune and guys who can run a companionable pass route. But he runs into a pack of naysayers in the press, boo-birds in the stands, and some doubting from the coaches on the sidelines.

"Even I had doubts at times," said Simms. "Was I ever gonna play as well as I thought I could? I was always confident, I thought I was good, but I was beginning to wonder."

In 1983, he lost the starting quarterback job to Scott Brunner. "And then I had lots of doubts," he said. "I thought, regardless of how much you work, how much you try, how much you want it, maybe it's just not in the cards for you to get it."

Then he began to speak like a living, breathing self-help book: "But the best thing was, I stayed right in with it, I hung in there, kept fightin' and got better."

But when he was on the bench, he was speaking in a way, he said, that now makes him wonder "why they even kept me around."

"I said I'd never again play for this organization, and for this coach," he recalled. In other words, he was as mad as a bull who has been called a cow. Then, he said, "I realized that I'd probably get another shot at quarterback, and so I told myself, 'Settle down.' But it might all have been a blessing in disguise. It was a terrible year—everything went wrong—and look, Scott Brunner's gone from the Giants. He played himself off the team. If I'd have started, I'd probably do the same thing."

There were injuries, of course, not just to him but to his receivers, and there were problems with running backs, and his protection did not make anybody compare it to the Great Wall of China.

"We all got better," he said now, "and I realize that on good teams you don't get beat up as much. I think I only hit the ground three times against Denver. Now I understand why some quarterbacks can last a long time in this game. Hey, maybe I'll play a few more years, too."

But even as the Giants got better and better, the doubts and aspersions about Simms continued.

Earlier in the year he had a poor game against Dallas, and it shook his confidence. He became more tentative.

It was Parcells who went to him and said, "Be daring. Don't worry about wrong things happening. Go out there and be that guy we know you can be."

Simms recalls, "I was a little down and getting ripped in the papers, and Bill said, 'We think you're great—we know you're great.'"

"Regardless who you are, you need support sometimes," said Simms. "And this was at the right time, and I needed it."

Which doesn't mean that everything goes swimmingly all the time. When Simms was sacked as the Giants were trying to score from the 1-yard line in the fourth quarter in the Super Bowl, Parcells was enraged. "Mostly at myself, for having called a lousy play," he would say, "but I took it out on Phil."

"I couldn't believe it," said Simms. "Bill is calling from the sidelines, 'C'mere, c'mere.' And he starts cussin' me out that I should have thrown the ball away rather than get sacked. And we're ahead, what, 33–13 or something? But that's typical, and he had a point at that."

Now, it's all done. Now, it's all in the past. He is still not Elway, nor, for that matter, is he Tittle or Conerly or Tarkenton. But there is hardly a Giants fan alive who, after Sunday, would want him to be anyone else.

THE RESPECT PHIL SIMMS HAS EARNED

January 4, 1994

IN THE GATHERING DUSK about an hour after the football game Sunday afternoon, with the last, orange ribbon of wintry light dissolving in the distant sky, the Dallas Cowboys had boarded their bus in the parking lot at Giants Stadium. It followed their 16–13 overtime victory over the Giants, and in his front-row seat, the Dallas coach, Jimmy Johnson, eased back. Suddenly he sat up. He had noticed, under the lights from the stadium that illuminated the parking lot, a man in a brown leather jacket.

Johnson summoned the bus driver to spring open the door, and Johnson, in his long black overcoat, hurried out.

"Phil," said Johnson. "Phil—I just saw you and wanted to catch you before you left."

"Oh, Jimmy," said Phil Simms, the Giants quarterback. Simms, holding a sandwich in tin foil, stopped walking and shifted the sandwich in order to shake hands with Johnson.

"You did a great job," said Johnson. "I know it's very little consolation after losing a game like this, but..."

"Nobody remembers any great job, Jimmy," said Simms. "They just remember that you lost."

"You guys really stayed in there," said Johnson.

"We've played better," said Simms. "We can play better. Say, Jimmy, tell me this. What would you guys have done if..." Then Simms looked around and saw a handful of people gathering around. He smiled and nodded to Johnson and they moved over to the side and for several minutes continued their colloquy in private.

The game, for the National Football Conference East title, had been as close to a bruising, heavyweight championship fight as football games get. Dallas dominated the first half. The Giants rose, in effect, not from the canvas but the artificial turf—led by their veteran quarterback—to tie the game and send it into a fifth period, decided unmercifully short, by Giants standards, by Eddie Murray's field goal.

"Phil's a tremendous competitor," said Johnson before reboarding the bus, "and a winner."

Johnson was eager to pay Simms, the 38-year-old quarterback, the respect that he has earned in his 15 seasons in the National Football League, 15 seasons of such highs and lows, such cheers and boos, that one wondered how he could keep his head. Indeed, one recalled that after the 1987 Super Bowl, in which he had had one of the greatest days any quarterback has ever had in a championship game, and was named the most valuable player in the game that the Giants won, he said, "After all the guff I've taken over the years, this makes everything worthwhile."

After 15 seasons of coming back from disparagement and demotions and injuries—one remembers how, for example, he lost his starting position in 1983 to Scott Brunner and in 1991 to Jeff Hostetler, and how he was out all of 1982 because of knee surgery, and out seven games last season with a smashed elbow, and how over the last couple years critics have said he was too old to be consistently effective—he was again seeking to lead his team through the playoffs.

After the game Sunday, he said that he wasn't looking back. "Guys are already talking about the Vikings," he said. The Giants will play the Vikings Sunday in Giants Stadium, in the first round of the playoffs. "The Vikings have really hit their stride recently. We'll have to play well to beat 'em."

The battering he took on Sunday, when he was sacked four times, will be a memory in his muscles, and in his chest, and maybe in the ringing in his ears. But his mind and heart must center not on the past but on the present—and imminent future.

Athletes, though, like many of the rest of us, are also driven to a large degree by the past, by all those who say one cannot, or will not. Did he feel redeemed in some way from having lost his starting quarterback job to Hostetler and won it back when Dan Reeves took over as Giants coach for Ray Handley?

"I got past the redemption and all that stuff a long time ago," said Simms. "Well," he added, with a little grin, "maybe at around the mid-point of this season."

He has learned that things "settle down," that what seems permanent today, or even at halftime, is, later, nothing but transient.

"In the huddle," said Rodney Hampton about the second half, "Phil didn't say much except call the plays, but you could see the determination in his eyes."

In the past, some said Simms would never be a Giants quarterback of the stature of Conerly or Tittle or Tarkenton. Now, anyone taking the measure of Giants quarterbacks—any team's quarterbacks, for that matter—must include Simms among the cream. The Vikings are sure to understand, as did the Cowboys, and their respectful coach, Jimmy Johnson.

FRAN TARKENTON:
NOT ALL NFL GREATS
ARE GIVEN THEIR DUE

December 6, 1995

TEN DAYS AGO, AS Dan Marino was breaking another one of Fran Tarkenton's passing records—this one for most touchdowns thrown in a National Football League career—Tarkenton, as one might imagine, was immersed in past glories. Those glories, however, had nothing to do with heaving footballs into end zones. He was checking out Michelangelo's David and the Colosseum in Rome, and the Palazzo Popadopoli in Venice. And the Old Scrambler was doing it in one place, yet.

It was in a Barnes & Noble bookstore in Atlanta, where Tarkenton, now 55, and his family may often be found browsing on Sunday afternoons. He was looking for a gift book about Italy.

At home later that night, a dinner guest told Tarkenton that Marino had tossed four touchdown passes in the game against the Colts, giving him 346 for his career to Tarkenton's 342. (Marino has since thrown two more.)

"I didn't have much reaction," Tarkenton said. "I knew he had tied my record last week. I love football, but when I left the game, I left it. I had other things I wanted to do."

After his retirement in 1978, after 18 seasons as a quarterback for the Vikings and the Giants, he went into the computer software business, where he thickened his wallet considerably. "Right now," he said, "I've got 14 different projects I'm working on." Once a scrambler, apparently always a scrambler, but he had enough time to offer misgivings about the handling of the record.

"This was football's equivalent of Henry Aaron breaking Babe Ruth's all-time home run record," he said. "A touchdown in football is like a home run in baseball, right? So one guy hits one, the other guy throws one. But football doesn't treat its roots, its foundation, its history, the way baseball does."

Baseball has indeed thrived on records, on its past, but football has seemed a more distant and impersonal game, with players often viewed as assembly-line parts and the operatives covered from head to foot in helmets and padded costumes. And there is the aspect of warfare in football, in which we simply move from battlefield to battlefield—often wagering, to be sure, on the outcome, to make it just that much more exhilarating.

"Last summer in Baltimore when Cal Ripken Jr. broke Lou Gehrig's record for most consecutive games played, it was wonderful," Tarkenton said. "I was glued to the television set. I watched every minute of it. And they brought Joe DiMaggio there, and Brooks Robinson, and even Johnny Unitas. But football isn't like that. The next call I get from the NFL will be my first. I hope this doesn't come off as sounding bitter, because I really feel I'm not. I'm just stating fact. You know, my quarterback heroes growing up were Sammy Baugh, Sid Luckman, and Otto Graham. These people are just part of the long-ago past as far as the NFL is concerned, and I think that's a shame."

Tarkenton, a member of the Pro Football Hall of Fame, asked a question. He wanted to know whether a center in the NFL who played every game for 20 seasons should be in the Hall of Fame, and if a defensive end who played every game for 17 seasons should. Well, it would be reasonable to believe that they might bear serious consideration.

"The first is Mick Tingelhoff and the other is Jim Marshall," he said. They were both teammates of Tarkenton's at Minnesota. "Neither one is in the Hall of Fame, but they should be. They were great players. And everyone knows Ripken's and Gehrig's records. Few know Tingelhoff's and Marshall's."

And an appreciation of Tarkenton, as well, seems to be fading into the dim mists of history. For those who remember Tarkenton, he often seems to be only the guy who ran all over the field like a suspect being chased by gendarmes. But he also wound up his career by throwing more footballs for more yardage, for more completions, and for more touchdowns than Unitas, Baugh, Luckman, Graham, Bobby Layne, Joe Namath, or Bart Starr. Most of those records have been broken by Marino, whom Tarkenton admires. "You can feel him burning inside to win," Tarkenton said.

"None of this is rocket science, or Bosnia, or the inner cities," he said. "It's just sports. And sports should be about fun. But I think we'd get more pleasure if we had a greater appreciation of history in football."

Looking around from Bosnia to the inner cities, it seems a greater appreciation of history beyond sports wouldn't hurt either.

Kerry Collins Turns Corner, On and Off the Field

January 20, 2001

EAST RUTHERFORD, NEW JERSEY—THE joke, so to speak, is that Giants quarterback Kerry Collins would be the first Super Bowl Most Valuable Player to win a car and not be able to drive it. Collins' driving privileges were suspended a year ago because he had pleaded no-contest to driving while intoxicated in 1998.

When the line about the MVP car was mentioned to him, he laughed.

"I hadn't heard that one before," Collins said yesterday, outside of the locker room at Giants Stadium after practice.

"It's not embarrassing?" he was asked.

"I think it's funny," he said.

Oh? "That's just me," he said, with an easy smile under a red Giants baseball cap. "You do the crime, you've got to do the time."

This is one of several ways Collins is dealing with problems that, just a year or two ago, seemed to be sinking a personable, strapping young man (he is now 28) and a gifted football player. He was called a drunk, a quitter, and a racist, among printable epithets.

"I was stupid and idiotic and chemically altered," he has said.

The idea that he would now be leading a team into the Super Bowl against Baltimore, that he'd be coming off a National Football Conference championship game against Minnesota last Sunday in which he rewrote the record books for passing excellence, that he'd be considered a team leader by black and white players, and, apparently, would turn his life around and become as sober as a soft drink, would have stunned many, including, surely, Kerry Collins.

In fact, he now drinks between 10 and 20 Diet Cokes a day. When he's not playing football, he amuses himself with watching movies, reading the playbook and being involved in charitable activities.

He takes part in activities for the Big Brothers, Big Sisters' at-risk program. He has been available for other good causes. As a new Giant in 1999, he learned about and visited pediatric patients at the Rusk Institute of Rehabilitation Medicine in Manhattan. He soon established his KC for Kids fund, which is a crusade to raise money for, among other things, a computer room that will cost $100,000. Among his donations, which have totaled $57,000, have been $1,000 for every touchdown he throws and $2,000 for every Giants victory.

"Sure, a large part of my motivation for these causes comes from what I went through myself," Collins said. "My story is now an open book. And if someone may be disadvantaged in some way, or has encountered problems, and hears about what I went through, and how I was able to change my life, it might give them inspiration. I hope it does."

He came out of Lebanon, Pennsylvania. When he was 14, his parents split up, and he and his father moved for the sake of Collins' high school career. He became a Heisman contender at Penn State, and was the first-round draft choice of the Carolina Panthers in 1995. All the while, he was developing a reputation as wild and hard-drinking. He lived life on the edge. Yet the next season, 1996, he was instrumental in Carolina's reaching the NFC Championship Game, where the Panthers lost to Green Bay.

At a party the next season in which he was said to be inebriated, Collins said a racial slur to one of his black teammates that he said was a joke. Problems escalated from there. In 1998, midway through the season, he told his coach that he wanted to be benched until the team "straightened itself out." He was derided by his teammates. "He's quit on us," said one player. "He's jumped ship." He was soon cut from the Panthers and wound up with New Orleans. He continued to stumble, getting the DWI citation. The league office insisted he go for rehabilitation, at the Menninger Clinic in Topeka, Kansas, and he did.

"That changed my life," Collins said. He said he hasn't had a drink since. He signed with the Giants as a free agent in mid-1999. The Giants gave him a four-year, $16.9 million contract. They were roundly thought to be nuts.

"Looking back," Collins said, "I'm proud of what I've accomplished. On and off the field. I guess my life today shows that if you can change—if you're willing to try to change—then good things can happen.

"I look at those kids at Rusk, some have been in accidents, some have problems stemming from other things, but they're there trying to rehabilitate themselves. I know that my problems seem small compared to theirs, but I tell them that in a way I was in a similar situation, and it's possible to get better."

Collins said the kids at Rusk are excited about the Super Bowl on January 28. "They've sent me banners," he said, "like 'Big Blue Wrecking Crew,' and 'Bring Home a Championship.'"

Collins will certainly be trying. If the dream comes true, it is conceivable that he'd even drive to Rusk on First Avenue for a visit in the MVP car. After all, he gets his license back on February 1.

DAVID BROWN HOPES
TO WEAR OUT GIANTS FANS

October 25, 1994

TWO GUYS RAN INTO each other in the rain in Giants Stadium on Sunday. They stopped and looked at each other. "Hey, what are you doing here?" one asked. "No," said the other, "what are *you* doing here?"

In fact, only one of them was supposed to be at that particular spot, which happened to be somewhere around midfield. The scheme that had been hatched called for the other individual to be somewhere else.

One of the guys was Howard Cross, a tight end for the Giants. The other was Mike Sherrard, a wide receiver for the same organization. And before they had time to rearrange their busy schedule, a ball was thrown to the spot where one of them was supposed to be. It was caught by a third party, one wearing a different colored suit than Cross and Sherrard.

This is recalled because it may shed some light on the Giants' offense, an offense that has been less than terrific, an offense with a lanky quarterback, David Brown, who has been blamed for most of the Giants' problems.

The coach, Dan Reeves, made a decision yesterday, a decision that many were waiting for, though many had not expected. He said, "I am not going to change quarterbacks." That is, not right now. The easiest thing for Reeves to have done was change quarterbacks, to give the football to the next in line, Kent Graham—the Giants' Prince William—who is willing and eager.

And while fans have been trained to seek miracles with quick fixes, like the firing of a manager or the dumping of a quarterback, Dan Reeves did what might be termed courageous. He stuck with the quarterback, who is only in his third season out of Duke. Reeves did so because he has confidence in himself and in his "system," which resulted in his Denver teams winding up in three Super Bowls. He did so because once upon a time he had a young quarterback who made a lot of mistakes and eventually got the hang of it. Name of John Elway.

This is not to say that Brown is Elway—and Reeves doesn't say that. But Reeves believes Brown can overcome.

He also saw guys running around in unprescribed fashion over the last several games. He saw a pass Sunday dropped in the end zone. He saw blockers blocking the wrong blockees. "I saw a lineman miss an assignment and the guy came right into Dave's face and he got off a good throw," said Reeves. "That's not easy."

Brown, as Reeves said, is "learning." Some fans think, "Yeah, but learn on your own time." Reeves, however, watched the game films over and over and decided that the guy had done enough things right, and hadn't done quite enough things wrong, to merit a demotion. Not right now.

Brown, though seemingly of gentle disposition, is obviously not, however, the wilting kind. In front of the news media yesterday—in baseball cap, blue-green sweater, khaki shorts, sandals that revealed a bandage for a turf toe he suffered scrambling on one play—he said with almost professorial aplomb that he must "learn under fire." He sounds convincing.

After a rousing start this season in which the Giants went 3–0 and there was talk of them going to football heaven, or the Super Bowl, whichever came first, they suddenly fell down a mine shaft, losing four straight.

While he must not take all the heat for the offensive offense, the quarterback accepts his share. He has been throwing some very good, strong spiral passes, with excellent form; unfortunately too many of the balls have been embraced by the enemy. Brown threw two interceptions to the Steelers Sunday. He has thrown 11 in the seven games this season.

Phil Simms, last year's quarterback, threw nine interceptions for all of 1993. But in his second season, in 1980, Simms threw 19. In the year Simms led the Giants to the Super Bowl, in 1986, he threw 22 interceptions, his career high. That same season, he threw four interceptions in one game, against Seattle.

"I had trouble falling asleep after the game," said Brown, who is from Westfield, New Jersey. "I kept seeing those two interceptions. But I know I have to forget about 'em. Have to go on."

And he talks regularly to Simms, now a sports broadcaster. "Phil tells me he went through the same thing, and how the fans used to get on him," said Brown. "But eventually they came to accept him. He said, 'They had no choice. I wore 'em out.'"

Reeves, properly, is giving Brown the chance to exhaust these fans, too.

JEFF HOSTETLER:
BRUSH WITH DEATH BONDS A FAMILY

June 14, 2000

MORGANTOWN, WEST VIRGINIA—ONE YEAR ago, Tyler David Hostetler, age eight, died. Last week, he played in a Little League game. This is the story:

The soft, spring rain had stopped and the evening sun angled through the clouds as Jeff Hostetler walked the family's six-month-old buff-and-white cocker spaniel, Rookie, down a path from his spacious house. It was about 7:00 PM last June 14 when they headed to Cheat Lake, which sparkled alongside his property. Hostetler moved with Rookie down a hill—this is West Virginia, after all, "almost heaven" as the locals often refer to it—and the hills and mountains are indelible to the majesty of the terrain.

At age 38, Hostetler, the former Giants quarterback who helped his team win two Super Bowls, had fashioned, surely, an idyllic life. He had married his college sweetheart, Vicki, and the Hostetlers had three boys: Jason, age 14 at the time, Justin, 11, and Tyler.

Tyler, the youngest and perhaps the most willful, was spending the night at a friend's house. He was tall and strong for his age, and had recently been chosen for his Little League's all-star team. Like his brothers, he was an honor-roll student, as well as a good athlete.

Hostetler, still sporting the mustache familiar to Giants fans, saw Rookie trot onto the tennis court. As Jeff was about to chase him off, he suddenly heard anguished screams from Vicki, up at the house.

"Jeff! Jeff! Hurry! Something terrible has happened! Tyler's hurt! Hurry!"

He ran toward the house.

"Beth Ann called," cried Vicki, in the doorway. "She could hardly talk. She said: 'Come immediately. Tyler had an accident.'"

Jeff and Vicki jumped into his white Suburban and flew down Eastlake Drive, up Sunset Beach and around to Snake Hill Road to the France farm, about six miles away, where Tyler had gone to stay with nine-year-old Charles France.

Charles and Tyler had hopped onto the Gator, a six-wheel all-terrain vehicle used for hauling lumber and other farm objects. Charles drove it a short distance, then jumped off and told Tyler to get on and follow him as he chased locusts. Tyler had never driven one before, but that would hardly have bothered him.

Tyler lost control and hit a fence post, and the vehicle flipped over on its side, pinning Tyler. A bar from the 1,000-pound vehicle wedged into Tyler's neck. Charles screamed for help and began running the 700 or so yards over a hill to the farmhouse.

Dr. John France, a local trauma injury and spinal cord surgeon who is Charles' father, does not usually leave the hospital until much later in the night. But by a quirk of fate this night he had come home early. He was speaking with a contractor building his barn when he heard his son's shouts.

"I didn't know what he was screaming about," John France recalled, "but it sounded terrible. I took off running in the direction of Charles." The contractor was at his heels.

"I found Tyler lying under the Gator. He wasn't breathing. It looked like his neck had been broken. His face had turned a purplish white, indicating cardiac arrest. I thought he might have either a spinal cord injury or brain injury. I don't remember how this other fella and I got the vehicle off Tyler, but we did. I gave Tyler CPR. He began to breathe again, and he had a thready, barely palpable pulse. I've seen a lot of cases of accidents where someone's neck is broken, and I wondered if I was saving a little boy who would be a quadriplegic the rest of his life, who might be ventilator-dependent the rest of his life, and was I doing the right thing?

"But I kept giving him breaths, and breaths, and breaths. And he opened his eyes. I stopped the CPR. Then his eyes shut and he stopped breathing again, began to discolor again. I applied CPR again. By this time my wife had called an ambulance, and within about 10 minutes it came. I had kept Tyler perfectly still to keep him stabilized, to keep from having further damage to his neck."

It had begun to drizzle again, and someone brought out a poncho to place over Tyler to keep the sandy-haired boy dry and warm. Tyler was now alert, and John France assumed correctly that he had got to Tyler within three to five minutes of the accident, otherwise the lack of oxygen to his brain would have been disastrous.

Tyler was carefully placed in the ambulance and the vehicle began to pull up the winding, mountainside roads from the farm when the Hostetlers drove up.

"We just knew that Tyler was in the ambulance, and we followed it," Jeff Hostetler said. "All the while we saw from the back window the medics working on Tyler. We still didn't know what had happened."

"I can't begin to describe what our feelings were, to see our little boy like this," Vicki Hostetler recalled.

When the ambulance arrived at Ruby Hospital, and Tyler was carried out in a stretcher, Jeff would remember the absolute fear in his son's eyes when they looked at each other.

"Daddy, Daddy," Tyler said.

"It's all right, Tyler," he said. "Everything's going to be all right."

John France emerged from the ambulance, and told Jeff and Vicki what had happened.

"How bad is he, John?" Jeff asked.

"He was dead, Jeff," France said. "He's alive now, but he's badly injured. There's some paralysis. We just don't know yet how bad it's going to be."

"Does he have a chance to recover, to have a normal life?"

"Yes, he's young, he's moved each extremity; the field's wide open for recovery."

Jeff and Vicki understood, of course, that there was also the distinct possibility of little or no recovery.

In bed now, with tubes in his arms and wearing a halo, Tyler asked his parents if he would get better. "Will I be able to play with the all-star team next week?" he asked.

"We'll have to see what happens, Tyler," Vicki said. "We're all praying for the best."

That night, Tyler took a turn for the worse. He stopped being able to move his arms, his legs, his fingers, his toes. He was completely paralyzed from the neck down.

Doctors told the Hostetlers that they could help by continuing to massage Tyler's feet, to keep the muscles limber, to give healing a chance.

For six weeks, either Vicki or Jeff or both were with Tyler every minute, day and night. They took turns sleeping overnight in his room, talking to him, trying to encourage him and kneading his feet to try to maintain muscle tone. Everything was devoted to Tyler.

Jeff, a free agent, had offers from the Tennessee Titans and the St. Louis Rams. "It would have been impossible for me to leave my son," he said. "There was simply no question about it."

Dr. Russell Biundo, medical director of the Healthsouth Mountain View Regional Rehabilitation Hospital in Morgantown, where Tyler was eventually sent, called the Hostetlers "two of the most devoted parents I have ever seen."

For six days after the accident, Tyler lay in the intensive care unit, his left side paralyzed totally and only the slightest bit of motion in his right hand and right leg. His nerve endings were so sensitive that a breeze could cause him pain. He yelped in agony when his mother's hair brushed against his bare arm.

"I hate my life," he said. "I want to die."

"You can't say that, Tyler," Jeff said. "You're tougher than that."

Jeff reminded Tyler about his own struggles in football, how he didn't give up. He talked about his injuries and the rehabilitation he had to go through, and his time as a second-string quarterback, just waiting for his opportunity.

"Quit has never been in my vocabulary, and it's not going to be in yours," he told Tyler.

Jeff recalled, "All of the lessons I learned in football—discipline, motivation, drive—all came into play in how I tried to deal with Tyler."

After eight days in Ruby Hospital, Tyler was transferred to Healthsouth for rehab. A little more movement appeared in his right side. In the third week, there was some motion in his left leg.

One day, Tyler's aunt Janie came to visit and asked if she could kiss him. "Okay," he said, not altogether thrilled. When she did, it appeared that he had moved the forefinger on his left hand, the hand that had remained paralyzed.

"Did you see that?" Jeff asked. They had.

"Tyler," Vicki said, "can you do that again?"

And he did. It was the first movement of an extremity in a week. "There was such joy, just for this little moment," Vicki recalled. "I turned away. I didn't want Tyler to see me crying."

After that, Hostetler said, "Tyler really took off." In the fifth week he started to try to walk again. "He had to relearn everything, every step," Hostetler said.

Tyler had the advantage of youth, but rehab was arduous, exhausting, and painful. He wanted to quit.

"You can do it, Tyler," Jeff said, with a decisive tone. "You will do it!" He helped him to take one more step than Tyler thought he could take. And then another. This went on day after day.

Several things helped Tyler's improvement, besides the various medications and, as Hostetler said, "incredibly wonderful care by the doctors." Visitors were important for Tyler, from his Little League teammates to his family—his brothers, uncles, aunts, grandparents—to family friends and even his beloved Rookie.

Calls came from a host of friends, and beyond. There were phone calls, from people like a longtime family friend Jon Miller, senior vice president of NBC Sports; as well as Barry Larkin, the Cincinnati Reds shortstop and a hero of Tyler's; and Michael Jordan. (All the tongue-tied Tyler could say to Jordan was: "Uh-huh...Uh-huh...Uh-huh...Okay.")

There were the stories Tyler enjoyed hearing, such as how his parents met, when Jeff was quarterbacking the West Virginia Mountaineers in the Gator Bowl in December 1982. He saw the pretty daughter of his coach, Don Nehlen, in a convertible. "Can you give me a ride?" Jeff asked her, and she said yes.

"And what about when you kissed her, Daddy?" he asked. Indeed, on that first day, there was a kiss. It seemed comforting to Tyler to hear of the romance of his parents, since he was feeling so apart from everyday things.

And he asked his father to tell him the football stories that he had heard on many other occasions. The story, perhaps, that he liked best was framed on the wall of Jeff's business here, Hostetler's Cafe, which specializes in bagels, a taste that he acquired not on the Pennsylvania farm where he grew up, but in Hillside, New Jersey, where he lived during football seasons with the Giants. On the wall is an article from *The Tampa Tribune*, written the day after Super Bowl XXV, on January 27, 1991, after the Giants' 20–19 victory over Buffalo. The headline read, HOSTETLER'S 7-YEAR WAIT WORTH IT NOW.

Jeff, who had been a career backup, passed for 222 yards, one touchdown, and no interceptions in the Super Bowl, filling in for the injured Phil Simms.

"The greatest thing about Jeff," George Young, the Giants general manager, said in the article, "is that no matter how frustrated, he hung in there and waited several years for his great opportunity, and he had it now."

Jeff indeed knew frustrations. He had a scholarship to Penn State, but after starting a few games and doing well, he was still second string to Todd Blackledge. The 6'3", 220-pound quarterback transferred to West Virginia; he starred on the football field as well as in the classroom, where he was a dean's list student.

In the pros, where Jeff also played for the Redskins and the Raiders in a fine 15-year career, he suffered a wide range of injuries, including a torn rotator cuff, a broken back, and several concussions. He also had three knee operations and ankle surgery.

Tyler was strong and tough like his dad, even to the point of being the lone third grader at Cheat Lake elementary school to pass the Presidential Physical Fitness test with, among other tests, push-ups, pull-ups, and a mile run.

"And something else helped, I want to believe," Jeff said. "And that is prayer. We're a religious Christian family. Every night, Vicki and I and the two boys knelt and said prayers for Tyler. Every night."

Six weeks after the accident, Tyler went home. The environment proved to be therapeutic. In a week, he was able to brush his teeth by himself. Two weeks later, Tyler was able to move about without help from anyone else. Shortly after, he started school with the rest of his classmates.

Dr. Gary Marano, a radiologist who is a neighbor of the Hostetlers, read the X-rays after the accident and observed the boy recently. "Tyler," he said, "is a little miracle."

But Tyler's head still did not sit properly on his neck. It listed ever so much. Last December, Jeff took Tyler to Miami so Dr. Barth Green of the Miami Project could operate on Tyler's neck, to straighten it out.

The operation was a success, and Tyler, Green said, "was walking around the next day like a champ."

Things have resumed a relatively regular pace in the Hostetler home. When Tyler was in the hospital, his two older brothers were eager to please, were even a bit deferential to him. No more.

"He's buggin' me again," Jason said, stating an older brother's time-honored position.

Bugging you about what? he was asked.

"Everything," he said.

Just a few weeks ago, Jeff turned down an offer to quarterback the Minnesota Vikings.

"My football days are over," he said. "Tyler's injury and recovery have been the most significant period of my life. And I realized that my time is much more valuable here, with my family, watching my kids grow up, being a part of it. I understand the frailties of life better than I ever have. How precious each day is."

What does Tyler think of his dad giving up football?

"I think he's crazy," said Tyler, not one to mince words. "We watched the Super Bowl between the Titans and Rams, and I thought it would be great if Dad was in the game. I'd play."

Not football, not for Tyler, or hockey. The regular pounding in those sports could cause a recurrence of problems for him. Basketball, baseball, golf, and tennis are permitted.

Tyler is back in the Cheat Lake Little League, playing first base and wearing No. 5 for the black-jerseyed BlaineTurner Advertising team. He is still not 100 percent back, the doctors say. He still has some problems with mobility in his left hand, for example, but he is almost there.

On a close play at first base in the first inning on a sun-splashed early afternoon recently, the runner stopped before he might have run into Tyler.

"I hold my breath on plays like that," said Jeff, sitting in the bleachers along the first-base line.

"You're always on pins and needles," Vicki said, "but the doctors said that Tyler could take a hit like that and still be okay."

Now Tyler came to bat, a left-handed hitter. In his age group, a pitching machine serves up balls to the batters. In his first three games of the season, Tyler had nine hits in 10 at-bats. He gets respect.

"Get back, Joey," the coach of the opposing team called to his center fielder. The words had hardly escaped from him when Tyler cracked a line drive over Joey's head. In the stands, Vicki and Jeff jumped up and clapped. The ball hit the wooden fence and bounced back, and Tyler David Hostetler, age nine, pulled up at second base with a double, standing there, under his black batting helmet, as if nothing much had happened.

II

A CLUTCH OF BIG BLUE COACHES

BILL PARCELLS:
WHAT'S A JERSEY GUY?

January 24, 1987

JUST WHEN EVERYONE HERE thought nothing more could be said about that game tomorrow, more of nothing was said.

It was one more day in which overkill held center stage.

After nearly two weeks the end has come to intense pregame interrogation of the participants with a concentration on analysis and psychoanalysis, on introspection, retrospection, and reflection. As well as the circumspect exchange of secrets regarding items from rolling zones (never mind, Mick Jagger) and pulling guards to recipes and what good movies you've seen lately—in other words, a profound dearth of news.

Now, finally, the two head coaches of the contending platoons, the Broncos and the Giants, were enlisted to speak at the last news conference before Armageddon.

In separate back-to-back engagements in a banquet hall of the Anaheim Marriott, Bill Parcells and Dan Reeves assured the assembled truth-servers and soothsayers that, yes, their teams are ready to go.

Yes, there is a high level of intensity. No, neither team is intimidated.

"Yes, we have to be concerned about the Broncos' offense because it contains a multiplicity of things," said Parcells.

"No, you don't stop Lawrence Taylor," said Reeves, "you hope you slow him down."

Someone asked Parcells, "What's your definition of a Jersey guy?" "A guy who lives in New Jersey," he said. True, of course, as far as it goes. A question was posed to Reeves concerning déjà vu of these two masses (the Giants are said to weigh 10,321 pounds as a group, some 200 pounds heavier than the Broncos): is there an advantage in one team's having played the other during the regular season?

"If any team has an advantage of playing each other twice," responded Reeves, "both teams would have that advantage." True, of course, as far as it goes. In the last workout, Reeves said his forces displayed a ferocity that was worrisome. "They were hitting each other so hard," he said, "I was afraid of getting somebody hurt. Made you hold your breath."

The Giants' last few days of practice have been, like some orange juices, high in concentration.

But like the Broncos, the Giants would find ways to relax.

In the training camp where the Giants have been ensconced, there is a dog—the clubhouse dog, he is called—and a game is sometimes played with him. A tennis ball is thrown at the door, and he jumps out from behind a garbage can and tries to snare the ball.

"He's kind of a goalie," said Parcells. "The players enjoyed playing with him. I did it for about a couple of hours myself."

Parcells did say that he was making sure in practice that "you cover."

He was talking about his defense, and not one of the most frequently asked questions about that football game tomorrow: will the Giants cover?

The reference is to the point spread, and not the defensive spread. Though the spread of the defensive cover could have a great deal to do with whether the Giants cover the spread. About the point spread for Super Bowl No. 21, the Giants are a 10-point favorite. "I don't pay attention to the betting lines," Parcells said. "It's a nonfactor. It's for someone else."

Like Coach Reeves? "An underdog could make a victory by them one of the greatest accomplishments of all time, considering the reaction when the Jets beat Baltimore," said Reeves. That was Super Bowl No. 3, in which the Jets were considered by oddsmakers almost three touchdowns inferior to the Colts.

Perhaps it was only inevitable that Parcells would be asked about his self-control, given that the day before he had noted that football "was not a game for well-adjusted people."

Was he concerned about his temper getting out of control on the sidelines?

"Out of control, no," he said. "Mad? Yes. Frequently? Yes. To the point where I appear out of control? Yes."

And he laughed. "I believe you're allowed to laugh," he said. "Otherwise you go crazy."

Reeves, made of stern stuff, was not all guffaws, and said he appreciated Parcells' sense of humor. "I like the way he gives names to some of his units, like the offensive line. He calls them, what, 'Suburbanites.' He's got a knack for that." Both coaches appear to have a knack for forthrightness, however. This came out when Reeves was asked about the time in 1979 when he was being considered for the Giants' coaching job.

"Mr. Mara asked me to come to New York and not tell anybody," Reeves recalled, referring to Wellington Mara. He was interviewed for the job, and then went home. "I got a phone call from Tim Mara, and he asked me if I had been in New York. I said no.

"I didn't know he had learned from Mr. Mara that I had been in New York. Well, it wasn't a good start of a relationship to be lying to somebody, and your chances of getting the job aren't real good."

It was an astute observation, and Ray Perkins got the job.

"But I take coaching real good," said Reeves, with a glimmer of a smile. "Mr. Mara told me to say no, and I said no."

Coach, will the Broncos have any trick plays? "The way people are considering our chances," he said, "if we gain five yards people will think it's a trick play."

Have the Giants done anything unusual in practice? "It was like we were preparing for a regular game," said Parcells.

A regular game? The Super Bowl? What a novel thought. News at last.

THE GIANTS' ROOKIE
HEAD COACH AND THE GHOST

October 1, 1991

AT RAY HANDLEY'S NEWS conference yesterday afternoon, someone asked him a question—virtually every question had something to do with how come the defending Super Bowl champs are in amongst the chumps in the standings—and on this question the rookie Giants coach remained silent.

"It's not that I don't have the answer to the question," he said at length, "it's just that I'm trying to find a way to say it."

Finally, he did find the words. The question was, are you angry with the team? The answer was, "No, I'm disappointed in the results." He also gave no indication that he was finished, either.

Right now, Giants players and Giants fans, and the rookie Giants coach himself, are eager to find the right words that will produce the victories that they all expected, especially after a championship year.

Instead, they've got losses in 60 percent of their five games this season.

The primary puzzlement is how come the Giants can't score touchdowns. They get inside what is known in current footballese as "the red zone"—that is, within 20 yards of the opponent's goal line—and they can't seem to take the ball in with any kind of consistency. They run and pass and gambol over the rest of the field, then there arises a barrier.

It's like the insurance salesman who gets the sale all ready to go, but he can't close the deal. The hand that holds his pen just won't ink the bottom line. Thus the Jints.

The news conference, at Giants Stadium, was held in a small, window-less room, and besides Handley and the reporters there was another party present, unseen but absolutely felt flitting around those yellow walls: it was the hefty ghost of Bill Parcells, the departed coach of the Super Bowl champs.

In training camp, after Handley had decided to go with Jeff Hostetler as his quarterback instead of the regular for many years, Phil Simms, it seemed a sign that Handley was seeking to make his own mark, and extracting the ghost from the Giants premises.

It is not easy to say exactly why the Giants aren't performing as had been anticipated, but Handley surely has to take some of the blame.

Is he too conservative in the "red zone"? Well, his predecessor was con-servative, too, but he eventually proved effective, though, like Handley, not right away. Parcells had a 3–12–1 record his first year. But of course he took over a losing team, not one that sported championship rings on their thick fingers.

The players say they are playing hard for Handley. In fact, Handley feels the running backs are playing too hard. "I've told them to calm down, to relax a little, and maybe they'll hold onto the ball better," he said, regarding the little problem of tumbling, fumbling footballs.

Handley is already taking heat from various sources, like fans and the press. A headline in a local tabloid, for example, called him a "wimp." For many, five games is an eternity. And for fans of a team that won a Super Bowl last year, it's even longer.

In person, one of the first things you notice about the rookie head coach is that he has what appears to be a solid jaw. One that looks capable of taking blows. And he's got a large neck, befitting of a former running back, and a good-sized body, too. And you notice his direct eyes. What one doesn't see, of course, is the inside of his head.

He mentioned that there have been three or four critical plays in these last Giants games that have made the difference.

Why must it come down to three or four plays?, someone wonders. So someone asks, "Well, it used to be—" The phrase hung in the air, carried, perhaps, from ear to ear by that bulky, ambulating ghost in the room. Handley responded to the question evenly.

To a question about what time he had got up this morning, the morn-ing after the third defeat of his professional head-coaching career, he grew slightly testy now. As if he was being questioned about having put in enough time with game films and chalk talks and all the other stuff coaches are known to fill their lives with. "Sufficient time," he said.

The players seem a little at a loss, too, though shy away from criticizing Handley. Sean Landeta, the punter, said, "We're not panicking. We're just a couple of plays from being where we want to be. And if we wind up 11–5, or 10–6, we'll be where we want to be."

That is, the playoffs. Meanwhile, the rookie coach had retired to check out the game films. Over his shoulder, whether he admits it or not, he was feeling the hot breath of the ghostly coach of seasons past.

DAN REEVES:
CAN 70,000 PEOPLE BE WRONG?

November 28, 1995

THE NEW YORK GIANTS, or the New Jersey Giants, or whatever they are, should demand their money back from the salary they're paying their head coach, or whatever he is.

It is obvious that the money would be better spent by spreading it around to the 70,000 or so fans who fill the stands of Giants Stadium. It is these people who generally think they know more than the coach, anyway.

And now comes word from the coach himself that, well, even if they don't know more about it, it doesn't matter, he'll heed them anyway. In this case, for him, ignorance is bliss.

On Sunday afternoon, in a crucial moment in the Giants-Bears game, the coach of the Swamplands Eleven, Dan Reeves, a man who has been a head coach for 15 years, with the local team as well as the Denver Broncos, had it in his mind to punt the ball. Then he thought better of it, he decided, because the fans wouldn't like it.

And guess what? He didn't punt the ball.

This was the situation: The score was tied, 24–24, with 55 seconds left in the final quarter. The Giants had fourth down and four yards to go for a first down. They were on the Bears' 32-yard line. They were going against a slight wind. Reeves decided, with good reason, not to go for a field goal—under the atmospheric conditions, he felt, it was too long a shot for the kicker, Brad Daluiso.

At first, Reeves said in a news conference yesterday, he was going to send in a play for Dave Brown to quick-kick. Brown is the quarterback, and he had done this once before this season.

But Reeves called a timeout. And then he changed his mind and went for the first down.

"You know what the biggest thought was?" he asked rhetorically. "It was, 'You aren't going to believe the crowd when they boo when they punt this football.' And that was the thing that went through my mind. I said, 'Let's talk about this and make sure this is what I want to do.'"

Reeves then explained why the coach, who is paid about a million dollars a season to call the plays, should follow not just what the crowd wants, but what he believes it wants.

"If you were in contention, you wouldn't worry about it," he said, referring to the crowd's anticipated reaction, "because you're more concerned about the game. But when you're at a position of 3–8, it enters into it."

Why should a losing record enter into a coach's decision on whether to bow to the crowd? His job is to win the football game, regardless of the team's record, and do it by his lights, not those of the butchers, the bakers, and the candlestick makers in the seats around him.

In other words, the coach would rather be loved than be right. Or he is tending toward that. And if he did it once, would he do it again? And if he does, who needs him?

The fact is, if his play works out, and he punts, and the Bears can't muster a drive in less than a minute and the Giants win in overtime, Reeves is a genius. As it was, the Giants didn't make the first down. The Bears took the ball and scored to win the game on a 37-yard field goal by Kevin Butler with seven seconds remaining.

Hearing this woeful tale from the coach, one's heart indeed bleeds a bit. Coaches are terribly harried people, it is true, and perhaps the pressures of New York make it even rougher. And he is certainly not the first coach or manager to bend to the perceived whims of the mob. (Seventy thousand people screaming a hundred different things is not exactly a science research lab.) But he is the first in memory to say that he was so influenced.

He gets a gold star for candor. He gets a kick in the rear for courage.

In 1952, at the end of another miserable baseball season for the St. Louis Browns, Bill Veeck, the owner of the team, and one always on the lookout for a gimmick, decided to give placards to the crowd—in the hundreds, if memory serves. When there was a situation that called for a bunt, or a new pitcher, or some other piece of strategy, he had the fans hold up the cards to make the decision for the manager.

As this was going on, not only the placards, but also the game itself had to be held up to find time to count the placards, since the fans themselves couldn't come to a unanimous decision.

This couldn't work at Giants Stadium. If all those fans made calls with placards, it might take three days to play the game, and television would never permit that.

Too bad. It would make Dan Reeves' job that much easier.

III.

ON THE LINE, OR
THEREABOUTS

LAWRENCE TAYLOR:
THE GREAT, FLAWED WARRIOR

November 10, 1992

HE FOUGHT NO FIRES, he defended no innocents, he performed no surgery, but he has been called by some a hero. His job was to jump on people and knock them down. And he did it better than anyone in recent memory.

His purest joy, he once said, was to hit someone so hard he could see the "snot bubble out of his nose." His was a brutal business, and he loved it. And many loved him for it. "I'm a wild man in a wild game," he once said with satisfaction. And the cheers in the stadium echoed and echoed in his ears.

On Sunday, though, all this may have come to an abrupt end for Lawrence Taylor, the indomitable, the indestructible, the invincible. "He's been pretty close to Superman," said the Giants' orthopedist, Russell Warren. But suddenly Superman was domitable, destructible, vincible.

In Sunday's game against the Packers, the star Giants defensive end ruptured his right Achilles' tendon, perhaps terminating his career. Taylor, now 33 years old, had said several weeks ago that this season would be his last, anyway, the end of a spectacular 12 years in professional football.

And so he went out not in a blaze of glory, but lying on a motor cart and being driven swiftly off the field, his arms covering his helmeted head as he writhed in pain.

In plain view, some 72,000 spectators in Giants Stadium saw now this warrior, this hero, this Superman, stricken, fallible, and flawed.

All cultures create myths larger than life, and often they are men of action. Ours not infrequently, and rarely wisely, seeks out sports stars for this purpose. Many of the subjects themselves fall into the bittersweet trap.

For all Taylor's bravado, however, for all of his crowing about "Living on the Edge," which was the subtitle of his autobiography, *L.T.*, written five years ago with David Falkner, he has been susceptible to frailties.

He has had drug and alcohol problems. And when he talked about life on that ledge, he had yet to face a second suspension from the league for having tested positive for drugs. One more time and he would be thrown out of the NFL.

But he maintained his super pose. When asked what he did during his 30-day drug rehabilitation stay, he said almost mockingly, "Played golf."

The hero described himself: "I live my life in the fast lane—and always have. I drink too much. I party too much. I drive too fast, and I'm hell on quarterbacks."

One seemed to equal the other. The Superman cloaked in this persona was similar off the field and on. The same rules, he figured, applied to both. But while one was a game that he played brilliantly, the other had the potential for disaster, and not just for himself. About his driving and drinking, he said, "If I don't care what happens to me now, can I really think about what might happen to others?" We wondered: what kind of a man is this?

Taylor had problems at home. There were paternity suits. There were his three young children growing up with a father who apparently didn't always have enough time for them, or his wife, Linda.

But the hero was in the fast lane: others beware.

Taylor was raised on the outskirts of a small town, Williamsburg, Virginia, and in what Falkner described as "little more than a shack." Whether the driving force under the tough veneer of the football man was the still insecure small, impoverished boy, it is for others to determine. What he has told us, though, is this: "I want to be the meanest S.O.B. who ever played the game. I want to be the best."

To be mean on the football field was a virtue, less so in private life.

"I think Lawrence has matured," said Steve Rossner, his business agent. "There are no more drugs, and I don't think he lives as much in the fast lane. It's like on the football field. As you get older, you can't do the same things you used to do. Things catch up with you. I think, for example, that he's giving much more guidance to his three children."

His son, T.J., is 11 years old, and his daughters Tanisha and Paula are six and four.

Rossner also said that Taylor's injury may change his plans: "A week ago I don't think anything would have got this guy out of retirement. Now he is rethinking the way he ended his career. The doctor said he would be healed for next season. I think Lawrence would rather finish on the field than on the sidelines."

It was announced recently by D.C. Comics that Superman—the original—would meet his Maker. Now there are second thoughts. Possibly like Lawrence Taylor. One primary difference, though, is that one man is made of steel, the other of flesh and blood.

GARY REASONS'
RATHER REASONED HEAD

January 6, 1990

THE HEAD IS A strange instrument, an awesome thing, a thing of multiple utilities. It can be used to cogitate; it can be used to ruminate; the skeletal remnant can be a memory device—"Alas, poor Yorick! I knew him, Horatio." And it can be used as a weapon—like being armed with your head.

When Gary Reasons used it as such a bludgeon four weeks ago, it may have saved the game for the Giants, saved their playoff chances, and helped create some of the optimism that they take into tomorrow's playoff game against the Los Angeles Rams in the Meadowlands.

Reasons, a Giants linebacker, tackled a man with his head. In fact, his head tackled the other guy's head in midair. It was such a spectacular collision that, Reasons said, people still exclaim about it.

"I was coming to practice earlier this week," he recalled, "and a CBS cameraman hollered from his truck, 'Hey, Gary, you jumped right out of my frame!' And the other night on Warner Wolf's 'Plays of the Decade,' he showed it and said it was 'The Hit of the Decade.'" On the screen, Bobby Humphrey, the Denver Broncos' tailback, was beginning his jump over the pile of players to try to score from the 1-foot line. Reasons anticipated the play and leaped, too. The pair, going in opposite directions in the same flight pattern, smacked face gear-to-face gear with such force that the ear flap inside Humphrey's helmet flew out—some thought it was his mouthpiece—and Humphrey was knocked back about a yard.

46

For Reasons, the crack of heads in midair was pure pleasure. "It got our offense on the field and everybody was high-fivin' me," he said. "This doesn't happen to a linebacker very often. It was like a Michael Jordan 360 slam dunk."

The game situation was this: in the third quarter at Mile High Stadium in snowy Denver, the Broncos, one of football's best teams, had the ball inches from the goal on fourth down. Denver had just tried three plays from within the 1-yard line, without scoring. The Giants were ahead—that word has a way of cropping up—14–0. If the Broncos scored, got pumped up, scored some more, the Giants might lose, drop to a 9–5 record, and perhaps disappear into the sunset of the season.

"I thought that that goal-line stand, and that play, were symbolic of our team, and our entire season," Reasons said this week. "We hung in there when most people didn't expect us to. We lost a lot of important people due to retirement and injuries, and a lot of people were picking us to finish behind Philadelphia or Washington or both in our division."

The tackle by Reasons made him only giddy, not groggy. "If you hit a guy right, use the right technique," he said, "it shouldn't be much of a problem."

The right technique, he explained, is accomplished with the face, or the forehead, or the nose, but not the top or back of the head. "That's when you can get hurt," he said. "That's when you can get that tingly sensation down the spine. The neck isn't made for tackles like that."

To a layman, or someone else sunk in a sofa and watching a football game, it is difficult to imagine how mighty are the collisions in the game, and how risky.

"But you can't worry about that," said Reasons. "You have to play aggressively. It's like a fighter pilot who goes up in an airplane. He may never come back. You know there's going to be contact, and there's always room for error."

"Sometimes after home games," said Terri Reasons, Gary's wife, "I'll be waiting for him outside the locker room and he doesn't come out right away. I start to worry. Deep down in your mind, you're wondering, 'Is he okay?'"

Now in his sixth season in the pros, Reasons has been playing with a sprained knee, but says he has suffered in his career little more than "the usual assortment of bumps and bruises and nicks."

"Oh, I've been shaken up, sure," he said. "I remember my rookie year with the Giants, and meeting John Riggins head on. He was a 250-pound running back and hitting him when he was in full steam made me a little wobbly."

One of the tricks of the trade, Reasons believes, is to stay cool. Before a game, he will keep his head even when some about him may be losing theirs. Some players through the years have been known to get up for a game, or harden their heads, by beating them against a locker.

"I don't," said Reasons, "and most of the Giants are fairly calm before a game. It's not like *North Dallas Forty*." This was a reference to the film in which football made war look like Simon Says.

Also, explained Reasons, he must stay cool because he has the intellectual responsibility of calling defensive signals on the field.

In the end, then, would he describe his head as a hard head, a soft head, or an egg head?

"I'd call it a suitable head," he said.

CALLOWAY OVERSTEPS THE LINE

October 4, 1994

CHRIS CALLOWAY, A PROFESSIONAL football player, got so excited at catching a pass Sunday afternoon in New Orleans that when he rose after having been tackled he flung the ball to the earth and appeared to say something, possibly uncomplimentary, to his tackler. Or maybe he was simply hyperventilating at his accomplishment. The referee immediately hit his team, the Giants, with a penalty, and the league said yesterday it would hit Calloway with a $2,000 fine.

"You can't do anything anymore," Calloway complained later. "It's becoming a boring league." He also said: "We need excitement in the league. They're taking away our opportunity to celebrate."

I thought this a remarkable statement. In days gone by, excitement came when there was a close game, or a guy made a fantastic catch, or run, or someone chased down someone racing along the sideline and nipped him just before he crossed the goal line.

But more and more, excitement to some of the players takes the form of high-stepping, like a guy leading 76 trombones; or shimmying, like a player with an ice cube in his pants; or boogeying with five teammates, as if they were a chorus line, arms across each other's shoulder pads, kicking up their cleats in a manic choreography, whenever one of their fellows makes a tackle, say, or a block. Or doesn't rush offsides.

The stuffy league officials, for some crazy reason, think all this is unseemly if not at times even devoid of couth, and have tried to temper the cha-chas, the tangos, and the taunts, which makes the likes of Can-Can Calloway dyspeptic.

I thought about "excitement" in pro football. I recalled that the most exciting performer on a football field that these bloodshot eyes have ever seen was Gale Sayers, the Bears' Hall of Fame running back, who once scored six touchdowns in a single game.

I called Sayers to learn how he felt about the so-called new excitement in pro football.

"I hate it," he said. "The refs should throw flags every time they see it. But TV made this happen. It made a monster of the whole game. If not for TV, we wouldn't have all that strutting and other stuff we see with Deion Sanders and all the rest of those idiots.

"All these fellas know they're on TV and go to sleep at night thinking, 'I have to do something spectacular when I catch the ball.' They have to be doing that, otherwise you wouldn't see these planned dances they do. I liked what Joe Paterno told his team about how to behave after scoring a touchdown: 'Act like you expected to get into the end zone.'

"I see them celebrating even when they're behind 25–0. Why are they celebrating? The guy I admire is Barry Sanders. He's so great. He fakes out five tacklers, spins away from three more, bangs over another two, and trots into the end zone. Then he either hands the ball to a referee or drops it on the ground. If he did a dance, it would take away from the beauty of his run.

"Some of these guys say that the league is taking the fun out of the game. I think it's the opposite. I think they're taking the fun out of the game."

Now, Dan Reeves, the Giants coach, did go to Calloway after the game and suggested that he try to contain his emotions after a big play.

How did all this begin? The sense here is that much of it started with Gorgeous George, who sprayed himself with perfume in the rasslin' ring. Muhammad Ali admired George and he saw how George sold tickets. Ali, however, was a natural showman, unlike some who came after, like Connors and Nastase and Neon Deion, who, as E.B. White said in another context, were full of fun, but not funny.

Or, as The Bard noted in Hamlet: "Suit the action to the word, the word to the action, with this special observance, that you o'erstep not the modesty of nature. For anything so overdone is from the purpose of playing."

The man makes a point. I would take Shakespeare and Sayers over Mr. Prime Time and his crowd any time.

THE SMELL IN THE
GIANTS' LOCKER ROOM

October 20, 1992

EAST RUTHERFORD, NEW JERSEY—THE Giants' locker room yesterday afternoon smelled just as it normally does. Not exactly like perfume. The nostrils of visitors, though, were particularly aquiver at this time because a player on the team, linebacker Steve DeOssie, said after Sunday's miserable 38–17 loss to the Los Angeles Rams that the team had developed a certain scent. "We stink," he said.

"We just have to face reality," DeOssie said. "We stink. That's the plain truth."

Soiled socks and football shoes and stained shirts from their workout yesterday were strewn about the locker room at Giants Stadium. The faces of some players were still pebbled with sweat. But here and there players, dripping from their shower, toweled and then began to spray themselves with deodorant and slap themselves with after-shave lotion.

While this couldn't change the play of the team, it radically improved the smell of the locker room. But no solace to Giants fans. Many of them had convinced themselves the Giants had a shot this season at the Super Bowl. They had convinced themselves that last season's 8–8 record and no playoff was an aberration. Giants fans can do this to themselves.

The Giants, meanwhile, are 2–4 this season and played Sunday as if they were intent on improving the reputation of the Rams, one of the least feared teams in the National Football League.

"When you don't play well," said Ottis Anderson, the running back, regarding DeOssie's comment, "you're entitled to any name they call you, in all honesty."

"Nah, the players didn't get mad," said DeOssie yesterday, in sweat pants. "If you were saying something that wasn't so self-evident, then I imagine there would be a problem."

"It was a heat-of-the-moment response," said Sean Landeta, the punter. "And we did play lousy. But look, it may not continue. I mean, we played pretty damn good against Chicago. And we played pretty damn good against Phoenix. What people don't understand, and they never will because they don't want to, is that there is only the smallest difference between the best teams and the worst teams in this league. Even in our Super Bowl years, we won about half our games because one or two plays went our way. Otherwise in both years we could have been 9–7."

All this rings true, and it may be how the players keep from thinking about how odoriferous the team is. Such a positive outlook is certainly what keeps them coming back for more punishment week after week. This, of course, as well as their million-dollar salaries.

While fans wish to recall that this team is a close kin to the Super Bowl champs of two seasons ago, the coach and the players try to see it otherwise. "Every team is different every year," said Landeta. "The teams they play are different. Everything changes."

At his news conference yesterday in a room near the locker room, second-year coach Ray Handley said: "This is not the same team as in the past. It's a different set of circumstances, and the players are not the same as they were in 1990. Taylor's older, Marshall's older. And unless we get a rush out of Lawrence and Leonard, we don't get pass-rush pressure."

He added, "A lot of these players are a year older than a year ago, and two years older than two years ago—you can probably handle the rest of it."

The coach smiled, something he hasn't been seen doing a great deal of lately.

He also answered many of the questions that he's been answering for several weeks now, saying he hasn't given up on the team, that the game Sunday against Seattle is the only game that occupies his thoughts, that maybe some of the players were trying too hard, that the offense is not shouldering enough of the burden.

"I think we're capable of being a good team," he said. "But it will take a great effort against the best teams to beat them."

Now, the coach's detractors seem to outnumber his supporters. And even when the team has one of its few good days, his reviews remain mostly bad.

Is he having any fun? "I'm striving to make it that way," he said.

He looked around. "Anything else?" he asked the reporters.

"It looks like you don't want to leave us and return to the locker room," someone said. "Is it us, or is it them?"

"Neither," he said. "I just have to go upstairs in a few minutes." He paused, and grinned. "Maybe I'm reluctant to do that."

It was a pungent remark, something even DeOssie surely would have approved.

EMOTIONAL PAIN AND A BULLET
DOOM EX-FOOTBALL STAR

November 5, 1984

PHILADELPHIA—A SHOUT FROM BELOW her window awakened Charlotte Smith. She had been sleeping in the bedroom of her second-floor apartment at 131 North 15ᵗʰ Street, a three-story red-brick building, in Center City here early Friday morning, October 26.

She heard, "Back against the wall! Back against the wall!"

It was still dark outside, around a quarter to three, and Charlotte Smith climbed out of bed. Her window was partly open because it was an unseasonably warm and humid night, and she pushed the window higher and leaned out.

On the sidewalk, she saw a large black man—she is also black—and the man was wearing a dark jacket or sweater and tan pants, she would recall. He was moving toward a policeman. The policeman, a white man and considerably smaller than the other, was hollering, "Back against the wall!" and slowly retreating from the advancing man.

She didn't notice a weapon or anything else in either one's hands. An empty police cruiser with a flashing blue light rotating on the roof was alongside the curb. The two men were now stepping into the yellow light on the sidewalk that spilled through the window from the night light in the closed luncheonette. Several yards away, at the corner of 15ᵗʰ and Cherry, two young black teenagers on mopeds watched. Otherwise, the street was deserted.

Charlotte Smith has on occasion been roused in the dead of night because, she told a reporter, "derelicts" come around that area—there are mostly office buildings, but the "derelicts" drift over from the bus terminal a few blocks away—and sometimes cause problems. Her immediate worry was that her boss, Murry Auspitz, might be in trouble. Murry Auspitz owns the luncheonette on the ground floor, where she works as a counter attendant. He arrives early to open the store.

When she saw it wasn't her boss, she said she "didn't pay it no attention," and got back into bed. A moment or so later, a loud crack rang out. "It was a gunshot," she recalled. "I've heard gunshots before."

She jumped up and looked out the window again and now saw the black man lying on the ground, bleeding. The policeman was at the squad car and, she recalled, "radioing in for help."

"I was hysterical in the window," she would say, "screamin' and cryin'."

She did not learn who the black man was until the following day, Saturday, when she saw the headline in *The Philadelphia Daily News*. It read: "Cop's Bullet Kills '50s Grid Star."

The dead man was Charles Fletcher Janerette Jr., age 45, an English teacher at the Daniel Boone School in Philadelphia and a former All-America lineman at Penn State and one-time player in the early 1960s with both the New York Giants and the Jets. For the last 12 years, Janerette had suffered from what was described by his parents as manic depression.

His killing would raise numerous questions and inflame passions, particularly in the black community of Philadelphia. In the official police statement, the officer would say that Janerette had gotten into the marked squad car when the policeman had stepped out to talk to the two youths on mopeds. Then, the policeman stated, he pulled Janerette from the car. He said that a scuffle ensued and his revolver went off. Janerette was shot in the back of the head. Janerette was taken to a hospital and died about 12 hours later.

Was Janerette, in fact, up against the wall? Was this a case of police brutality in extremis, or an accident, or did the policeman have no recourse in order to protect himself? How was it, if there was a scuffle, that he was shot in the back of the head? Had Janerette taken the medication that helped control his mental problem? Toxicology reports, which should show whether he had been taking the medication, will not be available for several weeks.

The police officer, Kurt VonColin, age 33, who reportedly stands about 5'7" tall and weighs about 160 pounds, bears a well-known last name in

Philadelphia. In 1970, his father, Police Sgt. Frank VonColin, age 43, was shot to death while alone at his desk in the Cobbs Creek Park guardhouse by a group of black men, members of a radical organization known as the Revolutionaries. The killing was considered by the police to be part of a conspiracy by the group to kill whites.

That crime touched off the largest manhunt in Philadelphia history. All but one of the assailants were caught. The only one still free is the one who is said to have pulled the trigger.

There are other questions that the story of Janerette raised: some deal with the adjustments of life after football, some with racism in American society, and others with the problems of the manic-depressive, a psychosis from which, according to his family, Janerette had been suffering for the last 12 years.

Charlie Janerette grew up in Philadelphia, first in the Richard Allen projects, and later in a better neighborhood in West Oak Lane, and became an all-city and all-state high school lineman. He went on to Penn State, where he was chosen a second-team all-American by *The Sporting News* in his senior year, and he played seven years in professional football. He was with the Los Angeles Rams in 1960, the Giants in 1961 and 1962, the Jets in 1963, the Denver Broncos for the next two years, and finished his career in 1966 with the Hamilton TigerCats in Ontario.

In 1956, Charlie Janerette became the first black class president of Germantown High School. He was popular, gregarious, and exceedingly bright. By the time he was a senior, he had reached his full height, 6'3", though, at about 240 pounds, not quite his full weight, which would go as high as 270 pounds with the Broncos. "Charlie," said a longtime friend, Garrett Bagley, "was a gentle bear."

Two of his boyhood friends were Harold Brown, now a North Carolina businessman, and the comedian Bill Cosby. Brown is believed to be the model for Cosby's comic invention, Weird Harold, and another Cosby character, Fat Albert, is believed to have been loosely based on Charlie Janerette.

Brown smiled when he recalled Janerette. "He was funny and he could take a joke," he said. "We said his shoe size kept up to his age."

Brown was asked if Janerette was in fact the inspiration for Fat Albert. "The guys have always thought he had a lot to do with it," said Brown.

"He was rotund, robust, as a kid," said Brown. "Not fat sloppy, but robust sloppy."

The boyhood friends kept in touch through the years. Last year, said Charlie's sister, Hope Janerette, when Bill Cosby opened a show in Lake Tahoe, he sent Charlie Janerette a round-trip first-class ticket to Nevada. Cosby told Charlie he'd have a Rolls-Royce waiting for him to use there.

Charlie told Hope, "I can't drive that thing. What if I had an accident? I could never pay for the repairs."

One of the many bouquets of flowers sent to the Janerette home bore this note to the family: "I'll see you later." It was signed, "Bill Cosby." Several attempts to reach Cosby were unavailing.

Charlie Janerette was the oldest of five children, and the only male, born to Charles Janerette Sr., now a retired postal office supervisor, and his wife, Lillian Ernestine. The five children—the other four are named Carol, Faith, Hope, and Charity—would all earn master's degrees, and two would earn doctorates. Charlie had dreamed of becoming a physician, and he enrolled as a pre-med student at Penn State.

But, he would say, the requirements of football didn't give him enough time to pursue the rigorous discipline of medicine, and he instead earned a bachelor's degree in science, and later a master's in educational counseling.

When he first went to Penn State, Joe Paterno, now the head coach but then an assistant coach, recalls that they thought there might be a problem. "He was a sensitive, shy kid and we wondered whether he was aggressive enough to be a good football player," Paterno said. "But he was very committed, and he wanted to make something of himself. He was very quick and had a lot of explosiveness, and he got tougher and tougher."

Janerette was thrilled to receive a scholarship from Penn State, but, he said in a newspaper interview a few years ago: "They didn't tell me I'd be the only black on the team. I didn't worry about that, though. I saw all the huge freshmen, and I just wanted to survive."

In the mid-1950s, blacks were just beginning to be recruited on a large scale for college athletic teams at major state universities around the country. It was no different at Penn State, the school tucked away in an area known as "Happy Valley." Janerette, though, seemed to make adjustments.

Janerette was drafted in 1960 in the fifth round by the Los Angeles Rams. His contract called for $7,500, and he received a $500 signing bonus.

It was enough for Janerette to put a $3,000 down payment on a house for his parents and sisters, a brick, semi-detached four-bedroom house on a street lined with spruce and cedar trees in the quiet, East Mount Airy section of north Philadelphia.

He started some games for the Rams, but at the end of the season, was picked by the Minnesota Vikings in an expansion draft, and then traded to the Giants.

In two years with the Giants, he would recall to *The Philadelphia Tribune*, a black newspaper, he played "a lot of defensive tackle when Rosey Grier was hurt, and I played on all the special teams. I even played with a broken hand. I had to."

Andy Robustelli, a defensive end on the team, remembers him as a "happy, jovial, always upbeat guy. But the Giants teams were so strong then and it was tough for anybody to break in."

In 1963, Janerette was cut by the Giants and picked up by the Jets. Weeb Ewbank, then the Jets coach, remembers him as a "nice person, never caused any problems, but we let him go because he was on the downside of his career, and we were building."

Janerette went to the Broncos as part of a nine-player deal with the Jets. "I remember Charlie getting up at a club we used to go to, called 23rd Street East, and doing great, funny imitations of James Brown," said Cookie Gilchrist, a teammate of Janerette's in Denver. But there was another side. "He didn't play enough, and he and I both thought he should have," said Gilchrist.

Denver, where Janerette earned his highest salary, $17,000, cut him and he played for a year in the Canadian Football League. He was 27 years old and finished as a professional football player.

He had married in 1965, and he and his wife, Joan, soon had a daughter, Dariel. There seemed no evidence of problems. He spent five years in the marketing department for General Electric in Syracuse, and it was in August of 1972, said Joan Janerette, when difficulties developed.

"He began acting strangely," she recalls. "Very hyper. His movements were very quick at times, and he began to say strange things. Like he was going to solve all the problems of the world."

He began to leave without telling her where he was going, and wouldn't return for days. She urged him to go to a psychiatrist, and he was eventually admitted to a Syracuse hospital and stayed there 10 days, she said.

She wondered about the source of his problems.

His wife believed he was suffering from manic-depression, in which there are sudden mood changes, surging from euphoria to deep depression.

The problems intensified. She went to a therapist, and she was told that he could be dangerous. "He was a big man, and I found it hard to restrain him," she said. In October of 1972, she left him, taking their daughter to Pennsylvania.

On October 18, 1972, he was charged with driving while intoxicated when he was involved in a car accident in which a pedestrian was killed. He pleaded guilty to a reduced charge and as a result his driver's license was suspended for three months.

"Charlie was so broken up by that accident," said Hope Janerette, "that every October 18 he would not go out of the house."

Following the accident, there were days of unexplained absence from work, and he lost his job.

Paterno, who stayed close with Janerette and knew of his problems, hired him as a graduate assistant. Janerette stayed at Penn State for two years and earned his master's degree.

But Paterno saw times in which Janerette would not be "acting right." And when Janerette next went to Cheyney State in Pennsylvania as an assistant coach under Billy Joe, there were more problems. "He was a good assistant," said Billy Joe, "and then on occasion he would do something completely out of character." At a football dinner, Janerette, the guest speaker, rose and soon, "began yelling out and cursing," said Joe. Janerette had to be led away.

He moved to Washington, where he sold computer software to federal agencies. He told a friend that one day he had been picked up off the streets by the police for no reason and jailed for four days.

He returned home to Philadelphia, where he got teaching jobs.

After his death, a student whom he had taught, named Angela Hurst, wrote a letter to Janerette's parents: "...I really do miss Mr. Janerette. He could joke with us, but he was also serious about his students getting to work, because he wanted us to learn. Even when I said, 'Mr. Janerette, I can't do this,' he would say, 'Yes, you can. Try it.'"

Although he took several jobs teaching in the Philadelphia public schools, he would continue to talk to friends about his dreams. "He wanted some kind of entrepreneurship," said Garrett Bagley, a friend, "or he wanted to get back into football. He missed football a lot, and he missed being a star. There were no more locker rooms, no planes to catch, no more autographs to sign."

Janerette was aware, of course, of his mental problem. "He always thought that the last episode—he called them episodes—would be his last," said his sister Charity. "He didn't really want to admit that he had a problem. And when he took his medication—lithium carbonate—he was fine. But when he didn't take it, and sometimes he didn't want to, he would be out of control. He was never violent, that we saw, but he'd be blinking his eyes and moving the furniture and talking fantasies."

He lived for the last three years in the house he had bought at the corner of Boyer and Horttler. But Charity said he considered it "only temporary."

"We knew he was in pain because of the illness, and he suffered with it and we suffered to see him that way," his sister Carol said. "But it was pretty well hidden. Almost no one outside the family knew about it."

His parents worried, too. "I hoped he wouldn't be a street person," said Mrs. Janerette, "and when he was out late, we waited for him, and when I finally heard the key in the lock, I could go to sleep."

He was working then at Boone, a remedial disciplinary school for boys. "He really related well to the boys," said the principal, Willie J. Toles, "and we had absolutely no problem with his performance or his attendance. And he always looked nice—suit and tie."

On Thursday, October 25, he did not report to school. The school called his house. He had not been home the previous night.

That afternoon, a student had seen Janerette in Center City, and the teacher gave him a few dollars, even though the boy hadn't even asked for it. Later, Janerette was reported to have asked a storekeeper he knew to lend him some money, and the storekeeper said Janerette berated him vulgarly for giving him so little.

At around midnight, Paul Jones, an old friend of Janerette's, and now a cab driver, saw him near the bus terminal.

"He didn't seem right," said Jones, who said he did not know of Janerette's mental problems. "He talked okay. We spoke about guys from

30 years back, but his movements seemed too quick, and his jacket and pants were disheveled.

"I said, 'Charlie, can I drive you home?'

"He said, 'No, but can you let me have a few bucks?'"

Jones did, and told him he had to get a fare and would come back in a little while.

He never saw him again.

It was a couple of hours later that police officer VonColin was in his cruiser near 15th and Cherry.

He stopped two teenagers on mopeds for a possible traffic violation. During the ongoing investigation of the death, VonColin is not speaking publicly. According to the formal police statement, one of the teenagers told him that someone was trying to steal his squad car.

According to the statement, VonColin moved toward Charles Janerette.

"Charlie once told me," said Hope Janerette, "that he had heard that if you ever have trouble, or don't have money, and need help, then you should get into a police car. He said, 'They have to take you home.' When Charlie was in a bad state, he always had some presence of mind. He was never totally out of control. And I wonder if his getting into that police car wasn't a kind of plea for help."

It was just about this time that Charlotte Smith heard shouts, and, soon after, the gunshot that killed Charlie Janerette.

Hundreds of people milled outside the gray-stone Berean Presbyterian Church on Broad and Diamond Streets last Wednesday at noon, before the services for Charlie Janerette.

People were angry about the way he died.

Willie J. Toles thought that it was a "classic case of misunderstanding."

Inside, in a gray steel casket strewn with flowers, lay Charles Fletcher Janerette Jr.

"I'm glad for one thing," said Hope Janerette. "I'm glad that now Charlie is out of that little private hell he was living in."

Charlie Janerette was eulogized by the Rev. J. Jerome Cooper, and then Cookie Gilchrist read a poem he had written for the funeral. Next, Faith Janerette, a dramatic soprano, shook the church with a moving gospel, "Right On, King Jesus." Some of the congregants moaned and sobbed.

The mourners then filed out, and some of them sang along with the church choir accompanied by an organist to the "Hallelujah Chorus."

As the funeral procession was about to leave for Northwest Cemetery, Harold Brown spoke to someone beside him. "When Charlie and I used to sit in church, and they played the 'Hallelujah Chorus,'" he said, "and on the last 'Hallelujah,' Charlie, under his breath, would add a '50s rock group ending, a little doo-wop. And today it was there. Damned if I didn't hear it. He was speaking. And it made me think, 'Charlie's okay now. Even with all the tears here, he can still play jokes.'"

LEAVE THOSE NOSE
TACKLES ALONE, LLOYD

December 20, 1988

MAYBE MORE THAN AT any other time of the year, this is the season for
the nose tackle, the guy in the literal middle of the belligerence that rages
in the football game, where the collision of helmets and shoulder pads is
a sound akin to bombs bursting in air.

The nose tackle is in the front line, running over people when he isn't
being run over himself.

And millions of people all across this favored land sit bundled up in the
stands or wrapped in their robes at home and root with all their heart for
their nose tackle of choice to either give it or get it.

And so when recently we read that the average salary of a nose tackle,
this most industrious and clamorous of working stiffs, was being held up
in negative comparison in order to hike the salaries of members of the
executive, legislative, and judicial branches of the Government, we were
quite naturally taken aback.

Lloyd N. Cutler, chairman of the commission looking into what he
states are the relatively low salaries of some of our top federal officials,
said during recent public hearings in Washington, "To illustrate in terms
most citizens will understand, we will have to decide whether the Chief
Justice of the United States should continue to be paid less than half of the
average salary of an NFL nose tackle."

With all due respect to the Chief Justice, and to some of the other judicial, legislative, and executive souls, the nose tackle who earns an average

of $254,000 a year makes it the hard way—by the sweat of his brow and the valor of his nose.

A few years ago, as the Giants prepared to enter the playoffs that led to a Super Bowl triumph, Jim Burt, the team's nose tackle—known as Sluggo for his grit—said of the trench warfare on the gridiron: "It's a good time to be there. The team is gelled. We're in the groove."

Burt won't be sharpening his beak for the playoffs this year, nor will any of the other Giants, of course, since they were eliminated on Sunday.

Other nose tackles will be at it instead, like Fred Smerlas of the Bills, Tim Krumrie of the Bengals, and Bob Golic of the Browns. Guys who are, as the saying goes, generally household names only in their own household. But who after a game are usually in need of half the contents of a well-stocked medicine cabinet to relieve the welts and bruises, not to mention the funny little ding-a-ling sound that won't shut up somewhere in a corner of the brain.

Now, Mr. Cutler did not say that nose tackles don't deserve the money they're getting, but there was an implication that something must be upside-down in the society if such disparity in salary between a brute like a Burt and a Chief Justice exists, or continues to.

Surely, Mr. Cutler does not mean to return Burt and company to previous salaries—low by most standards, lower by half, in fact, than what the Chief Justice earns—before the players' union fought the monolithic owners with strikes and other bargaining weapons to gain a better wage.

Surely, Mr. Cutler understands that in a free enterprise system people are paid what the traffic will bear—if they can get it, that is. And the football players wouldn't be getting it if the gate and TV and ancillary receipts wouldn't allow the owners to give it.

Interesting, though, that Mr. Cutler will use the nose tackle, or, as he did in other moments, the baseball player ("Don Mattingly is earning $2 million a year!") to illustrate that the federal officials are being underpaid "in terms most citizens will understand."

Most citizens have played football as boys, and baseball (as boys and girls), and perhaps can identify in a way that they can't with other entertainers—for the professional athlete is an entertainer, with a career life expectancy that is not only relatively short, but precarious, too.

It's harder to identify with movie stars and TV stars and rock stars. But they often earn incredibly more than nose tackles, or even first basemen.

In the last two years, according to *Forbes* magazine, Bill Cosby, for example, earned $84 million; Sylvester Stallone $74 million; Bruce Springsteen $56 million; Madonna $47 million, and Johnny Carson $40 million. Even that bag of bones, Arnold Schwarzenegger, did better than Burt, with $26 million over the previous two years.

In 1930, when Babe Ruth received the fantastic salary of $80,000, he was asked, "How do you feel making more money than the president of the United States?' Ruth supposedly said, "I had a better year than he did."

Burt and Smerlas and Krumrie and Golic had better years than some of those seeking more pay on The Hill. But if, as Mr. Cutler believes, heftier wages will lure better people into government, then we should give it serious consideration.

Meanwhile, leave Jim Burt out of it. He's got enough problems.

He's an Eagle, but Stan Walters' Family Still Roots for the Giants

December 27, 1981

STAN WALTERS, THE PHILADEPHIA Eagles offensive tackle, called his father recently. His father still lives in Rutherford, New Jersey, where Stan was born and raised.

His father was excited. "Well, son," said Stan Walters Sr., "isn't that something—the Giants are in the playoffs!" "Dad," replied Stan Jr., "what about us? We're in the playoffs, too." One step more, of course: the Giants, who call nearby East Rutherford home, are playing the Eagles in Philadelphia today in the wildcard round of the National Football League playoffs.

"I guess my family can't change," said young Walters. "They've been Giants fans for years and years. Oh, I know he wants me and my team to do well, but his heart deep down might still be with the Giants teams we grew up with."

Stan's father is a machinist in Jersey City. "I'm sure he's getting a lot of heat from his friends about the Giants game," said Walters last week by telephone. "It's hard for him, but I'm sure he's got mixed emotions."

"I was a Giants fan, too," said Walters "Of course, I've gotten over it." He stands 6'6" and weighs 275 pounds. He has an abundant head of curly hair and his eyebrows nearly meet, giving his eyes a dark, penetrating look. "But I remember the days of Y.A. Tittle and Kyle Rote and Del Shofner, and when Frank Gifford was a defensive back. I'd go to maybe one game a year at Yankee Stadium. God, it was exciting.

"I'd take the bus from home to the Port Authority, then take the subway to the Stadium. Everything was sort of dark and dreary until you got into the Stadium, then you'd come up from a passageway and then suddenly the spectacle would hit you. The huge crowded famous park, the bright green grass, the colorful uniforms. What a difference from my small high school fields. I dreamed of being down on that field one day."

Walters went off to Syracuse University, where he majored in business and offensive line. After his senior year, in 1972, he was drafted in the ninth round by Cincinnati.

"By then," said Walters, "I didn't care who drafted me, just as long as I could play in the NFL." Walters was confident but, as a fairly low draft choice, he was realistic. Before going to training camp, he had the Bengals send him a round-trip airplane ticket.

He made the taxi squad. But when Rufus Mayes was injured, Bengals coach Paul Brown elevated Walters to the regular team, and he started the last eight games of the season.

"I was lucky in the beginning because it happened that I didn't go up against the best ends is the league," said Walters. "I've seen rookie tackles start off against guys like Deacon Jones or Harvey Martin or Lee Roy Selmon. And they get blown out. Their confidence is so shot they never recover."

Walters, who was traded to the Eagles in 1975, went on to hold his own against the best defensive ends in the league, and he gained selection to two Pro Bowl teams, in 1978 and 1979.

Today, he will be assigned to defend against Gary Jeter, the Giants' outstanding end, who is fast and strong and seven years younger than the 33-year-old Walters.

"Walters is a cagey old veteran," said Jeter. "If you're going to beat him, it's got to be done on physical moves, either out-quick him or out-power him. You're not going to out-smart him. He knows how to set himself to throw you off.

"He does something else. He likes to talk. I like Stan personally. And I'm happy to talk to him off the field. But he's the master psychologist. He's out there saying, 'Nice move, Gary,' and 'Good show, kid.' I know he's trying to lull me into a false sense of security."

Does Jeter talk back? "Yeah. I tell him to shut up."

Walters says, "Well, no harm in telling a guy he makes a nice play, is there?" He laughs. He is not one of these linemen like Conrad Dobler, who luxuriates in a reputation as an offensive carnivore. Dobler has been known to bite an opponent's shoulder pads, when he can't get his teeth into the neck.

"A lot of guys like a reputation as a killer out there," said Walters. "But I like to think that you play as well as you can and you play right. Cheap shots are the easy way, but the most harmful to the team because they end up in penalties. I don't believe you have to draw blood to be good."

One player who drew Walters' ire was Coy Bacon of the Washington Redskins. Last year, after enduring an afternoon of rough play and rough language, Walters said: "The guy's an idiot. You play against him and you sink to his level. He doesn't realize it, but all of that mouthing off gets the competitive fires burning. It has the reverse psychological effect than he intended. In the fourth quarter I told him: 'Look at the scoreboard. You're 24 points down. What are you talking about?'"

This year, though, all was forgotten. Walters said that Bacon was "a phenomenal athlete." Walters was using his own favorite ploy—sedating the opponent with praise.

This season, Walters, along with the Eagles generally, have had their ups and downs. The Eagles, the defending conference champions, started the season with six straight victories, but finished 10–6, barely making the playoffs. Walters had strained knee ligaments early in the season and was sometimes off his game. The knee is much improved.

The Giants and Eagles have met twice this season and each team has won one game. This game, of course, will be the most important of their meetings. Some football players have unusual ways of getting up for games. Some bang their heads against lockers, some punch the wall. And what will Stan Walters, cagey old veteran do before the game?

"Put on my uniform," he said, "starting with my socks."

THE SURPRISING STORY OF
OBERLIN JOE AND GEORGE SAUER

May 24, 2013

WHEN I READ OF the death recently of George Sauer Jr., one of the New York Jets' Super Bowl heroes in the stunning January 1970 16–7 upset over the Baltimore Colts, a story told to me by Cass Jackson, a longtime friend of Sauer's, came to mind, and I gave Cass a call. It happened that I hadn't spoken with him in 39 years, or when I went to Oberlin College (Ohio) in 1974 to interview him—at the time, he was only the second African American head football coach at a non-historically black college in the National Collegiate Athletic Association.

Jackson remembered Sauer with fondness, admiration, and, well, amusement—especially about what transpired in a touch-football game they played in one day, and with an Oberlin guy named Joe. In the obituaries about Sauer, who died on May 7 of congestive heart failure at age 69, he is recalled not only as an All-Pro wide receiver for the New York Jets, and one of Joe Namath's favorite targets, particularly in Super Bowl III, catching eight passes for 133 yards, including one for 39 yards that kept a scoring drive alive in the third quarter, he is also remembered for having quit football at the end of the 1970 season, still in his prime at age 27, saying that pro football was "dehumanizing" and "fascistic"—"a grotesque business."

"He hated the system, the regimentation, was frustrated by it," said Jackson by phone. "But, you know, he loved football. Loved the game itself, even after he left the Jets." Jackson and Sauer had met in California after Sauer had quit professional football and Jackson was a defensive

69

back coach for San Jose State. Then Jackson was hired at Oberlin, and shortly after he brought in Sauer as a volunteer offensive line coach. "It was his first job after the Jets," Jackson said, "and he was with us for two years. Did a great job. Sweetheart of a guy. And could he run a pass pattern! It was a thing of beauty." In this regard, following is the story that Jackson, now 71 and acting head track coach at Monterey Peninsula College (California), told me all those years ago, and recalled again.

"I knew George still liked to play because when we both lived around San Francisco we'd toss the ball around in a park for three, four hours and then we'd stop and chat, and soon George would be up and running again, running pass patterns. He was like a kid. He almost wore my arm out.

"Sometimes we'd talk about the pros, and about all he'd say—and he mostly said it with his eyes—was, 'I wish it had been different, but it was fun while it lasted.'

"George stayed in shape. When he came to Oberlin to help me out, he jogged five, six miles a day. And he watched his diet. Sometimes he'd have just a couple of glasses of orange juice for supper. And he kept his head in shape by reading Camus or James Joyce.

"Since I knew he still loved football I thought when he came to the Oberlin campus I'd take him out to play in the local sandlot pick-up game. It was funny. You had to see this to believe it.

"The local hotshots, all of us black, played every Sunday evening in summer. This was serious stuff, although we had fun. A lot of us were high school or college heroes. And I even played defensive back for Saskatchewan in the Canadian Football League.

"We played just below Oberlin hill, with trees on either side of the field. It was a lovely setting, with the sun going down. And maybe a hundred people would come out to watch—wives, girlfriends, buddies, little kids.

"The week before I had brought an Oberlin philosophy teacher, who was white. It was embarrassing, he was so bad. He'd been chosen on the team opposing mine, and after the game one of the guys whispered that I shouldn't bring back any more white dudes like that.

"During the week, George arrives. I suggest he play on Sunday. He says okay. I bring him out to the field and guys are giving me dirty looks. George doesn't look like much of a player. He's 6'2", but he's kinda thin. He's wearing a sweatshirt and black shorts and he's tossing the ball real loose. And he's wearing his glasses the way he did down on his nose.

"Nobody realizes this is George Sauer. I keep quiet just to see what happens.

"There are about 20 players. Sides are chosen and George isn't picked. But one of the guys on the other team tells me, if you want your friend to play he's gotta be on your side. I say, well, okay.

"I throw the first pass of the game to George. It's an 80-yard touchdown. Nobody can believe what they've just seen, especially a guy named Joe, who was a star defensive player in our games.

"Joe figures there was a slip-up somewhere. He says, 'I got this new cat.' The next play we run, George does this fantastic move on Joe. George gets behind him, fakes toward the goal post. Joe lowers his head and starts chugging. George spins around and breaks for the sideline. I put the ball right on the money. Meanwhile, Joe is on the other side of the field. The crowd goes berserk.

"Now guys are on Joe. 'Hey, man, this cat's burnin' you up. Two TDs!' I figure now it's time, I got to fill 'em all in. 'This is George Sauer,' I say.

"The guys say 'Whooo?' I say, 'George Sauer.' And again, 'Whooo?' Someone says, 'Namath's receiver!?' I say, 'Yeah.' And Joe pipes up, 'I got him.'

"So George scores four more touchdowns. We win 60–0. It became the biggest story of the season in the black neighborhood in Oberlin. Joe was a great athlete and he was able to laugh about it, too. He could even laugh about his new nickname. Everyone began calling Joe, 'I Got Him.'"

JIM PARKER: SUNDAY'S WOES

September 10, 1969

ALWAYS ON A SUNDAY, during the football season, as the clock ticks closer and closer to game time, prodigious Jim Parker breaks out in a rash, welts form around his ears, and his nerve cords begin to quiver like plucked bass fiddle strings.

This pregame physical reaction has been occurring in Parker for the last 13 years, the first 11 of which were spent in the clubhouse of the Baltimore Colts. The former star offensive guard has been retired for two years now, but he still responds queerly on Sunday afternoons as he stands and fills orders in his package liquor shop in Baltimore.

"I start shaking like a leaf," he says. "Sometimes I think I'm going to get a heart attack. And I get these welts like someone beat me with a stick.

"Something in my body tells me it's game time coming up and I still got this urge to put on a helmet. I can't forget it. This nervousness comes from the mental strain of pro football.

"In the locker room before a game I'd get to thinking real hard about what was going to happen, and I'd get to rocking, from one foot to the other.

"I didn't know what the hell I was doing, and guys have told me that I started knocking tables over and crashing into lockers. Jim Mutscheller, he was an end for us, he used to say that he wouldn't come near me before a game because he was afraid I'd kill him."

When games are in Baltimore, the 35-year-old Parker gives his wife and daughter his tickets. He said he just cannot take being there. He never even goes to practice sessions.

"I went once, the first fall I retired," he said. "I was there for 30 minutes to pick up some stuff. I watched some of the scrimmage. But I had to get out of that place fast."

On a Sunday, as it nears 2:00 PM, Parker often bounds out of his store, lurches into his car, and drives around and around streets in a sort of daze.

"I can't stand still, I gotta move," he says. "I pop these Librium pills in my mouth, nervous pills, been taking them for 11, 10 years, while I'm driving. I don't want to know nothing about what's going on in the game—but I do turn the radio on and off, on the sly, to hear what's happening."

He recalls listening in ambush to a recent Colts game against the Rams and was concerned about how Sam Ball was blocking Los Angeles' rugged defensive end, Deacon Jones.

"I never did have no luck with Jones," said Parker. "I always needed help from Mackey and Curry and the backs. And I was glad I didn't have no part of that Jones anymore."

He remembers feeling sad for one of his ex-teammates, who was called for holding at a crucial moment in the game. And he could picture the reaction of the other Colts. "Eleven years I was holding half the time," he said. "They caught me only sometimes. Sometimes when I did and sometimes when I didn't. But the other players would never bitch at me. Never. But the guys would look at you with a funny look."

One of the hardest things to take now, said Parker, is when the offense and defensive starting teams are introduced and run onto the field. "I feel like driving my car right onto the field," he said. "But I gotta control myself. I gotta stay away. I tell myself, 'Parker, forget it. It's a young man's game. An old guy like you oughta sit quietly up in the stands.'

"I don't know. Maybe I'll be able to next season."

MIKE KARNEY:
A CHRISTMAS WISH REMEMBERED

December 18, 2004

NEW ORLEANS—THE LETTER WAS written 15 years ago by a little boy in Kent, Washington, some 25 miles south of Seattle.

> Dear Santa Claus:
> My name is Michael Karney. I am 8 years old. I have been a good boy. And I would like two things for Christmas. One is a football. And two is to play in the NFL. Thank you, and Merry Christmas, Santa.
> Michael.

The boy also drew a picture of a football, so Santa would not confuse it with anything else. After all, Michael did not know whether they played football on the North Pole. Like many of us, he was not sure what, for example, the elves did beyond helping Santa prepare for Christmas, so he thought he would add a hint.

The note was written in December 1989. Michael, a husky lad for his age with blond hair and blue eyes, loved football. Maybe it was the colorful uniforms, or the excitement of running and throwing or blocking and tackling, or the big, booming punts that caught his eye.

Whatever it was, his mother, Tina, remembered that as far back as when Michael was four years old, he would prefer to watch football games to cartoons on television.

Maybe, after all, there was something in the air, for, thinking only that it would make a sweet picture, a family photograph was taken of Michael at 15 months wearing a football jersey with the number 44.

So that Christmas morning, after his letter to Santa, Michael Karney woke up early, crawled out of bed, and hurried to the living room, where the family's tree stood.

And there, beneath the lights and ornaments and amid the gifts for his parents and two older sisters, the boy unwrapped a present marked for him. He tore open the bright paper to find, to his delight, a brand-new football. Santa had remembered!

As for his second request—to play in the NFL—well, that would have to wait.

Michael understood this. There was no record of an eight-year-old boy ever playing for the Chicago Bears or the Giants or the Green Bay Packers or even the neighboring Seattle Seahawks. So he knew he would have to be patient—if Santa would ever grant him his other wish.

But Michael Karney was not one to sit around with his head in the clouds. From his PeeWee football and junior high and high school days, he was, his mother recalled, surprisingly disciplined.

"He took the games seriously," Tina Karney said. "As he got older, he learned the best way to train, and he listened to his coaches. He also knew that if he was to get ahead, he would have to do well with his school grades."

Michael Karney excelled in sports—he was an outstanding catcher on his high school baseball team—and in the classroom.

His love remained football, and he was one of the better players, primarily as a running back and fullback. He was not particularly fast nor especially gifted, but he applied himself. As he grew older, he learned about myths and legends and what was true and what was not. He was, certainly, no longer the eight-year-old boy penning a note to Santa Claus, but he had discovered that if he were to realize his dreams, he would have to adhere to certain virtues. He had hoped to go to college and play football, and then—well, his dreams did not end there.

A number of colleges offered him football scholarships, and he chose Arizona State. He started for four years, mostly at fullback. He was a devoted weightlifter, and in his spare time, starting in high school, he pulled a weighted sled, ran with a parachute on his back, and pushed a car around his high school parking lot to strengthen his legs. Observers would ask if he was having car trouble and offered to help.

In years past, fullbacks ran with the ball, smashing into the line, a position made famous by the likes of Bronko Nagurski and Jim Taylor and John Riggins. Now, however, they were used primarily as blocking backs, to protect the quarterback or open holes for halfbacks.

There is virtually no glory for a fullback, other than the appreciation of other players, less often by fans. One rarely sees a fullback dancing in the end zone. The job of a fullback has sometimes been described as being in a car wreck on every play.

Karney took pleasure in it.

"Blocking is an art," he said. "There's the pancake block, in which you lay the defender flat on his back; there's the block where you cut a guy and make him lose his footing; and there's the cover, in which you maybe get a piece of the guy but redirect him away from the play. Some people look at you like it's beastly, but I see myself as a gladiator, like in Roman times."

Dave Atkins, the running backs coach for the New Orleans Saints, recalled how a young fullback once stood out during a film session.

"I was scouting the tailback for Arizona State and saw a punishing block by a fullback and wasn't sure I saw it correctly," he said. "So I re-ran the film. And there it was again. I wasn't even scouting the guy, and I was impressed. Then I saw another block and another. I turned off the projector and looked him up on the roster. Number 44. Mike Karney. He was only a freshman. I took note of it."

In the spring of 2004, Michael Karney, now 22, had grown to 5'11" and 254 pounds, and was a senior majoring in education, a few credits short of a degree. The NFL draft was to be held April 24, but first there would be scouting combines at which teams evaluate players eligible for the draft. Karney prepared for the combines in San Diego by working out with, and studying pro techniques from, Lorenzo Neal, the Chargers fullback, whom he had met when he was a senior in college.

In the combines, scouts and coaches test players for skills and football acumen. Karney did well, enough to solidify his rating as the best college fullback in the country.

"I studied all the teams that would need a fullback," Karney recalled. "And I saw that the New Orleans Saints had lost a good one, Terrell Smith, to free agency."

Smith had been a senior at Arizona State the year before Karney enrolled.

"But I wasn't sure what would happen, whether I'd even be drafted," Karney said.

On the first day of the draft, Karney was not taken. "I thought that if I had a chance, it would be on the second day, anyway," he said.

On the second afternoon, some 50 to 60 people gathered in the Karney home. "I had aunts and uncles and cousins and friends and neighbors and my high school coaches and teachers," Karney said. "We were watching ESPN, which was televising the draft. But my name wasn't coming up. It was now the fifth round. So I went outside to shoot baskets with a few of the kids. And then I heard my mother call out that there was a phone call for me. I went inside to take it."

It was Saints coach Jim Haslett on the phone. As Karney recounted it, Haslett said, "We're planning to draft you next, Mike. Are you ready to block for Deuce?"

That is, Deuce McAllister, the Saints running back.

"Oh, yes. Oh, sure," Karney replied.

"Good," Haslett said. "See you in camp."

Then Haslett passed the phone to Rick Mueller, the director of player personnel, and Mike McCarthy, the offensive coordinator, to congratulate Karney.

After the call, Karney turned to the houseful of people waiting to hear what was said. And it was about that moment that his name flashed across the bottom of the screen, relating that he had been drafted by the Saints.

"And then, everyone went crazy, jumping up and down and screaming," Karney said.

Mueller said he had seen films of Karney in college and had talked to his coaches.

"I knew he was our guy," he said. "He's a special kid."

In the Saints' first preseason game, against the Jets, Atkins, the running backs coach, told Karney that he would start. "I got chills up and down my spine," Karney said.

Now, he is not only the team's starting fullback, but the only fullback on the roster.

The second wish to Santa from the eight-year-old Michael Karney had been realized, 14 years later.

"You have to be completely unselfish to play Mike's position, and that's Mike," said Ernie Conwell, a tight end for the Saints and a nine-year NFL veteran who is from the same high school, Kentwood, as Karney. Their families know each other.

"I was happy that we drafted Mike, but I was concerned," Conwell said recently in front of his locker at the Saints training facility here, with Karney within earshot, several lockers away. "He had big shoes to fill, with Terrell gone. He was the new guy, and you never know. But right from the beginning, you saw how hard he worked. He's in the weight room on days off. He's watching film. He learned all the plays, even the ones that don't involve him. He just rammed into people, and he couldn't be denied. He'd run through walls if he had to. But he's made for it—look at him. No neck, no traps, just a solid block."

Conwell smiled, and so did Karney, sheepishly but appreciatively.

The Saints are struggling to get to .500 this season. "But Mike's been one of the positive forces for us," Atkins said. "He's made mistakes, but he doesn't make the same one twice."

And after the Saints beat Dallas on December 12, Mueller saw Karney sitting in the corner of the locker room, crying.

"He looked like he had gotten bad news, or maybe he was hurt," Mueller said.

Mueller went over and, as he recalled, asked, "Mike, are you okay?"

"Yeah, I'm fine," Karney said.

Then he got up and hugged Mueller. "It's just great to win," he told Mueller.

Mueller said: "The week before, Mike had missed a block on a guy, and Deuce fumbled. I know he took responsibility for the fumble. But against Dallas, he redeemed himself."

Karney, again swearing No. 44, had thrown a crushing block on Roy Williams, the Cowboys safety, opening a big hole for McAllister to complete a key touchdown run.

Late in the game, Karney said he stepped back from the huddle for a moment and looked around Texas Stadium. "It's a historic place, like Lambeau Field in Green Bay and Soldier Field in Chicago," he said. "And I thought, 'It's unbelievable. Here I am playing in the NFL and with and against guys I grew up following.' And yeah, after the game, I just couldn't stop crying. It all came true."

Karney recalled the letter he had written to the portly gentleman with the red suit and the reindeer. At some point, the letter was misplaced by his family, but they still have the football he drew for Santa at age eight.

"Do I believe in Santa Claus?" Karney said. "Yes, sir. No question about it. I believe wholeheartedly in Santa."

BRIAN URLACHER:
KEY TO THE BEARS

January 15, 2002

THE BLUE-AND-ORANGE FOOTBALL JERSEY, with No. 54 below the name, has been one of the top-selling jerseys in the NFL, and it contrasts the black and blue administered by its namesake owner, one Brian Urlacher, the singular middle linebacker for the Chicago Bears.

Urlacher, in just his second season in the league, has exhibited extraordinary traits: a swifter takeoff than a 747, a vertical leap to rival a trampoline champ, and the power on contact to cause the opponent he's aiming at to vibrate like a jackhammer. He has been instrumental in the Bears' stunning transformation from a team that finished 5–11 last season to one that went 13–3, captured the National Football Conference Central, and will play a second-round playoff game at home Saturday against the Philadelphia Eagles, Chicago's first postseason contest since January 1995.

Urlacher was named to the Pro Bowl as a rookie and was chosen the NFL's Defensive Rookie of the Year. He has been even better this season, making the NFL's first-team All-Pro squad and being selected a starter for the Pro Bowl. All this, at 23, has made Urlacher something of a household name in the Chicago area. It has, however, not quite made him a household face.

One evening earlier this season, the 6'3", 244-pound Urlacher, wearing a baseball cap over his short-cropped coiffure, went to an Aerosmith concert in a Chicago suburb. He pulled up in his black van at a specific gate. He was on the parking list. A young man was checking the list against the drivers.

"Urlacher," Brian Urlacher said to him.

"Like the football player?" the attendant asked.

"Yeah," Urlacher said.

The attendant perused the list.

"Here it is, okay, go ahead," he said.

As Urlacher drove in, he wondered to himself, "How many Urlachers can there be in Chicago?"

But there are surely at least two selves in Brian Urlacher.

There is Urlacher the star football player, who consistently amazes his peers. "You get a good sense of him in practice," said Danny Wuerffel, a backup quarterback. "Every defensive player has an area, and as a quarterback you get to learn how far and how fast they can cover it. Well, Brian has a very large area. I remember throwing a pass in the end zone and the closest guy to him was Brian. He was well behind Brian. But Brian not only sped to the spot, he had just an explosive leap and was able to slap the ball away. It was incredible."

Then there is the homespun, the earthy, the unassuming Urlacher. "He has this humility that's genuine," Bears coach Dick Jauron said. "You ask him about some exceptional play he's made, and he's really reluctant to talk about it."

Wuerffel added: "I've seen other stars in the locker room acting like they have a chip on their shoulder, or that you're just lucky to be in their presence. Not Brian. His attitude is more like a third-string college walk-on."

An example of this attitude is the fumble he picked up and returned for a 90-yard touchdown against Atlanta on October 7.

How did he feel when he came into the end zone for the score?

"Tired," he said. "It was a long way."

And when he scored another touchdown, December 23 against Washington, after catching a pass on a fake field goal, he celebrated by handing the ball to Bears kicker Paul Edinger.

"You spike it," Urlacher said, and the surprised Edinger did.

Urlacher later explained, "I didn't want to spike it because I don't like when guys spike it on me."

His most thrilling moment this season? "When Mike Brown scored that touchdown in overtime against San Francisco," he said of the Bears' dramatic 37–31 victory on October 28. "I was lying on the ground and thinking, 'We're actually going to win this game!'" The Bears came back from a 19-point deficit to tie the game in regulation.

What Urlacher doesn't say is that on the winning play, his looming presence may have unnerved 49ers receiver Terrell Owens, causing Owens to bobble the ball. It then squirted into the hands of Brown, the Bears' free safety, who raced 33 yards with the interception for the winning score.

Urlacher, from the pocket-sized city of Lovington, New Mexico, (population 9,471), may also have the perspective of the humble; he was drafted out of New Mexico in the first round, as the ninth pick overall in the 2000 draft, but the Bears slotted him as a strong-side linebacker.

He had played that position in college, as well as safety, and was also a receiver and return specialist. But outside linebacker didn't work for him with the Bears.

"Rosie Colvin beat me out," Urlacher said, referring to linebacker Rosevelt Colvin.

With fate playing its tricky game, however, the Bears' starting middle linebacker, Barry Minter, went down with a back injury. In a kind of desperation move, the Bears stuck the rookie Urlacher into the middle-linebacker position in the third game of the regular season.

In his first game as the starting middle linebacker, against the Giants in Chicago, Urlacher made an impressive 11 tackles, including eight solos, and a sack. He led the team in tackles in 10 games. Minter never got the position back.

"I needed more space to roam; I was too confined at outside linebacker," Urlacher said.

He needed to fly, which he has done for the Bears. But as good as he's been at middle linebacker—and many believe he is in the same class with the Baltimore Ravens' Ray Lewis, the NFL's premier middle linebacker—he still has a lot to learn.

"At first, I was just running around on the field, not sure where to go," Urlacher said. "So I just kinda followed the ball."

Jauron, though, appreciates Urlacher's work ethic and intensity. "Everyone progresses at different rates," he said. "Brian's progess has been pretty swift."

Urlacher no longer feels lost. He is now calling the signals on defense, and his teammates, according to Jauron, listen intently. "This season," Urlacher said, "I know where everyone is on the field."

He follows a great Bears tradition of outstanding linebackers, beginning with Bill George who virtually invented the position in 1954, when he dropped off the line.

But there has been no better middle linebacker for the Bears, or anyone else for that matter, than Dick Butkus.

"He's been pretty critical of me," Urlacher said. "But that's okay. He's a Hall of Famer. He can say anything he wants."

What Butkus said was: "To me, it seemed like he didn't run through a tackle. He doesn't punish the runner."

Butkus also didn't like the fact that Urlacher would knock a player down, then help the poor limp player up. It was good sportsmanship, Urlacher felt, performing a duty akin to a Red Cross aide.

"Quit shaking hands and patting everybody on the back," Butkus said.

Urlacher took this in. "I like hitting someone so hard that they don't know where they are," he said, "but I don't want to be a jerk about it."

Urlacher and the Bears are looking toward the playoffs, and perhaps the first trip to the Super Bowl for the team since the 1985 season of Walter Payton, the Fridge, and Mad McMahon.

As for the number of Urlachers in Chicago, there is one other listed in the phone book. Sandwiched between Urkovich and Urlab is Evelyn Urlacher on the South Side.

Otherwise, Brian Urlacher stands alone in Chicago. And football observers are coming to the conclusion that there is no one anywhere quite like him.

THE FRIDGE AT THE
THANKSGIVING TABLE

November 29, 1985

LAST THANKSGIVING, WILLIAM "THE Refrigerator" Perry was uncon-
cerned about his weight, which was zero on some scales. That is, he stepped
on the scale and when the needle zoomed past the maximum, 350, it came
to rest back on zero.

Last Thanksgiving, Refrigerator Perry enjoyed dinner at his in-laws,
the Broadwaters of Aiken, South Carolina. And what, Refrigerator Perry
was asked by phone yesterday, did they serve?

"You name it—it was there," he said. What did you eat? "A little of
everything," he said.

A little of everything, he was asked, or a lot of everything? "Both," said
Perry. This Thanksgiving at home in Chicago, it was, in fact, only a little
of everything—a little of the turkey that his wife, Sherry Perry, cooked,
and a little of the trimmings and the stuffing and the broccoli and the
cauliflower and the Brussels sprouts and the two sweet potato pies and
the two coconut pies.

Some philosophers theorize that Refrigerator Perry, who stands 6'2",
has a 22-inch neck and sports a 52-inch waist, has suddenly become a
beloved national phenomoneon because he is not only galloping for touchdowns for the Chicago Bears—coach Mike Ditka imports from the defensive unit when the team has the ball close to the goal line—but that he is
flouting our madness for thinness, and doing it with gusto.

Actually, Refrigerator Perry is on a diet and watches his behemoth's
weight like a hawk. He is down to 308 and holding steady.

The Bears, who drafted him as a defensive lineman in the first round out of Clemson last April, decided that his best playing weight was between 305 and 310. He was up to about 380 pounds last year, but reported to training camp in August at 325. It took him only a matter of weeks to slim down to his present poundage. Twice a week now, on Tuesdays and Fridays, the team weighs in.

It is in Perry's contract that at each weigh-in during the season he receives a bonus of $1,000 if he comes in at 310 or under.

He's thrilled about it. "I haven't missed on a thousand dollars but once," he said.

Mrs. Perry considered holding off Thanksgiving dinner until after the weigh-in on Friday, but decided against it. "William is careful at the table," she said.

What then are the diet secrets of Refrigerator Perry?

"For one thing," said Sherry Perry, "he doesn't eat as fast as he used to. I remember at a Wendy's when I first saw him eat a hamburger. He ate half of it in one bite. I said, 'Gosh, William, slow down.'

"And at dinner, I'd be amazed at him eating and eating and eating. I'd say, 'William, isn't that enough?'"

The Perrys have been married for three and a half years, and in the beginning, Mrs. Perry said, "cooking for William was very hectic."

"You have to remember," she added, "that I wasn't used to this kind of eating. I'm 5'5" and weigh 120 pounds and I've always eaten small portions.

"To keep William's weight down now, I put the food away after dinner, and don't let it set out. He used to love to finish dinner and then help himself to whatever was left over.

"And William used to sit in front of the television and drink cans of beer and snack the whole time on potato chips and cookies and what have you. There was no weight limit when he played for Clemson. Now, William is showing a lot of control. I'm proud of him. He doesn't snack at all. He says it doesn't bother him, and it seems to be true."

So popular is the Bears' hefty rookie that in Chicago many people have a picture of The Refrigerator on their refrigerator. Do the Perrys?

"All we have on our refrigerator," said Mrs. Perry, "is the door."

William says he has a lot to be thankful for this Thanksgiving. "I thank the Good Lord for giving me health and strength and my little girl"—the

Perrys have a three-year-old daughter, Latavia—"and my wonderful wife and a good family.

"I've been blessed. I'm thankful that Coach Ditka gave me a chance, and I'm grateful for all that's happened to me. It's crazy, and sometimes my wife and I sit down at night and look at each other and laugh about the whole thing. Do you really believe this? But it's been great. I mean, all the popularity, all the endorsement opportunities, all the good feelings. And I'm not going to change just because I got this and I got that. I'm still going to be the same old William Perry. It's me, as I am, same personality, same kid who grew up with a family of 12 brothers and sisters, same kind of character."

He was reminded that he wasn't quite the William Perry of old. There is a little less of him.

"Weightwise," he said with a laugh, "yes. But that's all."

The other change, of course, is that on occasion Ditka installs The Refrigerator in the backfield.

"I don't know all that much about football," said Mrs. Perry, "and when we were in college I used to say to William, 'I'd love it if you ran with the ball.' And he'd say, 'Sherry, don't even say that. It's something I'll never do.'"

At first this season, he was put into the backfield to plow holes for the lean running backs. Then, in a startling development, he was given a chance to carry the ball and ran for two touchdowns, each was for one yard—on the last, a week ago, he dived over the line like Walter Payton, or Walter Mitty. He has also caught a four-yard scoring pass, and leaped up with glee and spiked the ball.

"To tell you the truth," said Mrs. Perry, "I'd love for him to run a long one with the ball. I'd like to see him run through a whole team, meet 'em and knock 'em down flat and keep going.

"I love to see number 72 go in the game. I just wait to see what William's going to do next."

She is not alone. A goodly number of football fans, and other members of an intrigued and delighted citizenry, watch and wait with her.

DICK PLASMAN:
WITH A HOLE IN HIS HEAD

January 5, 1985

THE TALK WAS ABOUT hardnosed and hardheaded football players, and the name of Dick Plasman naturally came up. Not only was Plasman hardheaded when he played, he was bareheaded, too.

Dick Plasman was the last man in the National Football League to play without a helmet, as late as 1947. He also coached without a helmet in the National Football League, but that is beside the point.

In the early days of football, at least into the 1930s, playing bareheaded was not rare. But such historical players have been taking a bad rap in recent times. Perhaps the unkindest cut was made by Lyndon Johnson about Gerald Ford: "He played one too many games without a helmet."

Ford, in fact, wore a helmet—a thin leather covering, but a helmet nonetheless—as a center for Michigan in the 1930s. Plasman wore nothing on his head but a shock of blond hair, part of which covered a hole in his head, a result of a gridiron mishap.

Plasman, who died in retirement at age 67 in 1981, played for the Chicago Bears and the Chicago Cardinals, and later became an assistant coach with the Green Bay Packers and the Pittsburgh Steelers. With the Bears, he was, at 6'4" and 220 pounds, an offensive end, linebacker, and occasional kicker from 1937 through 1941, during the team's glory days as the Monsters of the Midway, and in the 1944 season.

Plasman served in the military during World War II, then joined the Cardinals and played with them for two seasons, 1946 and 1947. In the time he was away, the NFL had instituted a rule that made wearing a helmet mandatory, much to Plasman's dismay. He protested that this would cause a hardship on him, that this was an unfair labor practice. The league reconsidered and issued a special dispensation to Plasman, comparable to baseball's exempting the old spitball pitchers when rules were changed while they were still active.

Plasman was primarily a kicker with the Cardinals, and so didn't get much involved in head-to-head confrontations. Not so in his earlier days, when he received the hole in his head, which was actually a deep indentation in the acreage around his left temple.

It was obtained one fall Sunday in 1938 at Wrigley Field. Skull untrussed and hands outstretched, Plasman raced into the end zone for a pass, following the flight of a ball he would not catch. He never considered the outfield wall that jutted two feet into the end zone. In later days, the field would be resituated, and mats would be hung on the wall. Too late, though, for Plasman's pate. He crashed headfirst into the bricks.

When he woke up, a few days later, his head was finally covered, but with bandages. He lay in a hospital bed.

Sometimes there are indeed blessings in disguise. This was one of those times. An attractive nurse was ministering to him, and, if there was something wrong with Plasman's head at this point, there was nothing wrong with his eyes. When he left the hospital, he took the nurse with him, and married her.

Plasman soon returned to the football field, but still with no helmet, opting for more skull drudgery. But he had a reason: the leather chapeau of those days would drop disconcertingly over his eyes like the broken visor of a knight's armor. Besides, Plasman never liked to wear hats of any sort, and in the Army—he made the rank of captain—was nearly court-martialed once for strolling about the base with a denuded cranium.

Plasman was visited a few years ago while living in Arlington Heights, Illinois, a Chicago suburb. At the time, he was selling optical equipment, and he seemed to have weathered his days of playing without a helmet quite nicely. He said he thought of the crevice in his head only when he touched it. (Still, he did have a few other aches and pains. For one thing, he couldn't sleep on his right side, because of old football injuries—one of which was due to his never having worn hip pads.)

It seemed that his wife, June, considered the crash into the wall more than he did. When they had a disagreement, she explained to him, "You know something, you never recovered from that head injury."

Plasman recalled that only one opponent ever took advantage of his unhelmeted head. This was a defensive end with the Redskins who "kept bashing me with his elbow," said Plasman. One day the guy lay on the ground after a play, and Plasman stepped on him. "It worked," said Plasman, "and the guy stopped his antics." Plasman smiled, showing the bridgework that had replaced his football-lost teeth.

Hadn't Plasman feared injury as a player? He said no: "If you hustled and weren't lazy, you wouldn't get hurt." He added that if someone gave you a "real good shot," it wouldn't matter whether you were wearing protection or not. "The bells would be ringing," he said.

During his years as a coach with Pittsburgh, he was a favorite on the team, recalls Art Rooney, owner of the Steelers. "He was smart and had the touch with the ballplayers," Rooney said.

As a coach, Plasman still refused to wear headgear. And on the sidelines once he suffered frostbite of the ear.

Even though all modern players wear helmets, Plasman said he respected them. And he believed that they were bigger and smarter and faster than those in his day. Did that mean he'd have worn something on his head if he had played today?

"Yes," he said. "Earmuffs."

IV.

A CLUSTER
OF KICKERS

MATT BAHR: WHERE THE KICK FITS IN

January 25, 1991

GROWN MEN AND WOMEN turned from their television sets because the tension they felt was so great. Huge people in shoulder pads knelt on the sidelines, helmets bowed, as the game clock in Candlestick Park was stopped at ":04" in the final quarter last Sunday. The hometown San Francisco fans were on their feet in anticipation. The Giants, as the football world knows, were behind to the 49ers by 13–12, and were 24 yards from the goal line. Time for one last play, a play that would determine the outcome of the game, and which team would go to the Super Bowl to meet the Buffalo Bills.

In what appear to be kicking situations, Matt Bahr, the Giants' field-goal specialist, always sidles up beside the head coach, Bill Parcells, and waits to be told if he will be dispatched into the game. He now waited to learn if he would be sent in with the contest squarely his to win or lose.

"We put the ball in the middle of the field for you," Parcells said to Bahr. The assignment was clear. No "Win this for the Gipper." It was strictly a business proposition. And so Bahr trotted out to do his job.

What made much of this so gripping, and what often makes sports so captivating, is that much of what many of us do in our daily lives is crystallized on an athletic field in one moment, framed, as it were, for all of the spectators to see and hear and feel.

All of us endure pressure in many ways, sometimes many times, every day. But rarely is it so highlighted as in a football game on national television, and in the last seconds of a championship game. It is the magnification of the microcosmic.

Every day, most of us wrestle with issues and situations that are considerably heavier with consequence than the outcome of a football game:

What's the best approach to try to keep your kid off drugs? How do I make this sale to keep my job to feed my family? Should I walk the picket line? The surgeon better make the correct incision. The teacher has to make the book come alive. The munitions maker better tighten all the bolts properly.

But now in one high-profile moment many watched the flight of a football.

"I didn't notice the guys kneeling on the sidelines," Bahr said. "I guess you could say I was fighting the rush of adrenaline. Sure, I knew the score, and what this meant to the team. But I had to focus on my job. I try to take the same attitude to kicking an extra point in the first quarter of a game as I do kicking a field goal in the last seconds with the game on the line.

"I go out there and go through a kind of checklist: feeling the turf around the ball for my footing, and getting back in a comfortable position, and telling myself not to freeze in the starting position. I try to remember: head down, start slow and accelerate at the target, and follow through it."

It's funny, he said, that when he's on the field, he doesn't feel the nervousness in such predicaments as he has when watching someone else in them on television, like his brother, Chris, a former field-goal kicker for the Raiders in the Super Bowl. "I remember when I saw Chris in a similar situation," said Bahr, "I thought, 'How can he take the pressure?'"

In Candlestick, there was the snap, the hold, the kick.

"The ball was drifting a little bit left," recalled Bahr, "and when I saw that it was good, I didn't jump up and down. I just breathed a sigh of relief."

Then he turned to his ball holder, Jeff Hostetler, to slap palms with him in their great triumph. But it was inconvenient at that moment for Hostetler to slap palms with anyone since he was standing on his head.

Bahr is a seasoned pro—he has been kicking for several teams in the National Football League for 12 years—and his approach to his job, cool and narrowly focused in a kind of caldron of emotion, was noteworthy.

We tend to make heroes of such people in sports. But Bahr doesn't see himself in this light. "You're only as good as your next kick," he said. "This game is very ephemeral. You see players come and go all the time. And not just kickers, who are almost like gypsies in football, but everyone."

He has come and gone himself, from the Pittsburgh Steelers, from the Cleveland Browns, and, one day, certainly, from the Giants, too.

He has earned a master's degree in business, and one day will apply other skills in tense moments, as does his brother, Chris, who is now an attorney.

Matt Bahr has missed big field goals, too, but for one marvelous moment he was all of us, breathing a sigh of relief at having made the sale, or the incision, or opening a new vista of understanding for a child, or seeing your anti-missile missile explode on target.

The Super Bowl is Sunday. The pressure, as it were, mounts.

ERIC SCHUBERT'S WINDY SYMPHONY

November 5, 1985

IN THE HUGE, ECCENTRIC bowl that is Giants Stadium, the ribbons fluttering on the goal posts Sunday afternoon indicated that the wind was blowing in opposite directions.

For a meteorologist, this could cause concern. For a field-goal kicker, it could cause a coronary.

But not for Eric Schubert, the Giants' brand-new place-kicker—he had never played in a regular-season game for the Giants before, and had never played in the National Football League. Today, he is also the Giants' brand-new hero.

The raw wind was just one more obstacle that Schubert would have to overcome, and overcome it in front of a network television audience, in front of 72,031 fans in the stands, and in front of 11 large people from Tampa intent on, well, if not dismantling him, then at least distracting him.

Five times he was called on to send a football sailing straight between the uprights, and five times he did it, for 24 yards, 36, 24, 41, and 33. Eric Schubert's 16 points (including an extra-point kick after the Giants' lone touchdown) were instrumental—decisive, in fact—in the Giants' 22–20 victory.

Just before kickoff Sunday afternoon, the official reading of the wind was 13 miles per hour from the northeast. But that's in the parking lot. The wind swoops into the stadium and proceeds to swirl around the field as if lost in a maze. Schubert, unlike most field-goal kickers, didn't fidget. He didn't check the flags for wind currents; he didn't raise a finger to test velocity; he didn't inquire nervously about who was the holder, who was the center.

Schubert couldn't be bothered. He was there to kick, not to test atmospheric conditions.

In the relatively short, sometimes disappointing football life of the 23-year-old Schubert, the wind has not always, as the saying goes, been at his back.

When he was graduated from Lakeland Regional High School in Wanaque, New Jersey, he had several small-college offers to play football, but said he wanted to go to a big-time football school and then kick in the pros.

He went to the University of Pittsburgh, and made the team as a walk-on.

He was a good place-kicker for Pitt. Then in his senior year in 1983, he kicked off against Syracuse and his foot hit the newly painted insignia on the field, and he dislocated his right kneecap. He was not chosen in the NFL draft, and he was, he said, "very upset."

He then signed with the Pittsburgh Maulers of the United States Football League and made five of eight field-goal attempts. It wasn't enough to save the franchise. The Maulers folded.

"Then I tried out with the New Jersey Generals, and they cut me," he said. "I went to camp with the New England Patriots, and they cut me. I had done well in both places. I called other teams. They said not now."

In the exhibition season, he watched a Giants game on television, saw that Ali Haji-Sheikh, the regular place-kicker, was hurt, and the next day threw his cleats into the back seat of his 1970 AMX sports car and drove to the Giants' training camp in Pleasantville, New York, arriving 35 minutes later.

He announced he was there, and asked for a tryout. He got it, and kicked in two games. The last, on a Saturday night, was won in overtime against the Jets with a field-goal boot by Schubert. The players seemed to love him. Here was this cocky little stranger off the street who came in to win a game. "Schubie, Schubie," shouted Phil Simms and Lawrence Taylor, with delight. The veteran players invited him to play golf.

But on Monday, Schubie was cut, again.

"Sure," said Schubert, "I was upset."

Now, some three months later, Sunday Schubert was finally getting a chance in a real, live regular-season NFL game.

Small for a football player at 5'7" and 190 pounds, he had also been distant for a football player, working until a few days ago as a $36-a-day substitute high school teacher at Lakeland Regional, taking over classes in French or Latin or auto shop or mechanical drawing, or anything else, whether familiar with the subject or not, usually not.

After school he helped coach the varsity football team for $1,000 a season. Every day following practice, Schubert kept his leg trim and his pro football hopes alive by booting footballs off a tee into the darkening sky.

"He kept telling me that one day he'll kick in the NFL," said the varsity coach, Al Guazzo.

Last Tuesday night, he received a note at practice that Bill Parcells, coach of the Giants, had called. Schubert went to a phone and called Parcells back.

"Are you in shape?" Parcells asked. "We're looking for a kicker." Haji-Sheikh was suffering with a tender hamstring.

The following morning, Schubert, at Giants Stadium, booted while the Giants coaches watched and whispered.

When Schubert finished, Parcells said, "I'll call you tonight."

That night, there was no call from Parcells. The next night, Thursday night, Schubert went out to try his luck elsewhere. Shortly after he left the house—he lives with his in-laws, the Florios—his wife, Michelle, answered the ringing phone. It was Coach Parcells. "Oh no," said Michelle, "the little son-of-a-gun is out buying a lottery ticket."

Parcells laughed, recalling the conversation. "I guess she thought it would terminate the deal. But Eric called back five minutes later." The deal was on. And when the game was over Sunday, Schubert, said Parcells, made "one of the gutsiest performances I've seen in a long time."

It's possible but highly doubtful that Haji-Sheikh, on the injured-reserve list, will return to action this week. Teams don't normally keep two field-goal kickers.

"I hope that other teams saw what I can do," said Schubert. "And if I don't stay with the Giants, maybe I can get picked up someplace else."

And if Sunday's hero was back next week teaching Latin or auto shop at Lakeland Regional, how would he feel?

"Nothing against the high school," said Schubert, "but if that happened, I think I'd be pretty upset."

THE KICK NORWOOD CAN'T FORGET

January 22, 1992

SCOTT NORWOOD REMEMBERS IT, feels it—more than anyone else, surely, his 47-yard field-goal attempt with four seconds to go in the Super Bowl last year, a kick that sailed wide right by about six feet, and resulted in the Giants beating Buffalo, 20–19.

In the locker room afterward, stunned and shocked and deeply disappointed, Norwood was talking with a crush of reporters when Ralph Wilson, the owner of the Bills, broke through and grabbed his hand. "It wasn't you, Scott, remember, you didn't lose the game," said an insistent Wilson. "We had a lot of chances to win it."

The Bills held a post–Super Bowl party that night, but Scott Norwood did not attend. He was out with his wife, Kim, driving in a rented car around Tampa, Florida, aimlessly, distraught, she trying to console him. They stopped at a fast-food stand for a dinner of submarine sandwiches, then returned to their hotel. It was a mostly sleepless night for him, the failed kick seeming to burn in his brain.

The plane ride back to Buffalo was long and agonizing. Though his teammates were comforting, he still worried that he had let them down, let down an entire city, in fact.

"In Buffalo, the whole focus is on the Bills," he said recently. "Washington, for example, has politics and other diversions. Buffalo mostly has football."

At Niagara Square, on the steps of the Buffalo City Hall, the returning Super Bowl also-rans were, however, honored and cheered by 30,000 fans. Soon they sent up a chant: "We want Scott! We want Scott!"

"Scott? Scott? Is he here?" asked the master of ceremonies. Norwood was standing in the back, behind other players, seeming to wish to disappear.

He came forward. "We love Scott!" they cried. "We love Scott!"

Norwood spoke into the microphone on the podium. "I know I've never felt more loved than this right now," he told the crowd, and his voice broke and tears moistened his eyes. "I am going to dedicate the next season to all of you." And the cheers rang out again, and again.

Yesterday, though, at the Bills' news conference in the Metrodome, the site of Super Bowl XXVI, Norwood said that he wasn't looking back, that he had to remain positive about Washington and keep the same kind of confidence, mechanics, and perspective that has kept him, at age 31, kicking field goals and extra points in the National Football League for seven years.

"It was one kick in a career of a hundred kicks," he said about his final kick last year. "I went out and did the best I can." To other questions from the media: "No, it won't affect my play on Sunday. I'm glad we have a second chance to come back. Not many teams do."

He was asked if he dreams of winning the Super Bowl this year. His patient, narrow-set eyes gave a glimmer that said that was so, but his answer was more pat. "I just want our team to win," he said. "And if I can play a part in it, then fine."

Someone remembered a dream he had last year, and which Vic Carucci, a reporter for *The Buffalo News*, wrote about in his paper on the day before last year's game. He said he'd had a dream on Wednesday that he won the Super Bowl with a field goal. The headline of Carucci's story read NORWOOD CONFIDENT HE CAN WIN GAME IN FINAL SECONDS.

"I try to visualize the positive before I come on the field to kick," Norwood was saying yesterday. "I try to think about all the kicks I made, how they felt, how they looked. That's my mental approach on every kick. I also try to keep in mind the mechanics, the most important being to keep your head down and your eyes on the ball."

He had his good days and bad this season. Against the Raiders, he missed three field goals and an extra point. But in the AFC title game against Denver, he kicked a 44-yard field goal that would stand up as the margin of victory, 10–7.

His highlight this season, possibly, was against the Jets in Giants Stadium. And though it wasn't the Giants he was playing against, it was still their stadium, and it was the New York fans.

He had heard boos from them, and derisive calls. Then he kicked a 52-yard field goal and all of his emotion and frustration and exultation seemed to burst forth. Surprising even his teammates, he turned and pointed to each section of the stands and shouted: "That's for you! That's for you! That's for you!"

"You never step on the football field unless you think you can do the job," he said. "I know I can do the job."

Then he added: "No, I don't think about last year. I've put it totally out of my mind."

His mouth said it. His heart may have wished to believe it. But his eyes told a different story.

VINATIERI'S RARE MISS MAKES NO DIFFERENCE

December 27, 2004

EAST RUTHERFORD, NEW JERSEY—AN unusual moment took place with one second remaining in the first half of the Jets-Patriots game Sunday.

It was a quiet happening, and inconsequential. And while the crowd of 77,975 at Giants Stadium saw it all in the flesh—goose-pimply flesh, likely, considering that it was bitter cold—the teeth-chattering multitude may not have been quite aware of its eventual unimportance.

Adam Vinatieri, whose field-goal kicking is nearly as consistent as the sun coming up in the morning, lined up to attempt a 50-yarder. This is the same Vinatieri who had made 28 of 29 field-goal attempts this season, who had won Super Bowls with field goals in the final seconds in two of the past three years, and who has succeeded with 15 game-winning kicks in his nine NFL seasons.

He had made 23 straight this season, including two earlier in the game Sunday against the Jets.

He had been called on once again, after having kicked one from 28 yards and another from 29, both in the second quarter, and having accounted for seven (including an extra point) of his team's 13 points.

Going into the Jets game, Vinatieri was the league's leading scorer, with 127 points.

"We knew that if we had to kick a 50-yarder, it was going to be tough," he said.

Now, having discarded his blue sideline cape, his silver helmet glistening under the stadium lights, he saw the snap from center to Josh Miller, the holder.

"I take a big, deep breath," he said, "try not to think of the crowd, or the wind, or the circumstances of the game, and try to just concentrate on fundamentals. No matter if it's a 25-yard kick or a 50-yard kick."

Up rose the ball into the sky, and it began to blow wide left. Referees signaled no good, and the first half ended with the Patriots ahead, 13–0.

The kick was not needed, as the Patriots won, 23–7, with Vinatieri adding a 26-yard field goal in the third quarter. "It was an important game for us," Vinatieri said. "It gave us a bye in the first week of the playoffs."

In a locker room with an abundance of big shoulders and bulging biceps, the dark-haired, 31-year-old Vinatieri, at 6'0", 200 pounds, appears small. The opposite, of course, of how he plays.

How does this Patriots team (13–2) compare to recent New England teams? "We're solid," he said. "We've added an important part in Corey."

That is, Corey Dillon, the veteran running back who was obtained this season from the Bengals, and who established a Patriots single-season rushing record with 89 yards gained against the Jets to give him 1,519.

When the Patriots play in the postseason, it will not be surprising to see Vinatieri lining up for a kick that again could mean the difference between victory and defeat.

And what does his holder, Miller, say about this? "My job is not to screw Adam up," he said. "But he's a consummate pro. The biggest thing is when I place the ball down after catching it from the center, I keep it in the ballpark. Adam is not one of those head cases—a lot of guys want the ball placed down in the same spot every time. That's nearly impossible. Adam says, 'If it's in the ballpark, that's all I need.'

"He's money. I'd have to go out of my way to screw him up."

And that is hard to do to Vinatieri, even if he is only 31 for 33 now in field-goal attempts this season.

JUSTICE BYRON WHITE:
FRIEND AND MENTOR TO NICK LOWERY

April 21, 2002

NICK LOWERY WAS HAVING a tough time of it. He had been a fine place-kicker in college, at Dartmouth, and expected a career booting balls in the National Football League.

Not so quick. Lowery was cut 11 times from eight NFL teams before catching on with the Kansas City Chiefs in 1980. He beat out, of all people, Jan Stenerud, who to this day is the only place-kicker in the Pro Football Hall of Fame.

And things hardly got better for Lowery in his first training camp with the Chiefs. He was the butt of numerous pranks; he was not only a rookie but a rookie from the Ivy League, which carried with it a special kind of contempt in that bruising environment. One evening in training camp, for example, he found fresh cow manure in his bed.

He tried to talk to his new teammates, to be one of the guys, but he encountered resistance. Shortly after that, he went home to McLean, Virginia, and sought out his next-door neighbor on Hampshire Road, who had become a friend and mentor.

The neighbor was Justice Byron R. White of the United States Supreme Court. White had also been a football player, a 6'1", 195-pound all-purpose All-American back at Colorado. He picked up the nickname Whizzer while leading the nation in rushing, in scoring, and in total offense. He was also a star basketball player, and led Colorado to a National Invitation Tournament final at Madison Square Garden. And he was a standout baseball player and the valedictorian of his graduating class.

He went to Yale Law School and to Oxford as a Rhodes Scholar. In between he played football for one season with the Pittsburgh Pirates (later the Steelers), in 1938, and two seasons with the Detroit Lions, in 1939 and 1940. He led the NFL in rushing in 1938 and 1940. Then he joined the Navy and went off to fight in World War II.

So not only did Justice White know something of the athletic world, he knew something of the world.

"Nick," Lowery said White told him, his strong bearing carrying a sense of gentle strength, "the only way you are going to get respect from those fellows is not by anything you say, but what you can deliver, how you perform on the field."

It was a simple piece of advice, but when you are foundering, when emotions cloud your perspective, it is such advice, and coming from someone like Justice White, that will make an impact. It did make one on Nick Lowery.

That and other thoughts about Justice White came back to Lowery upon learning of the death Monday of his neighbor of 40 years. White, who served 31 years on the Supreme Court, was 84.

Lowery recalled the first full year he spent with Kansas City. He had a string of 11 field goals in 12 attempts, then kicked a game-winning field goal against the Lions. The guys who had been most vicious in riding him hugged him with tears in their eyes, he recalled.

"It was exactly what Justice White had been talking about," Lowery said.

Lowery said Justice White was reluctant to talk about his athletic career—"He would always change the subject"—and was perhaps happiest discussing history and people like Abraham Lincoln and Chief Justice John Marshall.

"I was curious to see what kind of football player he was," Lowery said, "and I was able to get a film of a game he played against Utah, my father's alma mater. It was amazing. There was this one kickoff return in which he almost ran backward in the end zone, then cut straight upfield—he cut like a knife—and broke about three tackles and completely faked out four or five other players and raced in for a touchdown. He was so fast, it looked like the other players were moving in slow motion."

He remembers Justice White talking about Bill Bradley a few years after Bradley became a senator. He said he admired Bradley because it was important to have balance in life, and not enough athletes do. Bradley had achieved balance as a student and an athlete, and he taught English in a Harlem school before getting involved in public service in government.

Lowery, now 45 and retired from football since 1997 after a superb 17-year career that included seasons with the Jets and the Patriots, has taken that advice from White to heart, too. He is a research fellow at the Harvard Project on American Indian Economic Development, and the first professional athlete to graduate from the Kennedy School of Government at Harvard.

On occasion, Lowery saw glimpses of the competitiveness that made White such a great athlete. About 1977 Lowery was playing basketball in the driveway with his two brothers—all of the Lowerys are over six feet—and White's daughter, Nancy, who was a field hockey star at Stanford.

"Justice White came by and we asked him to play," Lowery said. "He said okay. He took off his tie and rolled up the sleeves of his white shirt and played in his black dress shoes. He was about 60 years old. We played for over an hour, the justice and me against the three of them. He was tough, and we killed 'em. But we all had fun. The next morning I saw Justice White go to his car on crutches.

"I went over to him. What happened? He said, 'Oh, I hurt my feet a little bit, but I'll be all right.' And he was. A few days later I saw him out in his yard mowing his lawn in his shorts."

TOM DEMPSEY: STAR TO BUM

November 5, 1972

PHILADELPHIA—"LAST YEAR I WAS on top of the world," said Tom Dempsey. "Now I'm a bum." During the 1970 season, New Orleans Saints fans shook the stadium with cheers for Tom Dempsey, inspirational hero. This season they threw tomatoes that splattered on his back and beer cans that clanked off his helmet. He was finally cut from the Saints and dropped out of football for six weeks. He was then placed on the taxi squad of the Philadelphia Eagles.

Tom Dempsey, yesterday's hero, is a field-goal kicker. He is unique in his profession in that he was born with half a right foot. He must wear a special block-toe shoe. Some opponents last season even insisted that the shoe was an unfair advantage. Last year he kicked a 63-yard field goal for New Orleans to beat Detroit 19–17 in the closing seconds of play. It was the longest field goal in pro football history, breaking a 14-year-old record by seven full yards.

Tom Dempsey became an instant national celebrity by his record kick. He was the shiningest example of a man overcoming adversity. In the off-season he received awards ranging from New Orleans American Legion Most Valuable Player to Pro Football Writers Most Courageous Player.

"A lot of people said I was cocky and that I stopped trying," said Dempsey. "That burns me up. I pushed harder than ever because I wanted to stay on top."

His problems began the first day of training camp this summer. Dempsey reported in at 265 pounds, 20 pounds more than coach J.D. Roberts had wanted him to carry.

"Tom worked hard to get the weight off, but it was tough," said Saints publicity man Harry Humes.

In the exhibition season, Dempsey made but one field goal in eight attempts. Dempsey knew his job was in jeopardy. So did all the unemployed field-goal kickers around the country. Like vultures, they smelled the dying carcass. About 20 kickers showed up in the Saints' camp. Dempsey said that the boos and the beer cans did not bother him. "They booed others, too," he said. "The fans in New Orleans are the greatest. Really. They're rabid. They pay eight dollars a game to see a job done, and they deserve the best. I guess I put too much pressure on myself to stay on top, and that screwed me up."

Dempsey was cut a week before the 1971 season started. Coach Roberts said that, yes, it was a little emotional, with Dempsey being crippled and a hero from last season. "You always feel a little bad when you have to fire someone."

Dempsey said that he was sure he'd come around soon, that it was a temporary slump. But Roberts has noted that Dempsey has never in his four-year pro career been a consistent kicker, even though he led the Saints in scoring the last two years. Last season, despite three field goals from past 50 yards, Dempsey was 11th best out of the 13 regular field-goal kickers in the National Football Conference. His kicks were good 53 percent of the time. Curt Knight, who led the league, had a 74 percent field-goal-kicking average.

Dempsey, last season's hero, began selling insurance in New Orleans. He was hurt and embarrassed. "I was married in June," he said, "and I thought my wife married a hero. Now I was thinking she married a washout. But she stuck behind me."

Dempsey continued to kick nights at a nearby park. He would chase the ball himself. And he continued to call teams, trying to hook on somewhere. One day, six weeks after he was cut by New Orleans, the Eagles said they had a job open on the taxi squad.

A member of the taxi squad does not suit up for games, does not make road trips, is not on the roster. He practices with the team, which means, in the case of kicking specialists, that he goes off by himself. Kickers are the quirks of football teams. Noncontact players in a contact sport. Dempsey is there just in case, in case regular kicker Happy Feller starts missing or is injured.

"You go through a year like I went through," said Dempsey, "going from the top to the bottom, and you know that football is a plastic world, a fantasy land. And you come to realize that there are more important things in the world than football. You come to value your home life, for example, and feel lucky that you've married the right woman. But I still love the game. And I still think I'm a good kicker. I still think I can kick in this league."

.   .   .

In the following seasons, Dempsey became the Eagles' star kicker.

How Lou Groza
Changed the Game

December 10, 2000

NORV TURNER, HIS JOB as the Washington Redskins' head coach hanging by a chin strap last month, called Eddie Murray, the former field-goal kicker, to help save his job. Murray, 44, came out of retirement and, it turned out, was unintentionally instrumental in getting Turner fired. The dismissal occurred last Monday.

It came on the heels of two straight defeats by the Redskins—the second last Sunday against the Giants—in which Murray missed crucial field goals in the final minutes that would have either tied the score or given Washington a victory.

Murray had been one of football's finest field-goal kickers, but no longer. He was also the fifth kicker of the season for the Redskins, and each of Washington's six losses has been directly related to poor field-goal kicking or special-teams play.

The Giants, meanwhile, did not mount much of an offense either in the game as Brad Daluiso kicked three field goals for all of his team's points in a 9–7 victory.

The importance of field-goal kickers in football is hardly new. It is not as old as football itself, though field goals have been. In fact, when the National Football League chose its All-Pro squads of the decades from the 1920s on, there were no field-goal kickers listed for the 1920s, 1930s, or 1940s. On the 1950s team, finally, there appears the position "kicker" and the name "Lou Groza."

Before Groza entered the league in 1950, no player had ever kicked more than 10 field goals in a season. Groza kicked 13 in his first year, and continued kicking well and dramatically as the years rolled on. In 1974, seven years after he retired, he was inducted into the Pro Football Hall of Fame.

His funeral was last Monday. Groza, nicknamed the Toe for his prowess as a field-goal kicker, was dead at 76. Coincidentally, 76 was also the number he wore as a member of the Cleveland Browns for 21 years. And the 600 or so mourners for the mass in St. Mary's Church in Berea, Ohio, included many of his former teammates, several of whom played with him from the inception of the Browns in 1946 in the old All-American Football Conference, and who were with him when the Browns joined the NFL in 1950.

There was some discussion, to be sure, of Groza's remarkable record as a player, both as a terrific kicker and as an exceptional offensive tackle. Especially early in his career, a kicking specialist was a rarity. Rosters were not set at 53, as they are today, but at 32 to 36, and teams could hardly afford a specialist.

"If we got past the 50-yard line," Otto Graham, the outstanding quarterback of the Browns in the early years, said from his home in Sarasota, Florida, "we knew we had a chance to score because we had Lou Groza to kick a field goal."

Graham recalled the 1950 NFL Championship Game against the Los Angeles Rams, when Groza kicked a field goal from 16 yards with seconds left in the game to give the Browns a 30–28 victory. Groza's record of winning championships in team sports compares remarkably with the team titans like Bill Russell and Joe DiMaggio. In the two pro leagues in which the Browns competed, Groza played in 13 championship games and the Browns won eight of them. He led the league in field goals five times, which is still the record.

"Other than for his size, you'd never have taken him for a football player," said Bill Willis, a guard on the early Browns. "I mean, he was such a gentleman. He was a big guy—6'3", 250 pounds or so—and if he told a joke, it was never off-color, and it would never embarrass anyone. I was sensitive to that, and Lou was sensitive to my feelings."

Willis, a black man, was signed by the Browns in 1946, and it broke the color barrier in pro football, which had existed since before World War II.

"There were times in games when I'd be punched by an opponent after a play, or called a black S.O.B.," Willis recalled by telephone from Columbus, Ohio. "Lou and Lou Rymkus, another lineman, said to me: 'Don't let anybody excite you. If there's trouble, tell us. We'll handle it.' I never had to say anything. We were in the trenches together and they'd know. And the two would take care of the guy. It was comforting to have teammates like that, believe me."

In the Smithsonian Institution, there stands a pair of black leather high-top cleats, size 12, with white laces, that once belonged to Groza. They are part of an exhibit that honors achievement in a variety of American endeavors.

Those shoes, to be sure, had gone a long way, in more ways than one.

V.

ON THE RUN

ROB CARPENTER CARRIES THE GIANTS

December 28, 1981

PHILADELPHIA—UNDER THE FLOODLIGHTS, ROB Carpenter spent the greater part of this dark, misting afternoon running up and down Veterans Stadium with a bunch of people in green jerseys hanging all over him. It was quite a sight.

Not only did Carpenter, the blond, stocky fullback of the Giants, routinely lug a host of Philadelphia Eagles as he made his plunges and dashes through the line, but he was also carrying the playoff hopes of his team.

He wound up the day gaining 161 yards on 33 carries, and the Giants finished with a 27–21 victory in their wildcard playoff game. The victory sent them into the National Conference semifinal game next Sunday at San Francisco against the 49ers.

And it sent the home crowd of 71,611 drooping out of the stadium, their red-and-yellow slickers glistening and their green-and-white Eagles ski hats soggy.

Carpenter didn't score any touchdowns—he didn't have to. He got the yardage when his team needed it for field position, or to set up one of the three touchdown passes by the quarterback Scott Brunner, and, finally, to keep possession of the ball as the clock ran down.

Carpenter carried all but nine of the Giants running plays from scrimmage. His 33 carries was four more than that of the entire Eagles backfield. Ever since he came to the Giants in a trade with the Oilers earlier this season, he has been the most reliable runner they have.

Several times in this game, he had the wind knocked out of him. Once, it looked particularly grievous. Near the end of the second period, after being flattened after a gain, he lay supine for several moments. Then slowly, one limb after the other hooked back together, and he returned to the huddle.

The Giants jumped to a surprising 27–7 lead at the half, and then hung on. The Eagles, the defending National Conference champions, scored a touchdown in the third period, and again in the fourth. It was now 27–21.

"We were concerned, sure," said Carpenter after the game. "Not biting our nails concerned, but hey, we knew that the Eagles were hot now, and they have a potent offense. We knew we had to control the ball. If they got it again, they could score. And we'd be finished."

The Eagles kicked off, and Louis Jackson returned the ball to the Giants' 30-yard line. There was no question about the Giants' strategy. It would be Carpenter right, Carpenter left, and Carpenter over, under, and through the middle.

But wait. An Eagle was hurt on the field. It was Jo Jo Heath, who had made the tackle on the kickoff return. He was carried off the field on a stretcher. While Heath was taken from the field, men on horseback rode on. In the old days, they would have been the cavalry coming to the rescue. Today, they are the police in white riot helmets who are there to control the crowd at game's end.

Play is resumed. Carpenter gets a handoff and bangs through for a six-yard gain. On the next play, it is Carpenter again for a three-yard gain.

There are two minutes left in the game, and the Giants have third down and one yard to go for a first down, on their 39-yard line. The game hinges on the next play. If the Giants make the first down, they can run out the clock. If not, they would have to punt, and the Eagles have time to score.

Brunner, of course, is aware of the beating Carpenter is taking. He is also aware that Carpenter came into the game with an assortment of injuries, including a bad ankle.

"How you feelin'?" Brunner asks him. "Good," says Carpenter. "If he was hurt or tired," says Brunner later, "I know he would have told me. We couldn't afford a turnover at this point." Carpenter gets the call again. He follows the center Jim Clack's block and barrels ahead for five yards and a first down. As Carpenter gets up, so do the majority of Eagles fans, who sat until this, the bitter end.

In the locker room after the game, Carpenter sat on a table in his white uniform with artificial-turf stains and spoke to a large gathering of reporters.

His blond hair was in bangs across his forehead, and his wrists and ankles were still held solid with tape. "Yes," he said, "this is the best football day of my life. It's the greatest football game I've ever played in or been associated with."

He spoke softly, as though he were rocking on the porch of his farm near Junction City, Ohio, swatting flies in the summertime. "I'd have to say," he continued, his hazel eyes brightening, "that being born, getting married, and becoming a Giant were the three greatest days of my life."

SAYERS AND PICCOLO:
TIME TO REMEMBER A COLORFUL BOND

December 1, 2001

BRIAN PICCOLO LOOKED GOOD, from the outside, that is. He was sitting in pajamas on the edge of his bed in Memorial Sloan-Kettering Cancer Center in Manhattan and coughed. "That's a legitimate cough," he told me, with a little grin. "I've got a cold." He also had a cavity in his chest where a malignant tumor the size of a grapefruit had been dug out three months earlier.

This was in late February 1970. Piccolo had returned to the hospital for a checkup and chemotherapy. "All I have to worry about now is my thinning hair," he said, smiling and scratching his head.

He was hoping that his recovery would go so well that the following season he could return to the backfield of the Chicago Bears, where he had teamed with Gale Sayers, who was to running backs what Jascha Heifetz was to violinists.

Sayers and Piccolo were more than teammates, they were close friends. While visiting Piccolo, we recalled the relationship—he was "Pick" and Sayers was "Magic"—how the two of them had been rooming together on the road for three years, unusual in those days, since Sayers was black and Piccolo was white.

Piccolo, relatively small at 6'0", 205 pounds, was primarily a part-time player, but he had replaced Sayers, who was injured in the latter part of the 1968 season, and performed well.

Piccolo, during my visit to the hospital, added, "I won't know until June whether the doctors will let me play football again." And if he didn't play again? "Well, through this whole deal I've found that football is just not the most important thing in the world. All I want to do is lead a normal life.

"I'd love to get back to football. Sure, I was about to come into my own when this happened. And I'd love to be back there with Magic. I would be disappointed if I'm not with the team when training camp opens in July. But it's not the end of the world."

He continued: "I don't think about death now. Too many other things on my mind. Business—I'm a stockbroker in the off-season—and family. I have never looked at anything negatively. A man wouldn't be worth a hill of beans if he just sat around thinking about all the bad things in his life. No, I have no time to think about death."

Brian Piccolo never played football again, nor would he ever enjoy a normal life. On June 16, four months after that hospital visit, Brian Piccolo died. He was 26 years old. His wife and three daughters survived him.

The story has been told first in Sayers' 1970 autobiography, *I Am Third*, written with Al Silverman, and again in the acclaimed television drama *Brian's Song*. The movie has been remade, starring Mekhi Phifer and Sean Maher, and is scheduled to be broadcast tomorrow at 7:00 PM on ABC.

When the movie came out, in 1971, I asked Sayers his opinion.

"I didn't like a part of the movie because it made too much of the black-white thing," he said. "We were just two cats cuttin' up. Could've been two white guys or two blacks. Pick was just good folks."

Maybe Sayers was right, that there was too much made of "the black-white thing." But too often, unfortunately, too much is made of it in a negative context. From a broader perspective, the race aspect added significant texture to a heart-rending story.

One of the most dramatic scenes in the film occurred at an otherwise mundane football writers' banquet in May 1970 at the old Americana Hotel (now the Sheraton New York Hotel and Towers) in Manhattan. I happened to attend, and was about to leave after dinner.

For some reason, I tarried at the door when Sayers rose to receive his award as comeback player of the year. He had led the National Football League in rushing after a serious knee operation the previous season.

He spoke briefly about his friendship with Piccolo and then said: "He has the heart of a giant, and that rare form of courage that allows him to kid himself and his opponent, cancer. He has the mental attitude that makes me proud to be a friend who spells out the word courage 24 hours a day for his life."

Sayers had a tendency to speak quickly, and sometimes muffle his words. But the meaning to everyone in the banquet hall was clear, and unforgettably moving.

"You flatter me by giving me this award, but I tell you here and now that I accept it for Brian Piccolo," Sayers said. "Brian Piccolo is the man of courage who should receive this award. I love Brian Piccolo and I'd like all of you to love him, too. Tonight, when you hit your knees, please ask God to love him."

Tomorrow night we can relive that moment again, and, in the best of worlds, benefit from it.

FRENCHY FUQUA IS ALIVE AND STILL DOING SWELL

August 20, 1981

DETROIT—WHATEVER HAPPENED TO FRENCHY Fuqua's glass shoes with goldfish in them? Whatever happened to Frenchy Fuqua's white musketeer hat with red, white, and purple ostrich plumes? Whatever happened to Frenchy Fuqua? "The mad Frenchman!" said John "Count Frenchy" Fuqua. "The true and only and original black count! He's alive and still doin' swell."

He sat behind a desk with a sign that read COMMUNICATE, in his glass-paneled cubicle in *The Detroit News* office where he has, he says, the longest title in the company: carrier recruitment sale crew supervisor. That is, in charge of delivery boys and girls.

Frenchy has laughing eyes and a handsome beard. He has been at this newspaper job in his hometown since he retired as a running back with the Pittsburgh Steelers in 1977, after playing nine years in professional football and winning two Super Bowl championship rings and numerous dress-offs, or haberdashery clashes.

"Pittsburgh was destined to be a championship team when I was traded there from the Giants in 1970," he said, "but what they needed was a touch of class. And that was my contribution. I put a new trend in.

"I was awesome. One outfit that wowed 'em was the Pancho Villa, with a big black sombrero and black skin-tight jump suit and knee-high white moon boots. My caveman outfit floored 'em, too: red jump suit, fur poncho, and a hell of a little bow tie to go with it.

"Pretty soon everybody started getting into it. The better we dressed, the better we played. Even Chuck Noll, the coach, got into it. One day he wore white shoes."

Frenchy laughed. "Then I get a call from a friend. 'Frenchy,' he says, 'I got somethin' real sweet for you.' 'What is it?' 'How would you like some shoes you can put goldfish in?' I said, 'Hey, I got an outfit for it.'

"It was my count suit, with the musketeer hat and gold cane and lavender cape and my valet, which was Franco Harris, who carried the cape and never let it touch ground. And, oh yes, my wine-red knickers. That's why I switched from goldfish to tropical fish. The tropical-fish colors went better with my outfits.

"The shoes were actually fiberglass clogs with three-inch heels. I had two fish in each shoe. They were a little slippery to walk in, being glass, so you'd have to hold on to a rail when you went down stairs. But my biggest problem was that the fish kept dying. I kept running and adding water, and that just got my socks wet. I experimented with a small pump that ran up my pants, but that was uncomfortable. Finally I gave up the fish but kept the shoes—and put in a terrarium."

"I remember when I tried on my caveman outfit," he said. "I said to my wife, 'Doris, will this one blow their minds?' She said, 'John, you done blew mine already.' She was afraid to go out with me with some of those outfits.

"But I was the dress-off champ, she couldn't deny that. We had these contests in the locker room. One was on local TV in Pittsburgh. I went up against L.C. Greenwood and Chuck Beatty and Lee Calland. A sportscaster announced it like a fight: 'L.C. breaks out with hot pants, but Frenchy counters with fringed briefs; Beatty slugs back with a sock; Calland whips out a shoe.'"

"But it was no contest," Frenchy said. "I won every dress-off. Once, a defensive back for the Dolphins named Henry Stuckey challenged me. It was on the beach in Miami. I come out and see he's in a pink fur coat. I refused to compete. I said, 'A fur coat? If he can't dress for the season, I want no part of this.'"

Frenchy touched the knot of his quiet red tie, against a subdued peach-colored shirt. He wore black pin-striped suit pants. "Now I have to wear more conservative clothes," he said. "But sometimes when things aren't going too swell I'll go to my garage, where I keep my old clothes and artifacts, and think about those days. You got to have a little Walter Mitty in you to get through some days, right? But not long ago I wore my count outfit to a party, and I made the mistake of bending down for a drink of water. Instant ventilation."

He will wear his Super Bowl rings when he recruits for delivery personnel in junior high schools. "I was fortunate—to be a pro football player, to play in the Super Bowl, and to play on two winners," he said. "That's double the pleasure. When I make my pitch, it'd better be fast and good, because kids don't have a long attention span, and they don't want to work unless you can inspire them. Well, I say, 'Hey, any of you want to be pro football or basketball or tennis players?' Naturally. Then I go straight to the blackboard. I say, 'Did you know that every year 250,000 college kids are eligible for the pro draft but only 1,600 are drafted? And that only about 180 make the teams?' They say, 'Wow, is that all?'

"I say, 'I don't refer to football as a career. It's a stepping stone. I know too many ballplayers who were lost when opportunity didn't knock on their door.

"'But there's a way to prepare yourself. Now.' Now they're quiet, listening close. 'Start off learning a little something about business—and you can do that with a *Detroit News* route! You'll freeze your butt, you'll get mad when some people don't pay—but you're your own boss.' Then I destroy 'em with the prizes and gifts they can win. Sometimes I get so many applications I can't handle 'em all.

"It's challenging, it's fun. There were adjustments to be made after football—you're off the pedestal, the money takes a big drop. I know a lot of guys who've had grievous problems after they retired. But I've landed darned good. You know, I wrote a poem about my life."

And he recited:

> I swam the ocean and didn't get wet
> A mountain fell on me and I ain't dead yet.
> Horses and elephants trampled my hide
> A cobra bit me and crawled off and died.
> I hitchhiked on lightning, rode with thunder

Made people wonder. Whoa, whoa.
Yes, I'm a man of some ability, with much more agility
Often imitated, but never duplicated.

Frenchy Fuqua, the true and only and original black count, smiled, leaned back and loosened his tie. It had been quite a long journey.

JOHN RIGGINS AND
LIFE WITHOUT BLOCKERS

December 15, 1991

HE IS STILL ASKED on the street, "Hey, Riggo, how's Sandy baby?"

And John Riggins must answer in all candor: "Don't know. Haven't seen her lately." And he still hasn't heard from her, either, even after sending a dozen roses as an apology to her at her Supreme Court office.

The apology came after the last time—the only time—he saw her, almost seven years ago, in January 1985, when Riggins, then a star running back for the Washington Redskins and the hero of their 1983 Super Bowl victory, was seated across the table from Justice Sandra Day O'Connor and her husband, John, at the black-tie National Press Club dinner in Washington. Riggins, trying to make conversation while inebriated, called out: "C'mon, Sandy, baby. Loosen up. You're too tight."

Then he got up to talk to her husband, but never quite made it around the table. He collapsed and fell asleep under a chair, in his tuxedo and cowboy boots, pinning the wife of Senator John Glenn into her seat—"I must have been like an 18-wheeler lying there," he recalled. He stayed there, snoring, for about an hour, though the Justice was gone by the time he was awakened and escorted from the premises by the security guards. (He also sent a dozen roses to Mrs. Glenn and the three or four other women at the table that night.)

Riggins spoke about his life and times earlier this week in the quiet of a Manhattan restaurant. Upon arrival, the 6'3" Riggins, following the maitre d'hotel as he once followed blockers, easily made his way between tables, busboys, and waiters as easily as he shed tacklers on the football field. He weighs 240 pounds, just five pounds more than in his playing days, and it appeared that all he needed was to remove his turquoise bolo tie and black corduroy sports jacket and don helmet and pads to take his place in the Redskins backfield for their game this afternoon against the Giants in Robert F. Kennedy Stadium in Washington.

"In those days," said Riggins, "I thought people in Washington didn't allow themselves to enjoy a party. They were stiff. That wasn't my idea of a real hoedown good time. I liked to have people swinging from the chandeliers. I'd like to think I've grown up a little since then."

The speaker when Riggins was motivated to take his snooze under the table happened to be the vice president of the United States, George Bush. "He wrote me afterward," said Riggins, "and said something like, 'Well, John, we all have our bad days.'"

Riggins, now 42 years old and retired from football for six seasons, told this story with a bit of a sheepish grin on his face, a broad, intelligent face with eyes that look as though they still, on occasion, might covet a chandelier.

Much has happened for Riggins since his last game in pro football, in December 1985: a recent divorce, difficulties accepting separation from his four children, living for a reclusive year and a half in a trailer on the Potomac River, and perhaps some problems with alcohol. He has begun a career in radio (he does commentary on football on a radio talk show in Washington). And now, he hopes, to begin one in acting, too. He plans to move back to New York from his home in northern Virginia. Meanwhile, he still keeps an eye on football.

He wondered about the motivation of the Redskins for the Giants game today, one that is meaningless in the standings. "I know I'd be bored to tears right now if I was on the team."

Somehow, one got the feeling that he would, as he usually did, find something to relieve the boredom, as he usually did. He has been called variously "independent," "boorish," "witty," and, to be sure, "bibulous." One time he wore an Afro, later a Mohawk, and sometimes he shaved his head bald.

He held out for all of one season, 1980, because the contract the Redskins offered wasn't to his liking. "And something else. It was a kind of revenge against the owners. There's a seamy side to football. There's the thing about when you're hurt and they stick a needle in your arm and say, 'Okay, go back out there.' And there's the way they treat the players, like some of my friends, who were dropped when they weren't of any more use. I had just gotten fed up with some of that stuff."

Riggins was a country boy from Kansas, from the small town of Centralia (population: 500), but had learned that he didn't have to do things in a small-town way, or the way others wanted him to. And that if he could carry a football, eventually people would come around to him. And it happened. The season after Riggins sat out, the Redskins paid him close to what he asked for and he would repay them by becoming one of their finest runners. He led them to Super Bowl XVII in January 1983, in which he made a spectacular 43-yard run against Miami that broke open the game in the fourth quarter and helped the Redskins win, 27–17. He ran for a total of 166 yards, then a Super Bowl record.

"Not many athletes have a big game in the biggest game there is," said Riggins, "and it changed my life in a number of ways. One of them was that it made Washington kind of a small town for me, Centralia all over again. I'd walk down the street and people would be calling, 'Riggo.' You have to remember, Washington only has two things that most of the people there care about, government and the Redskins. And a lot of the time they don't care for the government."

Sometimes, Riggins' way of relieving his boredom was not always in his best interests. John Riggins, as he admits, likes to drink, although he says that he is not an alcoholic. He is able to stop for long periods of time and then return to moderate drinking. "I've heard that an alcoholic is someone whose life and work is affected by drinking," he said. "I don't think my work was. I mean, I played 14 years in the NFL, and I was the oldest running back, at 36, to gain more than 1,000 yards. Me and the woolly mammoth."

He still holds records for most touchdowns scored in a season, 24, in 1982, and his 104 career rushing touchdowns are third behind Walter Payton's 110 and Jim Brown's 106.

He drank regularly after practice. "To celebrate," he said. "I was always looking for a reason to celebrate. And the Redskins understood that I did what they wanted me to do on the field, so they put up with my off-the-field stuff."

But his drinking did get him into a problem with the law. In one publicized case, in 1985, he was arrested as an intoxicated passenger in a car in Reston, Virginia. "At least I had the good sense not to drive in my condition," he said, "but the police stopped the car because they felt my friend was too drunk to be driving. And when they were going to arrest him, I said, 'Hoo, I'm not going to let him take the rap.' So I got into trouble, too."

He said he didn't think his problems with his divorce had anything to do with drinking. "My ex-wife may disagree with me," he said, "but I think she might disagree with me on a lot of issues."

When they separated in January 1989, Riggins bought a 21-foot trailer and went to live in it on a piece of property that he owns along the Potomac River in Virginia. "When I moved out of the house, I couldn't see myself renting an apartment," he said. "I wanted to try living alone, isolated, like that." But he said he also lived in the trailer "for pecuniary reasons." "I had money from football," he said, "but I was never sure how far it would go."

He retired from football after the 1985 season and had not thought much of his future. He had a lot of time to think about this in his trailer, as he hauled water to drink. And he wondered about all this on freezing mornings in his sleeping bag when all the heat was off and the frost was on the window.

"And I thought, 'Well, what do I do now?' The one thing I knew I didn't want to do was get out of that sleeping bag."

He seemed, to an outsider, the classic case of the man-child ex-athlete who can't grow up, and who was lost in the so-called real world. "I don't know about whether I had lost my way," said Riggins. "It was more like I never knew my way."

His whole life, he said, was playing football. "And playing football for as long as I did can give you a distorted view of life. I mean, I was fast and big and had good balance. I was a better animal than most. And I didn't even have to practice hard. But when you retire at 36, and everyone else is more or less just getting their legs in other endeavors, you wonder about yourself. I've often thought that a pro career should never go more than four years, like in college. Then you're forced to get on with your life in something else."

He had no real skills, other than being an entertainer. "That's what a football player is, isn't he?" asked Riggins.

In the summer of 1990, Riggins moved out of the trailer and into an apartment. He came up to New York, a place that had awed him and attracted him ever since he played for the Jets from 1971 to 1975. Riggins found a place to live in Chinatown and stayed there for about six months. He then moved back to Virginia. He was searching for something, and wasn't sure what.

He soon came to another realization. He wanted to be closer to his children. He sees them now once a week and sometimes on weekends. "Sometimes it's disruptive for them," he said, "and you see them going on with their lives, and you're not always a part of it. And I feel maybe I'm letting them down. It can make you melancholy."

Riggins has four children: two girls ages five and 12, two boys, 17 and eight. The oldest, Bobby, is a high-school senior and a wide receiver on his high school football team in Virginia.

"Now that I'm out of the game," said Riggins, "I realize more than ever how dangerous it is and how lucky I was to get out of it with relatively few injuries. I thought about this when Mike Utley of the Lions became paralyzed for life while blocking a few weeks ago. I'm not sure I want Bobby to play in college. But that's up to him."

Riggins has decided that he will try to be an actor. He has signed on with a theatrical agent, J. Michael Bloom of Manhattan, and plans to take acting lessons. He dreams of becoming an actor like Robert Duvall. "I want to play real people," he said, "not those larger-than-life guys that Schwarzenegger and Stallone play."

Riggins said that he often thought that he played football to please his father, Gene Riggins, a depot agent, who was an avid sports fan.

"I know he dreamed of me or either of my two brothers becoming a pro," said Riggins. His brothers, Frank and Billy, were, like John, running backs for the University of Kansas. "And I think I wanted to make my dad's dream come true. But acting I feel is for me, and me alone."

And if that doesn't work out? "Maybe I'll go back to Kansas and buy a farm, or a ranch. But I want to give this acting a real shot."

With dinner over, and most of the restaurant cleared of patrons, Riggins rose to leave. "You know," he said, "I wonder about Justice O'Connor sometimes. I did make a fool of myself that night, but I wonder if, on the flip side, she's a little more festive at a party. All I know is, she gave me a little smile when I suggested she loosen up. It was one of those Rodney

Dangerfield looks that says, 'Cute kid. Now I know why tigers eat their young.'"

He laughed, and, in turquoise bolo tie and black jacket and black kangaroo cowboy boots, walked out into the cool New York night, the old football player, but still a young man, in search of a cab, and maybe of himself, too.

LARRY CSONKA:
MONSTER? HARDLY

November 14, 1971

WHEN HE WAS A high school senior, Larry Csonka was supposed to have nearly broken his house apart. He had been told that the way to strengthen a forearm was to keep banging away at something hard. "He smashed three walls and knocked one door off its hinges," said his father.

Years later Csonka was sleeping in a tent on a camping trip and was awakened by a neighborhood bear. Csonka reportedly elbowed the bear in the belly, and the intruder fled.

Before this season, Csonka, the Miami Dolphins' fullback, vowed that nothing short of a head injury would keep him out of the lineup. "If it's a broken bone or a muscle tear," he allegedly said, "I'd grab the doctor by the throat and say, 'Make it well, by God.'"

Then there is Larry Csonka on the field. Look: he is a 6'2", 240-pound block of rock. His full face is dominated by a nose broken nine times over the years. Watch: two Buffalo safeties at the 5-yard line hit Csonka simultaneously from each side. They bounce off. Csonka enters the end zone standing up. Again: Csonka piles into mountain of Denver defenders, disappears, emerges out the other end to score, dragging defenders. And note: midway through the season Csonka leads the American Football Conference in rushing.

"My brand of football is different from my lifestyle, though a lot of people don't want to believe it," Csonka said. "I'm really an easy-going guy off the field. But everybody likes to promote the football player as a flesh-eating monster, dragging knuckles on the ground, wearing a beat-up sweater and sneakers that don't match."

Csonka is soft-spoken and articulate. He chooses his words carefully. A grunt does not seem to be in his vocabulary. His wife, Pam, says that Larry is usually very even-tempered at home. Larry also plays the harmonica to relax. None of which seems very flesh-eating or knuckle-dragging.

"Funny how stories grow," said Csonka. "Like the one about knocking walls down. That's not true. It was just one wall. It was in our kitchen. The wall had weak plaster. It wasn't that big a thing."

Does he still hit walls?

"Once in a while when I get angry. But doesn't everybody? Besides, I don't hit walls too hard anymore," he said.

And what about the bear story?

"Nothing special. It was a small bear."

And the one about grabbing a doctor by the throat and demanding that an injury be made better immediately?

"Another exaggeration. I wouldn't grab anyone by the throat. Oh, sometimes you'd like to take hold of a defensive end and throttle him. But you don't. Football is so complicated, you've got to keep your cool to win. But I've found that you can hurt him just as much by impact, running smack into him."

Sometimes Csonka strikes back another way. He may be the only player in history to have been penalized 15 yards while carrying the ball. On that play he forgot that the tackler was not a wall and knocked him silly with a forearm.

"Every time a ball carrier runs he gets hit from 11 different directions," said Csonka. "And sometimes you've got 1,600 pounds of humanity crashing down on you. You've got to protect yourself.

"But football is very gratifying. Like when you're called upon to go toe-to-toe in a tough, tight situation. I guess it dates back to prehistoric times, when mind and body combines to accomplish something special. And after it's through and you're so tired—well, it's like what Vince Lombardi said on the eve of his death, 'There's no better feeling than to lie on the field exhausted but victorious.'

"After football, I'm sure I'll never feel the same kind of satisfying self-expression again. I don't think you can ever feel that total mind-body exhilaration of accomplishment in the business world.

"Football is digging in and belting. I've enjoyed it since I was in junior high school in Stow, Ohio. I think about those days. We played on a dirt field behind the school. There were no bands at halftime. The only spectators were a few concerned parents. The bleachers were raggedy. So were our uniforms. They were old hand-me-downs from the high school. The right half of your shoulder pad usually didn't match the left half.

"We played hard because we loved it, and because we wanted to win. And until I began playing so much on artificial turf, I didn't realize how much fun dirt was. When I was a kid I really enjoyed the dirt in my ears and eyes. I guess I was always a dirt-faced kid.

"Yet I've always been concerned with the niceties. I mean, if I don't like what a person says, I probably wouldn't say anything because I wouldn't want to hurt his feelings.

"The only time I get mad off the field is, well, like when I get up in the middle of the night for a glass of water and I step on a sharp toy left by one of my little boys. Then I get excited. I jump around and holler obscenities.

"Or like when my car stalled three times in heavy traffic. The third time, I punched the dashboard. I broke the air conditioner. I also cut my hand open. I was bleeding all over the dash. I just sat there for 15 minutes feeling like a tool."

VI.

RIVAL QBS

JOHNNY UNITAS:
AN IMMORTAL DOESN'T LOOK BACK

February 13, 1973

SAN JUAN, PUERTO RICO—FROM the front, Johnny Unitas is still a young man despite last season. He has a cowlick, an almost mischievous gleam in his eyes and a good hunk of teeth in his smile. His belly is flat.

Yet he is nearing 40, an ancient age for football, a game as brutal as time, which exposes "immortals" for the vulnerable human beings they are.

Johnny Unitas is one of these so-called football immortals. He was voted by sportswriters the greatest quarterback of all time, during the commemoration of the National Football League's 50th anniversary. He was named football player of the decade, in the 1960s. He has three times been the Most Valuable Player, six times named All-Pro quarterback, and led the Baltimore Colts to a handful of championships in his 17 seasons. He has set dozens of passing records.

Unitas, however, is aware that, like Orpheus, one gains nothing by looking back.

"People don't even ask what have you done for us lately," he said. "They ask, but what have you done for us five minutes from now."

Unitas says he is no complainer, not his nature. But he has just come off what he calls "the worst year of my football career" and there is uncamouflaged bitterness in his voice.

Midway through last season he received a phone call while in the Colts' training room that hit him the way few linemen ever have.

The caller was Joe Thomas, new general manager of the Colts.

"He said," recalled Unitas at the recent American Airlines golf classic here, "that they were going with youth and that Marty Domres was going to be the quarterback from now on."

Unitas hung up, and went to John Sandusky, the new coach who had replaced Don McCafferty in the team shakeup.

"I told John Sandusky I'm not going to be one of those run-out-the-clock quarterbacks," said Unitas. "He told me he didn't want me to be either, but that his orders were to play me only if Marty got hurt."

Domres got hurt on one play. It was a nationally televised Monday night game against San Francisco. Unitas was called in. He trotted onto the field. The crowd caught its breath. There was great sympathy for the old god, who had withstood the siege of the mod age by maintaining a short hairstyle and black high-top cleats.

Unitas was also the tough-fibred man's man, poised and unbowed in the greatest of adversities. Even the story that he had recently kicked a locker-room towel in anger was hotly denied by him ("When I pitch a bitch, I'll do it to a man's face").

He dropped back to pass, was hit from the blind side, and fumbled. The other team recovered. Unitas came out of the game for good. It seemed that the pillars of the Temple would fall next.

Unitas, on the gold course of the El Conquistador Hotel, was asked to reflect on that faraway moment. Was it embarrassing?

"No. Somebody missed a block. I wasn't embarrassed, but I was unhappy."

He said that for the first time, football was no longer fun for him. Hope was gone. He felt that the Colts had "thrown in the towel on the season." He came to practices the way a factory worker punches the clock. It was a chore. Back in 1955, when he was cut from the Pittsburgh Steelers as a rookie, he was sad but there was hope. He was a young man just out of college. That fall he played for the Bloomington, Pennsylvania, Rams, a semipro team, for six dollars a game. But there was hope. Next season the Colts invited him to a tryout. He made the team. It was the dawn of a dream-come-true.

There also had been calamities through those years, of course, like losses in two Super Bowls, and broken ribs, a punctured lung, shoulder contusions, knee injuries, torn tendons in his throwing arm, a torn Achilles' tendon. Surgery on several occasions.

Joe Thomas saw not a god, after 17 years, but an aging football player. He traded Unitas to San Diego at the close of the 1972 season.

A personal services contract with the Colts that calls for Unitas to get $1 million over 10 years after he retires has complicated the deal. Unitas is waiting to see what the Chargers will do to pick it up.

Unitas, though, will play more football because he feels he can still do the job. "And it is a job, but it's also been my whole life."

The rigors of the life—the 17 pro years of being slammed on football fields across the country—are revealed more from the back than from the front.

As Unitas walks away down the fairway, one notices his deeply sloping shoulders and funny bowed legs. The walk is determined, but it is not frisky.

TERRY BRADSHAW: PITTSBURGH'S BENIGHTED KNIGHT

October 21, 1971

PITTSBURGH—TERRY BRADSHAW ENTERED PROFESSIONAL football last season as the greatest thing since Sir Lancelot. As the season progressed, he came more and more to resemble Don Quixote.

He strode onto the football field as if it were the lists of Camelot. He was heralded as the dashing and noble embodiment of the future grandeur of Pittsburgh Steelers football. Ramrod tall, blond, with chiseled features, square and dimpled chin, ingenuous in the gilt-edged tradition of chivalry, and possessing a right arm that was expected to lance defenses. Then the visor of his armored helmet clanked down before his pool-blue eyes, and the hero rode gallantly off in the wrong direction.

He set some sort of record for muddledom by being tackled for three safeties in the first three games of the 1970 season. Instead of exalting in the polite applause of Guineveres, he was suffering the boos of Sancho Panzas. He wound up the season breaking an NFL record with his 24 interceptions.

Bradshaw admits now that last season he was confused by the rush and forgot to concentrate on the defenses. He backpedaled into the pocket with trepidation, watching not his receivers but the defensive linemen waving their arms like windmills.

"Before a game last year," he said recently, sitting in the locker room before a practice session, "I would get scared. I felt it in the pit of my stomach. I didn't sleep. I didn't eat. I didn't play well. It was a horrible nightmare."

He soon was spending most of a game on his well-padded fanny. When not being dumped on the playing field, he was dumped on the bench; Terry Hanratty took his playing place.

But it is a new ballgame, a new tilt, so to speak. Bradshaw is now conquering. This season he is the first-string quarterback without question. He is no longer being divested of his epaulets in broad daylight. The team has been winning, and has a chance for the American Football Conference title.

Bradshaw says quarterback coach Babe Parilli has helped him read defenses, call better plays, throw short with "touch" instead of rifling balls that pierced his receivers like spear jabs, and run only when it helps the team and not out of sheer fear.

"Plus we have a better, more experienced team than last season," said Bradshaw. The offensive line holds, the defensive line bruises, and running backs like Frenchy Fuqua can bust open a game.

"I dream of being the best quarterback in the game and playing with the best football team in the game," said Bradshaw. "I guess I would like to be the kind of quarterback Joe Namath is. He's probably the most courageous guy I've ever seen. The way he can play with those crippled knee. And he's got great poise, but I think that comes with confidence and achievement. I also would like to have that quick release that Joe has."

Bradshaw was asked if there was anything else Namath has that he'd like.

"Sure," said Bradshaw, smiling a very blond, blue-eyed All-American smile, "his phone numbers."

Returning to less-frivolous matters, Bradshaw said he would like to meet Namath some day and ask him how he is able to handle the pressure of fanfare. He admits that "people aren't bothering me as much this year," but he seemed to leave open the possibility of publicity madness in the future.

"Of course, I still get lots of letters," Bradshaw said. "Mostly from kids. Usually they write a whole long letter saying how great I am as a quarterback, how much they admire me, how they'd like to be me. They blow my mind, and then ask for an autograph. Except for one letter recently.

"Some kid asked for three footballs, 12 jerseys, one pair of cleats, a car, and $10,000 in small bills. Oh, yes, and an autograph."

The original Sir Lancelot had it easier. All anyone ever asked of him was cheap chivalry.

BEN ROETHLISBERGER: STEELERS' SECRET WEAPON NEARLY REMAINED ONE

October 12, 2004

THE 6'5", 240-POUND ROOKIE quarterback came off the Steelers' practice field and went into the locker room, his cleats clicking on the tile floor. He looked every inch as if he had chosen the right profession: hair clipped neatly to fit into a helmet, a trimmed goatee that any spy might covet, shoulders that could rival most linemen's, eyes that even at age 22 apparently do not miss much.

Ben Roethlisberger, fresh from Miami of Ohio, where he earned All-American status, has suddenly, unequivocally, and confidently made a splash in the National Football League.

Thrust into the starting lineup for the last three games, after an injury sidelined Tommy Maddox, Roethlisberger has led Pittsburgh to three victories, the last a 34–23 decision against rival Cleveland, and elevated the Steelers, with a 4–1 record, to the top of the American Football Conference North Division.

He is just the sixth rookie quarterback to win his first three starts since the NFL-AFL merger in 1970. Among the others were Phil Simms, who won his first four starts in 1979, and Mike Kruczek, who went 6–0 as a fill-in for an injured Terry Bradshaw on the 1976 Steelers, who were midway through their Super Bowl dynasty run.

"I had thought about one day becoming an FBI or a CIA agent," Roethlisberger said, pulling up a chair in a room in the Steelers' training complex on a recent afternoon, and setting on the floor an armful of playbooks and other information. "It intrigued me. But I thought that being as big as I am, I might stick out." He smiled. "Wouldn't be so great for going undercover."

Being big in the NFL, especially when hunching over the center in anticipation of a ball being snapped into his large hands, is a virtue. He can, for one thing, readily scan the defense to see what it has in mind, and where he can make adjustments in his play calling. At least equally important, he said, is reading the eyes of the opposing linebackers, who are intent on thwarting the novice's objectives.

"I think I'm a pretty scary judge of character—kind of the spy thing," he said. "And I look into eyes of the linebackers for clues. Sometimes a guy won't look at you and you know he's trying to throw you off and he's probably going to be blitzing. If they look you in the eye, they probably want you to think they're blitzing, and they won't be. And sometimes you see an excitement in their eyes, and you know they're coming at you. Sometimes they try to fake excitement—they want you to think they're coming at you—and they drop back. In a split second, more or less, you have to determine what's fake and what's real in their eyes. Sometimes I'm right, and sometimes I'm wrong. I'm still learning."

In the first game he started, on September 26 against the Dolphins in Miami, he seemingly guessed wrong. His first pass was intercepted, on an improvised play.

What did the head coach, Bill Cowher, say?

"Didn't say a whole lot," Cowher said in his understated manner, "except to make sure Ben understood that he has to be more careful, and to use good judgment."

But when Roethlisberger came back to the sideline after that errant throw, he comprehended, with the would-be CIA or FBI agent's instincts, something deeper in the coach's eyes.

"He said something like, 'Okay, keep your head up,'" Roethlisberger said. "He was calm on the outside, but I knew he was upset. I'm sure he was thinking, 'What did I get myself into?'

"But everybody said something: 'Throw it away.' 'Be smart.' 'You'll get 'em.'"

And so Roethlisberger did. On a sloppy field in the rainy aftermath of Hurricane Jeanne, he went on to complete 12 of 22 passes for 163 yards. He did not fumble, and he was not intercepted again. He put the finishing touches on a 13–3 victory midway through the fourth quarter when he rolled out and threw a 7-yard touchdown pass to Hines Ward, who made a diving catch.

After the game, he gave credit to his teammates, especially to Ward and his spectacular catch, but he also called attention to his first pass of the game.

"It was a pretty good pass," he said. "It hit Surtain right in the chest, I think." Unfortunately, Patrick Surtain plays for the Dolphins. "I just laughed at myself," Roethlisberger said. "There was nothing else I could do. I couldn't take it back. You just laugh at it, shake it off, put it behind you, and learn."

It was his ability to learn quickly, and to demonstrate poise under pressure, that convinced Cowher, from as long ago as training camp, that Roethlisberger might well be up to the task of assuming a pro quarterback's responsibilities.

"When I was growing up," Roethlisberger said, "I admired Joe Montana and John Elway in how they handled difficult situations. Never getting thrown off their game."

But few quarterbacks, even one like Roethlisberger, who was a first-round draft pick and chosen 11th overall, make an impact in their rookie season, let alone have a chance to start. Roethlisberger was the third quarterback selected in this year's draft, behind the No. 1 choice, Eli Manning of the Giants, and the No. 4 selection, Philip Rivers of the Chargers.

Manning and Rivers watch their games from the sideline. But when Maddox was injured in the second game of the season, Roethlisberger stepped in as the starter.

Most rookies take time. Quarterbacks like Dan Marino and Peyton Manning did well in their first year in the NFL, but they were exceptions. Even Elway was benched as a rookie.

Joe Galat, a former linebackers coach with the Giants and the Oilers, and, like Roethlisberger, an alumnus of Miami, has followed Roethlisberger's career closely. He said: "A rule of thumb for quarterbacks in the NFL is, the first year, you find out what you're supposed to do. The second year, you find out what the defenses are doing. And by the third year, you're ready to put the two together. But Ben, with his powerful arm and ability to make plays out of the pocket if he has to, and with obviously a keen intelligence and a drive to succeed, is way ahead of the curve."

On Sunday, at home against the Browns, Roethlisberger was just that, ahead of the curve. He completed 16 of 21 passes for 231 yards, passed for one touchdown, and ran for one. One of his most impressive moments came immediately after he threw a pass that was intercepted and returned for a game-tying touchdown in the first quarter. On the next series, as he was about to be slammed to the turf by Ebenezer Ekuban, he completed a 48-yard pass to Plaxico Burress. Two plays later, Roethlisberger ran six yards into the end zone to put the Steelers ahead for good.

While it was not cloak-and-dagger stuff, it was dramatic, and understandably gratifying to Roethlisberger. And, in the eyes of Steelers fans, Big Ben, as he is called, surely wound up choosing the right profession.

NOT TIME FOR FLUTIE TO RIDE OFF INTO THE SUNSET

November 11, 2003

IT HAS COME TO this: age, as Shakespeare might have put it, cannot wither Doug Flutie.

On Sunday, two weeks after he turned 41, Flutie flew around a football field—passing, running, directing the proceedings—as though he were 20. Okay, maybe not 20.

"I feel as good as I did when I was 30, that's for sure," he said after he led the San Diego Chargers to a 42–28 victory over the Minnesota Vikings.

At an age when most football players—make that ex-football players—are home popping anti-inflammatories for ancient injuries and swigging beer to expand an ample midsection, Flutie started in place of Drew Brees, who is a mere 24.

Flutie did nothing more than complete 21 of 29 passes, throw for 248 yards and two touchdowns, run for two more touchdowns, and make men watching the game on television in nursing homes rap their canes on the floor with excitement.

Other fans share that ardor. "There's something romantic about an old guy being able to play a young man's game," said Marc Bernstein, a lawyer and proprietor of Cafe Indulge on Second Avenue in Manhattan. Bernstein is hardly ready for a retirement home, but he is, like many of us, somewhat past his dewy-eyed youth. And he marveled at Flutie's performance. Why not? Flutie sprinted like Jesse Owens, threw like Willie Mays, commanded the team like George Patton, and did it all in the guise of Methuselah.

It was Flutie's first start in two years, and it adds to a remarkable pro legend, which began when he was considered too small—he's 5'10"—to play in the NFL. In his second pro season, when he was a part-time player with the Chicago Bears, he was disparaged by many, including the Bears' starting quarterback then, Jim McMahon, who called Flutie "America's midget."

Obstacles for Flutie, in his 19ᵗʰ pro season, are, however, nothing more than something to be scaled. Ageism was simply another one of them. He just shuts up and performs—and prevails. At his stage, you know what you can or cannot do. In the arena, there is no way to fool yourself or anyone else.

At home, you may apply the law of geriatrics: "The older you get, the faster you could run as a boy." Or, as the voiceover on the old Lone Ranger programs used to say, "Return with us now to those thrilling days of yesteryear." The yesteryear, that is, that we might only be conjuring up in our daydreams, like castles in the sky.

It doesn't hold, however, on the athletic field. If, like Flutie, you can keep yourself in condition and your wits about you—and by the grace of a coach who either has confidence in you or, like the Chargers' Marty Schottenheimer, had little choice since the kid quarterback was laying an egg—then you have a shot at success. Never mind the ton or so of human-kind galumphing after you.

When Muhammad Ali, in the ripeness of years, defeated the whipper-snapper George Foreman, who was also the reigning heavyweight champion, with the Rope-a-Dope tactic, it was viewed as astounding.

When Arthur Ashe, on older legs, beat Jimmy Connors, in the spring-time of his wonderful career and ranked No. 1 in the world, with guile and lobs and drop shots to win Wimbledon in 1975, it was justifiably hailed as a triumph squared.

When Jack Nicklaus, at the doddering athletic age of 46, scored six birdies and an eagle on the last 10 holes on the final day of the Masters in 1986, to win the tournament 23 years after he won it the first time, it seemed to give everyone over 30 hope that, maybe, anything is possible.

One night last season, Michael Jordan, having returned after his sec-ond or third or fourth retirement from basketball, and again emerging as a legitimate All-Star, scored 43 points at age 40, doing it when he was no longer Air Jordan. The earthbound, mortal Michael made some of us consider again our position and potential while splayed on the living-room couch.

Coming out of Boston College, Flutie was selected in the 11th round of the 1985 draft by the Los Angeles Rams, the 285th selection overall, and this after having just won the Heisman Trophy. And he never played for the Rams.

He wound up with New Jersey in the United States Football League, and in 1986 signed with the Chicago Bears, although he played little in a season and a half. He was traded to New England in the NFL, was released by the Patriots in 1989, then went to the Canadian Football League, playing for British Columbia and Calgary and Toronto, and, operating as though "no" had no application to him, became a star, winning the Most Valuable Player award six times in eight years.

He returned to the NFL, had some good years with Buffalo, but by 2001 he was considered a fossil and was released. But he signed with San Diego, where more recently his primary duties have been to keep the bench heated. Until now, where he is surely answering a question that Satchel Paige, himself no lambkin when he pitched in the major leagues, once posed.

Paige said, "How old would you be if you didn't know how old you was?"

TROY AIKMAN:
SO STRONG, SO VULNERABLE

November 7, 1994

UNDER THE HARSH STADIUM lights and in front of an assemblage of ill-tempered men who are intent on knocking him down or knocking him out, Troy Aikman, peering across the green field and about to take the snap, must block out the possibilities of catastrophe.

Monday night in Texas Stadium, the Cowboys quarterback must look at the 11 Giants across the line and think only of X's and O's and not of X-rays or optical and cerebral damage.

In fact, to be effective, he believes, he must consider neither the bruising recent past, in which he has suffered two concussions in games—the first last January, the other two weeks ago—nor must he consider a possibly incapacitating future, in which there could be memory loss, headaches, speech problems, loss of balance, and fuzzy vision.

Also, he must not allow himself to contemplate the cracked ribs and torn ligaments and cartilages he has suffered and the back, knee, shoulder, elbow, and finger surgeries he has undergone.

"You can't be scared," he said one day last week. "Am I concerned to a degree? Yes. But I can't afford to be scared. I have to go back to pass and focus on my receivers as the play develops in the secondary and feel the rush. But if you play scared in this game, you're as good as gone."

Twice in the past eight months he has suffered concussions—the first was in the National Football League championship game against San Francisco last January, the second against Arizona two weeks ago.

Twice in the last two weeks, he has taken vicious hits from defenders steaming into him like locomotives. The first, the Cardinals' Wilber Marshall, escaped a fine even though he cracked into Aikman's jaw with his helmet lowered. The second, the Bengals' James Francis, incurred a $12,500 penalty. The National Football League determined that Francis had deliberately gone for the quarterback's head.

The fine was levied by the league in apparent hopes to minimize the increased assaults on Aikman and his brethren, the endangered quarterback.

And while Aikman, who stands a solid 6'4" and weighs 230 pounds, looks as though he can withstand a lot of corporal punishment and has, he understands that there must surely be limits. "You know that there are possibilities that one more hit could result in permanent damage," he said.

Aikman drew a comparison to living in California: "You love living there and you know that one day the Big One might hit and destroy everything. But you stay and take your chances. And I know I'm the kind of quarterback who is more vulnerable to hits than some others because of my style—the way I stay in the pocket and will take the hit to throw if it means a completion—but I can't change."

He sat in a schoolroom-like desk in a windowless room and was wearing gray sweats after a workout at the Cowboys complex. In his sixth season in the NFL, Aikman, who will be 28 later this month, still retains the blond, strong-jawed Saturday Football Hero good looks that many remember from his days at UCLA.

He said that while the millions he earns as a quarterback are significant to him, it is hardly the sole reason he remains in the game.

"The primary fact is, I love to play football," he said. "I love the competition. I love the atmosphere, from the locker room to the games. And I can hardly say that my continuing to play is an aspect of manliness. I don't think it's unmanly to be concerned about your health out there. I do know that if I did, it would inhibit my work."

Looking back, though, Aikman realizes the risks he took in playing in the Super Bowl last season. He suffered a concussion in the NFC Championship Game against San Francisco two weeks before that.

"I still was having some headaches and blurred vision, but I wanted to play in the Super Bowl," he said. "I mean, how many times in a lifetime does a guy have a chance to play in the Super Bowl?"

Though Aikman played decently in the first half, he seemed to just walk through the paces and primarily hand off to Emmitt Smith in the second half, which was plenty good enough for the Cowboys to beat Buffalo and win their second straight Super Bowl.

"I was terrified when I realized later that I hardly even remember playing the second half of the Super Bowl," he said. "I was lucky I wasn't hit seriously in the game because that could have been disastrous."

He was also knocked out of the game last week against the Cardinals.

"But I'm feeling okay now," he said. "I'm not experiencing any of the post-concussion effects that Merril Hoge and Al Toon and those guys talked about."

Hoge, a running back for the Bears, quit the game earlier this season when he complained of lasting effects after a blow to the head. Al Toon, a wide receiver for the Jets, retired two seasons ago after suffering multiple concussions over his eight-year career. Today, on his farm in Wisconsin, Toon says he still experiences the woozy effects of those blows. And two years ago, quarterback Timm Rosenbach, after several injuries including a concussion, retired from the game because, he admitted, he had become frightened of further harm.

With all of this, there are recurring questions about whether team doctors should allow players like Aikman to continue playing. And while the players often insist on going back into games if they can stand up, others like the announcer and the former coach John Madden say that the extent of a head injury should be a matter for a doctor to decide, not a player.

In the Arizona game, it was the doctor's decision, and not Aikman's.

"I've been on the sidelines and it's the worst feeling," said Aikman. "You want to be a part of things and you're not."

When Aikman came to the sideline after the Marshall hit, the Dallas team physician, J.R. Zamorano, asked him three questions: "What day is it? What month is it? What year is it?"

"I think he scored 33 percent," Zamorano recalled. Aikman knew it was Sunday, but that was all. The doctor wouldn't let him back in the game.

But Aikman returned to the field the following week, when he became the generous target for James Francis.

Aikman is aware, however, that team doctors—paid, of course, by the ballclubs—might rush players back on the field, and some have even lied to the players about their extent of their injuries. Tony Dorsett, the former Cowboys running back, recently recalled how he had been told by a team doctor that the pain in his side was just a muscle pull, but learned after the season that it was known he had a cracked rib.

"No question, players with injuries are often sent back onto the field long before they are healed," Aikman said. "It's the medical staff whose job is to get them back in the game, and it's the players who often are afraid of losing their jobs to someone else.

"But I feel I've been adequately informed. I make my decisions based on that. And I have received medical clearance to continue playing football. But people ask about suffering all the injuries, 'When's enough enough?' And right now I'd have to say, I don't know."

JIM PLUNKETT: WHO WAS "READY"

January 20, 1984

TAMPA—ON THE SIDELINES IN the heat of the game, Matt Millen, the Raiders linebacker, turned suddenly to Jim Plunkett, then the second-string quarterback, and shouted, "Get ready! Get ready!"

Plunkett, pulling on his black-and-silver helmet, said: "I'm ready! I'm ready!"

Telling Jim Plunkett to be ready was like telling Paul Revere to make sure his horse was shod. Wasted breath. The scene on the sideline with Plunkett took place last November 6, late in the third quarter of the Raiders' game against Kansas City.

Marc Wilson, the Raiders quarterback, had just been injured. He would not be able to return to the game. Plunkett entered the contest with his team losing, 13–7.

Plunkett, now a month short of his 36th birthday and one of the oldest players in the National Football League, trotted onto the field and promptly led the Raiders on two long scoring drives, one of which included a 19-yard touchdown pass. The Raiders went on to win, 28–20.

"It was an important game for us," said Plunkett, the Raiders' starting quaterback again. The Raiders had lost two out of their last three games. "And it was important for me."

Plunkett, who will lead the Raiders against the Washington Redskins Sunday in Super Bowl XVIII, had been the starting quarterback when the season began. But he lost his job to Wilson in the eighth game of the regular season. Before coming back against the Chiefs, he hadn't played in the previous two games.

But this was nothing. He once hadn't played for most of two years, and then, when called upon, led the Raiders to the Super Bowl championship. That was in 1981, when the Raiders beat the Philadelphia Eagles.

"I guess my lowest point was when I was released by the 49ers," he said, referring to 1978. "I thought about quitting football then, and going into business. I'm not sure exactly what kind of business. But I had lost confidence as a football player."

This was after he had been a Heisman Trophy winner, emblematic of the best player in college football, with Stanford in 1970, and then a top rookie in the National Football League with the Patriots in 1971.

From that point, his pro career has had many "hills and valleys," as he termed it.

Even after leading the Raiders to the Super Bowl victory over Philadelphia, with three touchdown passes, and being named the most valuable player in the game, he would lose his starting job on at least two more occasions with the Raiders, and then battle back to regain it.

"This last one was pretty rough," said Plunkett. "I don't think I was solely at fault. But I don't want to point any fingers, so that's all I'll say. But whatever it was, it was a team effort."

Coach Tom Flores said that he had replaced Plunkett because he thought the quarterback was trying too hard to make the big plays, and thus throwing an inordinate amount of interceptions.

"Sure, we had those," said Plunkett, "but I thought that after all my experience, they'd go with me longer. Something else. When I was replaced, we were in first place, with a 5–2 record."

Flores said that if he hadn't had anyone as capable as Wilson to replace Plunkett, he wouldn't have. No solace for Plunkett, however.

"For the first week after that I really had trouble concentrating," said Plunkett. "My mind would wander and I really had trouble concentrating. I couldn't believe it. I said, 'Not again.' And my mind wandered and I'd ask myself, 'Will I ever get another chance?'"

Then Wilson went out. Then Plunkett came in. And the Raiders moved. Plunkett, starting again, went three and a half games without an interception, and the Raiders won six of their last seven games, and added two more victories in the playoffs.

What is this ability that Plunkett has to bounce back?

"I couldn't tell you," he said, "except that I've always been a stick-to-it kind of guy."

Possibly, he added, it came from his parents, both of whom were blind. He remembers that they never complained. He recalled watching his mother cook. "She never thought twice about it," he has said. "She knew where all the utensils were and reached for them as if she had sight." He said that when he was growing up, in San Jose, he often was the last one picked in games in the street. "I was always determined to prove that I belonged," he said, "and that I was anyone's equal."

And that led to dreams. Even now he can envision scenarios of the Super Bowl game. "I think about how I'll react to certain situations. The scenarios are always changing."

What about the end of the game, does that change, too?

"No," he said, "that always comes out the same. We win."

JOE NAMATH AT CANDLELIGHT

February 22, 1972

DORADO BEACH, PUERTO RICO—TWO women circle and stop and peek, like curious kittens, and ask themselves in quiet excitement, "Is that really...*him?*"

Joe Namath at dinner with three male companions raises a wine glass and toasts, "Health," when the two bejeweled middle-aged women interrupt. "Joe, may we bother you for an autograph for our sons?" One extends a cloth napkin.

Namath is giggly. He pushes back his chair, slowly rises. "Want me to write something special?" he asks. He laughs shyly, like a tickled schoolboy trying to cover a giggle from the teacher. "You won't get this napkin through customs," he says. The ladies are delighted.

Namath is one of the most immediately recognizable men in the United States, also one of the most controversial. Everyone has an opinion on Joe Namath, and it seems almost everyone wants his autograph, too.

Namath's mood is changed now from the time two years ago in 1970 when he received a crank threat on his life. He seemed more puzzled than frightened by such a vicious response to his carefree lifestyle. For a time, it appeared he wanted to shrink from the limelight. But Namath is too spirited to remain hunched in dark corners.

One of Namath's dinner companions said he had recently talked with George Sauer, the former Jet who retired. "George said one reason he quit was that he was sick of people pawing and drooling over him because he was a football player," said the companion.

"George say that?" asked Namath. "Well, some people just don't want it. They don't like it. Steve Thompson wanted to go back home to work. So he up and quit the Jets, too."

Namath, his black hair in bangs, bent his head and dug into a steak. He looked up and smiled again, the candlelight on the table accentuating his deep dimples.

"I was supposed to have a date tonight," he said. "I met this beautiful blonde last night in the hotel casino here. I mean bee-yoo-tee-ful. I walked over to her and said, 'A beautiful woman like you shouldn't be alone.' She said she wasn't alone, exactly. But she didn't want to be with the guy she was with. I said, 'Well, that can be fixed.' She said not tonight. She was going back to her room—alone. I asked her about tomorrow night. She said yeah. I told her I'd call her at 6:00. I called. She wasn't in. I left a message. She never returned the call. I'd sure like to see her. I'd like to know what she was thinking about."

A man and his wife come over and got an autograph. They left.

"I noticed," said a dinner companion, "that you always stand when women come over to the table."

"Sure," Namath said. "That's the least I can do. I mean, if my mother asked for an autograph, I'd want the guy to stand for her."

His thoughts drifted to his hometown, Beaver Falls, Pennsylvania.

"When I was in high school," he said, "a guy named Poolhead nicknamed me Joey U, 'cause I idolized Johnny Unitas. Those were the days. Did you know I worked one week as a shoeshine boy in a hat-cleaning store? They paid 50 cents a week. A week! I quit after the first week. I knew I was cut out for bigger things, even then." He pushed back his chair and bent over and laughed boyishly.

Joe came up for air, and his close friend and traveling companion, Becher Khouri, said, "I'll check the messages at the front desk, see if the girl called."

For all of the "Broadway Joe" headlines, Namath still seems to choose his friends the way he must have in Beaver Falls—are they straight? Are they loyal? Do they make him laugh? He mentioned a New York friend named Mickey. "He's in a couple small pizza restaurants with his father," said Namath. "I've known Mickey for several years, and I didn't know until recently that he never went past the ninth grade. I can dig that. I went to college, I told him, but I didn't learn much past ninth grade anyway."

Khouri returns. No message from the blonde. Namath then pours more wine. More people come for autographs. The intermittent conversation rambles. Namath talks about how much he still admires Unitas and watches him on television whenever he can to steal some of the old master's tricks. "And he's still got 'em all," said Namath.

He asked about protesters he had recently read about. "People were picketing in New York about the Irish problems," he said. "I don't understand that. If people want to do something, why don't they just go to Northern Ireland and talk face-to-face with the people there who can do something about it? What good is picketing in New York?"

He lamented the theft of his $10,000 full-length mink coat from his New York apartment. "Funny thing is," he said, "I never wore it, I didn't pay for it. I got it for doing some P.R. But I loved it. I may buy another one."

He was laughing again, pouring more wine.

Just then, there was a tap on his shoulder. He turned. "I don't believe it, I don't believe it," he said into his napkin to muffle his surprise. He stood.

"Hello, Diane," said Joe. He pulled up a chair for her. It was the young woman with shoulder-length blond hair.

He sat back down and crossed his legs, leaned back in his seat, smiling quizzically at her. The flicker of the candle lit up his boyish blue eyes and he uttered a barely audible "wow."

DOUG WILLIAMS AND JOE GILLIAM:
HISTORY IS TIDY; LIVES AREN'T

January 9, 1997

TWO SMALL ADJOINING NEWS items on the sports page reported separately on events Tuesday relating to two former football players. It was curious to see their names more or less linked in this fashion.

The players had both been National Football League quarterbacks, both from black colleges, and both of them with historical significance. But Doug Williams and Joe Gilliam went in opposite directions after their playing careers, one positively, one tragically.

Nine years ago this month, Doug Williams, from Grambling, became the first black quarterback to play in the Super Bowl, when he led the Redskins to a 42–10 victory over Denver.

Yet it was 13 years before that, in 1975, that Gilliam, from Tennessee State, became the first black quarterback on a Super Bowl team, though he was a backup to the Pittsburgh starter Terry Bradshaw and did not see action in that game, or in the Super Bowl the next year.

Williams, 6'4", broad-shouldered and with a terrific arm, said before his Super Bowl that Gilliam was one who "had helped open the door for me, and if you don't want to call it a door, say it's a wall."

For a long time, the last place on a football team that one would see a black man was quarterback. Pro owners and college heads had been loath to have a black man as the anchor of their team, for fear white fans would not relate to them. They worried that white teammates would refuse orders from them in the huddle. And, finally, black quarterbacks were considered—"I know," said Williams, before the 1988 Super Bowl, "some people thought we weren't smart enough."

All that has changed dramatically, though not completely. But colleges like Auburn, Louisiana State, and Oklahoma have or have had black quarterbacks in recent years, as have many pro teams, and many of those ignorant fears have dissipated.

Gilliam, goateed, spindly, 6'2", was an electric player who could run and throw and became the first black quarterback to emerge into the national spotlight. On a Monday night in 1973, before a national television audience, he started for the Steelers in place of the injured quarterbacks Terry Bradshaw and Terry Hanratty.

"A lot of people will be watching me," he said before that game against Miami. "I feel I'm representing the black people, showing them and whites that a black man can play this position in the pros."

He did not have a good game, and Bradshaw returned to the lineup. "But I'll get another chance," Gilliam said. "I'm too good to let something like this discourage me."

He never made it to the top rung, going from the Steelers to the Saints, playing sandlot football, returning with the United States Football League, and retiring in 1984.

Williams had begun his career by making a splash with Tampa Bay, then foundered, was released, played in the USFL, was picked up by the Redskins, played one down in 1986, then won the quarterback job, lost it, won it again, and tied a record for throwing four touchdowns in a Super Bowl, and was named the game's most valuable player. A year later, Williams was released. His playing career over. He returned to his hometown, Zachary, Louisiana, and became the high school coach there. He later became an assistant coach at Navy, and then a scout for the Jacksonville Jaguars.

Gilliam began his battle with drugs while a player. After football, he worked on the docks in New Orleans, tended bar, and had other odd jobs. He lived on the streets, bumming dollars. He went through many drug rehab centers.

Last September he was given a volunteer job as an assistant coach at Tennessee State, provided he stayed clean. His father, Joe Sr., had been an assistant at Tennessee State and now teaches in the physical education department.

"I'm an addict," Joe Gilliam Jr. said before taking the volunteer's job in September. "But I'm fighting it as hard as I can fight, but man, it's tough. I take it one day at a time. I can't afford to look ahead to tomorrow."

Last Tuesday, Williams, 42, was named head football coach at Morehouse College in Atlanta. On the same day, it was reported that Gilliam, age 46, had been arrested in Nashville on drug-possession charges. He had been holding a pipe with crack cocaine in it. He was given a six-month jail sentence, which was suspended on the condition he complete six months of probation, undergo random drug tests, and perform 48 hours of community service.

PERSEVERANCE PAID OFF
BIG FOR JOHN ELWAY

April 27, 1999

AS QUARTERBACK FOR THE Denver Broncos for the last 16 years, John Elway has lost two miles and maybe three city blocks during football games, or 3,780 yards. This is a National Football League record for going backward.

He has had more people pounce on him more frequently than any other quarterback in NFL history, having been sacked 516 times. Another record. This means that no one wearing the livery of an NFL team has ever had to rise—head inside his helmet ringing like the Liberty Bell, bones jiggling like a Halloween skeleton in the wind—and wobble to the huddle to try again, and again.

Then there were the notorious Super Bowls. His first was in 1987, when the Broncos lost to the Giants. His second was in 1988, when the Broncos lost to Washington. His third was in 1990, when the Broncos lost to San Francisco.

He may have been excused for thinking at times, "I should have stayed with baseball." He was the Yankees' first draft choice in June 1981. He played one year in the Yankees minor league system, after his junior year at Stanford, and surely learned valuable pro lessons about disappointment and redemption.

John Elway, who will be 39 years old on June 28, has announced that he will officially retire Sunday. It would have come already but for the high school tragedy in the Denver suburb of Littleton. He believed rightly and sensitively that his announcement might draw attention at a totally inappropriate time.

Looking back, not only did Elway return to games in which he was repeatedly knocked down, physically and otherwise, but he also became the winningest quarterback in history, with a record of 148 victories, 82 losses, and one tie, a .643 winning percentage, just ahead of the Dolphins' Dan Marino in victories and percentage.

"I may not always play my best," he said after the third Super Bowl, and looking for some light at the end of the tunnel, "but I always play my hardest. I'm competing all the way until the scoreboard clock reads zero-zero-zero."

And it is no secret that he returned for a fourth time to the Super Bowl, in 1998, and won it, at the tender age of 37, risking loin and limb, to scramble and dive for a crucial first down late in the 31–24 victory over highly favored Green Bay.

The Broncos' owner, Pat Bowlen, was so moved by Elway's professionalism, resilience and, well, dotage, that when handed the 1998 Super Bowl trophy after the game, he said, "This one's for John."

"You wonder if you're going to run out of years," Elway said. "But fortunately I hung on." Then Elway came back to lead Denver to a second straight Super Bowl championship over Atlanta in January.

If a sports figure can legitimately be viewed as a model of something positive—an increasingly difficult stance in today's sports world—John Elway is a prime candidate. Elway has become a living symbol of refusing to be defeated by defeat. As a pro, it began in baseball.

Elway was an outstanding outfielder and hitter for Stanford, and with, not surprisingly, a bazooka for an arm. In the summer of '82, after his junior year in college, he signed with the Yankees for a $140,000 bonus. He would return that fall to again play football at Stanford. But at Oneonta, New York, the 6'3", 205-pound All-America quarterback wondered early on what he had got into, a kind of harbinger for his football career.

For the first week and a half he had just one hit in his first 22 at-bats. "And the fans were on him—some of it was pretty vicious," Suzanne Nader, then the team general manager, said, "and the paper here, *The Daily Star*, each day had a 'Where's Our Golden Boy?' story."

The Golden Boy showed up. He played an excellent right field, throwing runners out with the accuracy of his touchdown tosses. And he wound up batting a promising .318 in 42 games, with four homers and 25 runs batted in.

The question after his senior year was: would it be baseball or football? "It's a thrill to throw a touchdown pass," he said, "but there's nothing like hitting a home run." He was the No. 1 pick in the 1983 NFL draft, and decided on football. Perhaps that was where his heart was, and his dad's—Jack Elway was head football coach at San Jose State.

"We hated to lose John," George Steinbrenner recalled yesterday. "He was a good ballplayer and a good citizen. While he didn't have all the tools of a Derek Jeter, he had the right ethics and the right understanding, and he would have made himself a star in baseball."

Did he believe Elway made the right decision? "Are you kidding!?" Steinbrenner asked.

Yes.

DETROIT FANS CHEER FOR THE
QUARTERBACK WITHOUT THE UNION LABEL

January 6, 1992

THE LAST GUY ANYONE in Detroit would have considered a football hero became an unabashed, unmitigated, unquestioned hero yesterday. In this town that wears the union label so proudly, he was considered a strike-breaker. In this town that has boasted such quarterback stars as Bobby Layne and Earl Morrall and Tobin Rote, the guy who came to camp this summer as the team's No. 3 quarterback, who has played in things like the Potato Bowl while attending a community college, who wasn't even drafted by the National Football League after his senior year in college, this guy is today's hero here.

And in this grizzled, battered town, this blue-collar, lunch-bucket town, the guy with the dark, tousled hair and the gentle eyes and the unprepossessing build of, say, a high school chemistry whiz, this guy was cheered wildly by the 78,290 football fans in the Silverdome.

What Erik Kramer did to deserve all this was lead the Detroit Lions to a spectacular 38–6 victory over the Dallas Cowboys in the divisional playoffs, placing them in the National Conference championship game Sunday against Washington and giving them a chance to go to the Super Bowl and win their first football championship in 35 years.

Kramer led Detroit simply by completing 29 passes in 38 attempts for 341 yards and three touchdowns. He did it after he was goaded and baited and derided by the Cowboys. The Cowboys defense stacked up on the line, virtually daring him to throw, and anticipating that he would give the Lions' ace runner, Barry Sanders, handoff after handoff.

Earlier in the week, a pair of Cowboys defensive players, Tony Casillas and Jack Del Rio, were outspoken about Kramer, calling him a scab for having crossed the picket lines to play for Atlanta during the strike-interrupted season in 1987.

Del Rio kept up the verbal barrage during the game, or part of it, anyway.

"I didn't hear him make any more remarks after the first quarter," said Kramer.

On the first series for the Lions in the first quarter, Kramer took the Lions 68 yards for a touchdown on five plays, all of them passes, concluding with a 31-yard toss to Willie Green.

"I took the remarks that were made about me as a challenge," said Kramer. "They didn't show me respect; they didn't show our team respect. When I woke up this morning I didn't even feel any jitters. I just wanted to get to the stadium to play."

When it was all over, Kramer said: "It's been a dream season, and this was a dream game. Now we gotta keep it going."

Kramer got his chance this season in the Lions' eighth game, also against the Cowboys. Their first-string quarterback, Rodney Peete, suffered a torn Achilles' tendon on the first series of plays and was lost for the rest of the season. The Lions called on Kramer, who had moved past Andre Ware on the depth chart. Kramer had played three games in the strike season right out of college, had then spent two seasons in the Canadian Football League, and at this time last year, after spending most of the season on the injured reserve list of the Lions, was out of a job. He had traveled a long way to get to this point, from Pierce Junior College in California to North Carolina State to disappointments in the pros.

But against Dallas in that first game, Kramer responded handsomely. He threw two touchdown passes and the Lions won, 34–10. He went on to play a large role as the Lions won six of their next eight games going into yesterday's playoffs. "He's won some games for us," Lions coach Wayne Fontes said of Kramer. "He's made the big play."

In regard to his once having crossed the picket line, Kramer says: "I had to do it. It was probably the last opportunity I'd have to play in the NFL. It was a hard thing to do, but you have to do what's best for you."

Kramer, meanwhile, has demonstrated resilience and poise and skill this season—his teammates call him "Brass" for his independence and coolness under pressure—and in a curious way he seems to personify aspects of this city, the part, anyway, that consists of doggedness.

"Times are tough around here, as tough as most people can remember," said Ted Wagner, reduced to part-time work on the assembly line at the Ford Escort plant here. "So that's why a lot of us overlook it that Erik Kramer was a scab. He's our quarterback, and it's the Lions. We're rooting for him."

Motown, from "The Motor City," depends hugely, of course, on one particular industry, automobiles, which is reeling. In a depressed national economy, cars have been hit as hard as any product.

In this area, though, as in many others, sports has often been a great rallying point. And while the Lions have been down for a long time, they remain beloved. Then suddenly this season they began to win again, behind Kramer.

Nevertheless, nobody, even in Detroit, had thought of Kramer in the class of Elway or Marino or Kelly. Or Samuel Gompers.

Ted Wagner shrugged when asked about the non-union quarterback. "Right now," said the part-time assembly-line worker, "we're hoping for two things here. We want the Lions to win and for George Bush and the Big Three"—representatives of General Motors, Ford and Chrysler—"to come back from Japan with good news about trade barriers. If that happens, there will be such a warm glow around here you'll see flowers growing in February."

And, oddly enough in this union town, maybe echoes of cheers, too, for Erik Kramer, who once crossed a picket line.

FOOTBALLS JUST KEPT DISAPPEARING

December 8, 1990

THE SCORE OF POSSIBLY the most lopsided championship game in the whole history of sports was 73–0, when, exactly 50 years ago today, the Chicago Bears beat the Redskins in Washington for the National Football League title. The score might very well have been 74–0, but Sollie Sherman cannot be blamed for this. He was no longer in the game.

Sollie Sherman was the third-string quarterback for the Bears, behind Bob Masterson and the starter and star, Sid Luckman. The Bears led at the half, 28–0, and Luckman didn't play after that. Masterson took over at quarterback and remained into the fourth quarter. Then George Halas, Bears coach, summoned Sherman, with the score, Sherman recalled, "something like 60–0."

"I wasn't nervous," Sherman said yesterday from his home in Chicago, on the weekend of another Bears-Redskins game in Washington tomorrow. "I had played a little earlier in the season. And besides, we had a pretty comfortable lead."

Sherman, then in his second and final pro season, led a drive in which the Bears soon scored again, on a two-yard run by Gary Famiglietti. "And then the thing happened that got me into the Hall of Fame," Sherman said.

"The head judge, Red Friesell, came over to me and said: 'Better not kick the extra point. We're running out of footballs.'

"In those days, there weren't nets up behind the goal posts as there are today, and the fans kept the balls. And we had kicked so many extra points that we were running low. In fact, I don't think we were even using a regulation ball by the end of the game. It felt too big and inflated, more like a beach ball.

"But rather than line up in our regular T-formation offense, we lined up as if to try to kick the extra point. I was holding. The ball was snapped and then I got up and threw a pass that Joe Maniaci caught in the end zone. That made it 67–0. If you go to the Pro Football Hall of Fame in Canton, Ohio, you'll see a reprint of the scoring on that day. And if you look closely, you'll see my name for that extra-point pass."

Sherman came out of the game after that, replaced by the fourth-string quarterback, Bob Snyder, whose pass failed on the attempt for the extra point after the Bears' final touchdown.

Sherman, now 73 years old and chairman of the Allied Products Corporation, recalled that only three weeks before that championship game, the Redskins had beaten the Bears, 7–3. "And there had been a controversial play at the end, in which we thought we had scored," he said. "George Marshall, the owner of the Redskins, said that the Monsters of the Midway were crybabies. Well, Halas was a master psychologist, and with the greatest use of cuss words—of which he was also a master—really got us up for the game.

"Bill Osmanski ran around left end on the second play of the game, an absolutely perfect play, and George Wilson, a lineman, blocked two guys at one time and they flew into the air, and Osmanski ran 68 yards for the touchdown. The Redskins came back right after that and Sammy Baugh, a tall, skinny guy who could thread a needle with a ball, hit Charley Malone near the goal line with a pass, but Malone dropped it. After the game, Baugh was asked if that play made a difference in the game. Baugh said, 'Yes, the score otherwise would have been 73–7.'

"But at halftime Halas gave us a big pep talk. He said, 'We can't let up. The Redskins are too good a team. They can come back!' Halas was a real emotional guy, and at one point in the second half he had a stunned look on his face at what we were doing.

"Pretty soon everyone wanted to kick an extra point and get in the scoring column. Jack Manders was our regular kicker, but Dick Plasman kicked one, and Joe Stydahar and a rookie named Phil Martinovich. Bulldog Turner tried one and missed."

Each winning player received $873.99 from the game. "Which was good, considering I was making $150 a game," said Sherman, "and Halas didn't pay us for the exhibition games. We got per diem meal money, which was $3, and I managed to save a quarter."

For Sherman, who had played at the University of Chicago, that Redskin game was his last. He left pro football to enter business. "I had gotten married and had to earn a living," he explained.

Recently, a T-shirt with a picture of the 1940 team appeared in Chicago stores and Sherman sent one to Luckman, who still lives there.

"Sid called to thank me," said Sherman, "and he sounded sad. He said, 'You know, Sollie, more than half the guys on that team are gone.'

"He didn't recognize one of the players. I told him, 'That was Martinovich, Sid.'

Sherman then returned to the day 50 years ago. "On the train back from Washington after that game we had quite a celebration," he said. "It was all something to remember, really something to remember."

VII.

COACHES ACROSS
THE FIELD

VINCE LOMBARDI:
SUPER BOWL LOCKER ROOM ORATION

December 1, 1970

NEW YORK—A PARENT RECENTLY complained on a Steubenville, Ohio, radio talk show that the local high school football coach not only used bad plays but, throwing salt on the wound, he used bad grammar, too. In support of the coach, some members of the student body painted a huge banner which they displayed at the next game. The banner read: WHAT DO YOU WANT? GOOD GRAMMAR OR GOOD COACHING!

Assuming that coach Abe Bryant's tongue did indeed trip over restrictive clauses and subjunctives, how serious is that? Particularly since his teams have been successful in one of the country's toughest football conferences.

To determine the cause and effects of grammar on the gridiron, Vince Lombardi's pregame locker room Super Bowl speech (January 14, 1968) was read by the eminent grammarian, Dr. Bergen Evans of Northwestern University. (Evans confessed he had never heard of Lombardi—"Did you say Lombardo?"—before this).

LOMBARDI: *It's difficult for me to say anything. Anything I could say would be repetitious. This is our 23ʳᵈ game this year. I don't know of anything else I could tell this team. Boys, I can only say this to you: boys, you're a good football team.*

EVANS: So far, this sounds like the king's English—if the king had stayed sober. Of course, the coach contradicts himself by saying anything he says will be repetitious. But rhetoric has to go in for repetition. Besides, you begin any effective speech by denying what you're going to say. The Supreme Court does it all the time...

LOMBARDI: *You are a proud football team. You are the world champions. You are the champions of the National Football League for the third time in a row, for the first time in the history of the National Football League.*

EVANS: When you see it in print, there may be a confusion in the prepositional clauses. But writing is stodgy and pompous, while speech is mercurial and improvisational. You see, everybody speaks well, or they couldn't survive. If you get your point across, then you're speaking effectively. Lombardi succeeds here.

LOMBARDI: *That's a great thing to be proud of.*

EVANS: School teachers have been earning their living for years by frightening people into not ending a sentence with a preposition. But I love what Winston Churchill said when he was corrected on it: "That is something up with which I shall not put."

LOMBARDI: *But let me say this: All the glory, everything that you've had, everything that you've won is going to be small in comparison to winning this one. This is a great thing for you. You're the only team maybe in the history of the National Football League to ever have this opportunity to win the Super Bowl twice. Boys, I tell you I'd be so proud of that I just fill up with myself.*

EVANS: He mixes the subjunctive with the indicative, but is it confusing to the ear? No. American people are the most scared people in the world about using their language. We don't have an aristocracy or a peasantry. Ours is an economically upward-tending society, and this middle-class society has transferred the sacred chalice to our language.

LOMBARDI: *I just get bigger and bigger and bigger. It's not going to come easy. This is a club that's gonna hit you. They're gonna try to hit you and you got to take it out of them.*

EVANS: "Gonna" is a common colloquialism. A word like "going" has two "g's" and the formative tendency is for the tongue to elide one of those two consonants. The word "pilgrim" had a similar growth as "gonna." Pilgrim is from "peregrine," meaning, traveler. The "r's" in peregrine were too hard to say, so our mouths just said the hell with it.

LOMBARDI: *You got to be 40 tigers out there.*

EVANS: Technically, the compound verb should be "should be" or "must be" or "ought to be." He could also have said, "It is essential that you aspire with feline ferocity." Some impact, that.

LOMBARDI: *That's all. Just hit. Just run. Just block and tackle. If you do that, there's no question what the answer's going to be in this ballgame. Keep your poise. Keep your poise. You've faced them all. There's nothing they can show you out there you haven't faced a number of times.*

EVANS: He did drop the pronoun "that" after "nothing." "That" introduces a noun clause. But really, a football coach to be effective in his environment just cannot be hoity-toity.

LOMABRDI: *Right?*

EVANS: Correct.

VINCE LOMBARDI JR.:
"IT'S HARD TO BE ME."

December 20, 1972

(Around Super Bowl time, the late Vince Lombardi, who died two years ago in 1970, is always news. First, he coached the winning team in the first two Super Bowls ever played. Second, the winning team now receives the Vince Lombardi Trophy.

And Lombardi lives in another way. Perhaps no other coach has had the impact on the philosophy of modern-day coaches—from Little League to the NFL—that Lombardi has had).

"IT'S HARD, REALLY, TO be me," said Vince Lombardi Jr. "Father is with me all the time—constantly. People miss him. People always remind you of that. But under no circumstances do I try to be his carbon copy. I'm a product of my generation, he was a product of his. My philosophy is different from his."

Possibly the most legendary bit of philosophy held by Vince Lombardi, the late Green Bay Packers and Washington Redskins coach, is that "Winning isn't everything—it's the only thing."

"A lot of people question that now," said Vince Lombardi Jr., in his law office in Minneapolis. "I guess I'm not willing to sacrifice all that he did for winning. Like I'm not willing to be away from my family as much as he was. He had his way. I have mine."

Lombardi, now 30 years old, was recently elected to the Minnesota House of Representatives. His party affiliation was Independent, but he said he will caucus with the Conservatives. He represents the Lino Lakes suburban area, where he lives with his wife and three boys, ages six, five, and one and a half, and one daughter, four.

"I guess parents always say that they will bring up their children different from their parents," said Lombardi. "So did I. For one thing, I was not going to be as physical with my kids as Father was with me, not as strict. He was not one to spare the rod." Lombardi laughed. "Where did he hit me? Anywhere he could catch me.

"But I find myself saying some of the same things to my kids—'If I get hold of you, you won't sit down for a week!'

"The thing he emphasized most was schoolwork. If I fell down in grades, he wouldn't let me out of the house until the next marking period. I had nothing to do except study. But I remember one time I was a sophomore in high school, when we still lived in New Jersey. I got thrown out of school for a day, for a very minor matter. I was told to bring my father and mother to see the principal the next day.

"I was really in trepidation, waiting for my father to come home. When I told him what happened, he didn't say 'boo.' I was steeling myself for the worst. But he knew that I felt bad enough, so he didn't have to say anything. He had a great sense of timing. Though I wish he had been a little more nonphysical like that a little more often."

When Lombardi was 16, his father got the head coaching job at Green Bay, and so the family of four (including a younger sister) moved to Wisconsin. It was here that young Vince began to feel the pressures of being the son of a legend-to-be.

"I played football and the report around the high school, a Catholic school named Premontre, was that I was supposed to be the greatest thing since sliced bread," Lombardi recalled. "They figured, if he's the coach's son, he's got to be great. They had me up to 6'2", when at my very best I was 5'10", 195."

Lombardi became a starting fullback on the team, yet he felt his father never really cared very much.

"I'd come home and I'd say, 'Dad, I scored a touchdown today.' He'd say, 'Oh yeah?' I thought he wasn't interested in me as an athlete, only as a student. But later I'd hear that he was pleased when I did well on the football field.

"In retrospect, I guess it was good that he never pressured me to be an athlete. He probably sensed that there was enough pressure on me—by myself and by others—and he didn't want to add. Everyone expected big things of me, including me, because I was Vince Lombardi's son. I used to feel very, very tense before games."

Lombardi received a football scholarship to St. Thomas College in St. Paul, Minnesota. He eventually became starting fullback and captain of the football team. One of the few times he remembers his father interceding in his college career was at the beginning of his sophomore year.

"I took a room off campus," said Lombardi. "Father called the dean of men and told him to send me home. He didn't want me living off campus. Well, I got a room in a dormitory."

Lombardi recalls something else about his college days. "I may have been the only kid in school who hated to go home for summer vacation." Lombardi laughed again. "Father always found the hardest jobs for me to do at home—construction, loading boxes into semitrailers in a pickle factory. He made it a point never to find me an easy job.

"He learned about the value of hard work from his father. My grandfather was strict, too, in the ways of the old country. I remember Father saying that he always had to do a lot of busy work around the house. They lived in Brooklyn but they had a barn, and Father remembered having to tear up the barn floor and then Father made him put the planks down again. And it had to be a good job! Or my grandfather would be mad and get physical."

"So Father learned early the philosophies that would carry him through his life: appealing to an individual's pride, integrity, singleness of purpose, commitment to excellence—winning.

"Some of those things I have accepted and live by, too. But there are pluses and minuses. I had great respect for my father. I was in awe of him. And because of this we weren't what you'd call buddies, never really the closest. He was dedicated to his work—and he was a great success at it. But he wasn't home that much. He was very busy. We'd talk on occasion, but you mostly had to fend for yourself.

"But life was exciting, to be in the center of it. And for a kid, to go to training camp with a pro football team—wow!

"I saw that his philosophies at home were the same with his football team. He drove them like he tried to drive me. But he was also aware that everyone's an individual. He had to take everything into proper context. He has been a great influence on a lot of coaches—not just in the pros—but on the lower levels, down to pre–high school football coaches. And from what I've seen and heard, I'm not convinced that younger kids are prepared for the strain that some well-meaning coaches place on them. Maybe you can't overemphasize the striving for excellence, but I think you can overemphasize the striving for victory.

"What made Father so unusual was that he was so articulate and so successful. And you know, it wasn't until his last year or so of life that he realized that he had more to offer people than just football. He realized that people wanted to hear the things he had to say about malcontents and misfits receiving too much emphasis when the achievers and doers should get it. He was surprised at the impact.

"One thing I take a tremendous amount of satisfaction in is that Father didn't realize his dream of becoming a head pro coach until he was 46 years old. I think of this when I'm feeling impatient about not having accomplished all I've wanted. And I'm only 30. So Father's greatest example for me, possibly, is that you've got to serve your apprenticeship—put in your time, make your mistakes."

·　　·　　·

Today, Vince Lombardi Jr. tours the country as a motivational speaker.

MARV LEVY: HOW THE BILLS BUILD THEIR VOCABULARY

January 23, 1991

IN TEAM MEETINGS, BUFFALO Bills players sometimes turn to each other with a blank look on their faces when listening to their coach.

"What did he say?" they whisper.

"I think the word he used was 'extrapolate,'" one of them recalled. Another time, the word was "salient." And again he might make a historical reference, such as their having to "cross one river at a time, like Hannibal."

"Sometimes," said Darryl Talley, a Bills linebacker, "we get together later and try to piece together what it is he said."

Marv Levy is the slight, soft-spoken, silver-haired coach of the Bills who looks as though he took a wrong turn and wound up on the sidelines in a football stadium instead of in the carrel of a library. Levy would never be mistaken for Mike Ditka or Art Shell, or any one of numerous colleagues who played pro or big-time college football, or appear to. While Levy is never referred to as "hard-nosed," he's not called "soft-nosed" either. Descriptions like "scholarly" and "erudite" are more common. Levy in fact earned a Phi Beta Kappa key from Coe College and a master's degree in English history from Harvard.

"Some of us have thought about bringing a dictionary or thesaurus to team meetings and look up the words as we go along," said Kent Hull, the center, "but that might take up too much time."

Levy, though, gets his message across. One of the most significant examples occurred in the second game this season. The Bills were losing by a considerable margin to the Dolphins about midway in the fourth quarter. At this point, Levy removed some of his first-line players. One of those players was the 6'4", 275-pound All-Pro defensive tackle Bruce Smith.

The huge Smith was angry about it and confronted the coach. One observer said that Smith said, "Why are you quitting?" Smith recalls that it was more like, "Why are we coming out?"

If the question by the fearsome lineman is a little cloudy, in retrospect, the response by the coach is crystal clear. "You do the playing," he said, "and I'll do the coaching."

It was Levy's view that the game was beyond redemption, and that there was no need to risk injury to his top-drawer players. It was also a chance to give some work to the sous chefs of the line and the backfield.

"It was probably the best thing to happen to us," said Smith yesterday, "It was like a wake-up call. Maybe we were reading too many of our press clippings. We licked our wounds and regrouped."

From that point, the Bills began to rip through the opposition, highlighted by the 51–3 triumph over Shell's Raiders Sunday in the American Football Conference championship game. They now find themselves in the Super Bowl.

Levy is seen by his players as low-key, to be sure, but not indecisive, like some Buffalo Hamlet. "He can be stern, and a real disciplinarian," said Steve Tasker, a wide receiver. "One of his sayings is, 'If you don't pay attention to details, you'll have the job of having to convince everyone that you're a tough-luck team.'"

His attention to detail is so great he missed the traditional photo-interview day at Tampa Stadium yesterday because he was reviewing films of his rival Sunday, the East Rutherford Giants.

"I don't think of myself as an intellectual," Levy said the other day. "I do enjoy reading books that don't contain pictures, however." The book he has on his night stand currently is a 900-page, one-volume history of the Civil War era, *Battle Cry of Freedom*, by James MacPherson. "But a lot of people read books," said Levy. "The truth is, I see myself as a football coach, even if I don't read books like Bear Bryant's *How to Build Championship Teams*, and Bud Wilkinson's *Secrets of the Split T*." He smiled. "But I used to."

Levy, 62 years old, had his first job as a football coach in 1951, at the St. Louis Country Day School, followed by college coaching, including at the University of California, and then in the pros, first as an assistant coach and later as a head coach in Canada and for the Kansas City Chiefs.

"There are moments," he said, "when I look out on the field and say to myself, 'What the heck are you doing here? What's so important about all these men banging into each other?' But I love the game and the challenge of it all. I remember when I got fired from my jobs at California and Kansas City. I thought, 'I know I'm a good coach, and I'm going to prove it. I'm not going to wither up and disappear.'"

And on Sunday about half the nation will see that he hasn't, as he stands on the sidelines, cogitating like crazy.

"My favorite word that I learned from Coach Levy?" said Ray Bentley, a linebacker. "It was 'pontificate.' He pontificated for 15 minutes on how he was not going to pontificate."

"He said that?" Bentley was asked.

"No," Bentley said, "he did that."

MIKE DITKA AND THE
HEART OF GRABOWSKI

November 15, 1988

GRABOWSKI LIVES! LONG LIVE Grabowski! Grabowski understands, though, that to keep on living he must exercise a little less Grabowski, for Grabowski two weeks ago suffered, as the nation knows, a heart attack.

Grabowski—actually, the head Grabowski—is also known as Mike Ditka. "We're a bunch of Grabowskis," said Ditka a couple years ago, implying that his team, the Chicago Bears, was an assemblage of tough-minded and tough-nosed working stiffs.

He has been as tough as any of them, and looks the part. He is a brawny man with brown hair combed straight back, a small brush mustache, and with a manner that depicts the kind of player he was. As a tight end for the Bears in the 1960s, he was called The Hammer because he didn't just stiff-arm would-be tacklers. He clubbed them. Yet there is a gentleness and a sense of humor, if not even an appreciation for the absurd, about this Grabowski. When the recent heart attack was diagnosed, Ditka didn't want to go to the hospital. Finally, doctors won out. "Well," he said, "I was going to visit a friend there anyway."

Grabowski has shown before that he can be funny even in the face of a serious setback. In 1983, he made an impassioned locker room speech and broke his hand while pounding a metal uniform chest. He came back at the next gathering of his team, held up his arm in a cast, and said, in Knute Rockne fashion, "Let's win one for Lefty."

Ditka struggles, he suffers, he rants, he raves, he fights, he laughs, he cries, he exults in victory, and admits it when he does something dumb. He wears all of his emotions on his rolled-up sleeve.

The charm and the joy and the considerable attraction of Ditka, one of the reasons that he has received letters from all over the country after the news of his heart attack, and why local broadcasts in Chicago were interrupted with news about the coach, is that this Grabowski is no coaching automaton, no briefcase toter with aviator glasses, no cool customer. He's much like the rest of us only, it seems at times, more so.

On Sunday, the 49-year-old coach was on the sideline for the Chicago Bears game at Washington at a stage, noted a cardiologist, when other patients are walking up and down the hall of a hospital.

Ditka wasn't coaching, he was just observing, and often from a relatively uncustomary position: horizontal. He wanted to be there, but had the good sense to purchase a ticket for his cardiologist, who sat alongside him, and took his pulse when the game got heated and the coach felt light-headed.

Ditka said we won't see Mike Ditka screaming at players on the sidelines anymore, won't see Mike Ditka throwing clipboards, won't see him pulling his hair out.

His intensity, though, has marked his style. The Bears, with a 9–2 record this season, have responded to him, from the punk-rock quarterback to the ambulatory Refrigerator. In Ditka's first year as a head coach, in the strike-abbreviated 1982 season, the Bears finished 3–6. Three seasons later they were Super Bowl champions.

Ditka has been in pain to win for as long as he can remember, longer than when he was All-Pro with the Bears, longer than when he was All-America for Pitt, and as far back as when he was in the Little League, in the steel-mill town of Aliquippa, Pennsylvania.

"I don't know where it came from," he once said, "but I had this attitude, this competitiveness. I was never a good loser. I was the captain of my Little League team and the best player. And when someone made an error, I'd kick him out of the position and I'd play it. If the pitcher walked two guys in a row, I'd come in and pitch. The manager didn't say anything. I was terrible. I didn't have many friends in the Little League."

There will be, he says now, a new Grabowski.

There have been several attempts by him at constructing such a new personage. One came several years ago after he had retired as a player and underwent a hip replacement because of an old football injury. The doctors told him to go easy, go slow, let it heal properly. But Grabowski was eager to get back to his old ways, and went to the golf course and to the racquetball court and beat balls he should not yet have been assaulting. The hip didn't mend as it should have, and now he walks with a little limp.

A couple years ago, believing that he should demonstrate composure on the field, he took to wearing neckties. It was Grabowski's theory that if you're wearing a necktie, you must conform at least somewhat to polite society.

Though Grabowski never rents his tie, he did vent his spleen. And he continued to comport himself on the sideline as though he were himself fit to be tied.

It is clear now that not only does his career depend on his exerting self-control, his life depends on it.

Some Grabowski watchers believe that even in his most heated moments there is awareness. They recall that incident, after a heartbreaking loss in overtime to the Colts in Baltimore in 1983, when he suffered his coaching injury.

"We are going to get better!" he told his team in the locker room, his fist thumping the metal uniform chest in front of him to punctuate his sentences. "We are going to learn from this defeat!" Thump. "And next time we'll win a game like this!" Thump. "Now, Vince," he said, turning to the quarterback, Vince Evans, for their postgame ritual, "you lead 'em in prayer. And Doc," he said calmly, to the team physician, "you come with me. I think I broke my hand."

AT ONE TIME, PAUL BROWN JUMPED FOR JOY, TOO

August 7, 1991

PAUL BROWN'S MOMENT OF ultimate triumph was surely on the day before Christmas in 1950 when the team he founded, owned, coached, and named for himself, the Cleveland Browns, beat the Los Angeles Rams for the championship of the National Football League. The Browns had been losing, 28–27, when, with 20 seconds left in the game, Lou Groza, in his plain white leather helmet and dirtied white uniform, lined up to attempt a 16-yard field goal for the Browns.

It was a gripping moment, not only in Municipal Stadium in Cleveland, where the action was taking place, but through much of the Midwest, where the game was being televised (it wasn't until the following year, when the Rams turned around and beat the Browns, that an NFL championship game was nationally televised).

I was a 10-year-old in Chicago and watched the game closely. When Groza sent the ball through the uprights I got pretty excited. Not as excited as Paul Brown, though, who, as *The Akron Beacon Journal* reported the next day, "went into the nearest stage to berserk."

Brown was known as an unsmiling, mechanical man, a robot-like creature who, if he didn't exactly invent the X's and O's of professional football, at least expanded and honed them. When you saw him prowling the sidelines, in his snap-brim hat and long winter coat and knotted tie, he looked like my idea of Digger O'Dell, the undertaker on the radio show *The Life of Riley.*

But the "mechanical" man, sober as steel, was human underneath it all. And Brown's satisfaction came not just from winning that game, to be sure, but proving something. It was the first season in the NFL for Brown and the Browns, and some observers felt that they would be lucky to win even one game in the "big league."

The Browns were one of the original teams in the old All-America Football Conference, which lasted from 1946 through 1949, when it merged with the NFL. Brown's team was composed of such wonderful players like Otto Graham and Marion Motley and Dante Lavelli and Mac Speedie and Dub Jones and Bill Willis (one of the first black players signed in pro football's so-called modern era, and signed, of course, by Paul Brown).

After being inspired by that 1950 championship game, I went outside on snowy Springfield Avenue and kicked my football, with the fraying, rubber-exposed ends, and dreamed of being Lou Groza in the waning seconds.

All this business occurred to me when I heard Monday that Paul Brown had died at age 82 of pneumonia.

He had been a tremendously successful coach on the high school, college, and pro levels, and then an outstanding general manager for the Cincinnati Bengals.

Brown's innovations were great, including his concern for detail, from playbooks to studying game films, which he always called "movies." He even instructed his players in table manners at training camp, "Don't eat with your elbows on the table and eat quietly."

"I coached for Paul for five years with the Browns," said Weeb Ewbank yesterday by telephone from his home in Oxford, Ohio. "And I remember one of the first things he told me. He said, 'You'll coach the tackles.' I said, 'But I played quarterback in college.' So I coached the tackles. The reason, I imagine, is that he knew I'd work very hard on it, and that it being new to me I'd bring a fresh approach."

Brown was also successful because of his motivational techniques. The Browns' first game in their first season in the NFL was against the Philadelphia Eagles, the defending champions. "Today," he told his team in the locker room, "you will have a chance to touch the great Steve Van Buren."

The prideful Browns did more than just "touch" the Eagles' star full-back, they slowed him up and won, 35–10.

Brown wasn't wild about some of the new stuff in pro football, like dancing in the end zone after a touchdown. He told his Bengals players, "Act like you've been there before."

Though he loved winning, it seemed that he loved the game of football even more.

I remember a locker room scene at the Silverdome on that Sunday in January 1982 after the Bengals had lost to the 49ers in the Super Bowl, 26–21. Forrest Gregg, the Cincinnati coach, was talking to reporters when an elderly man with a snap-brim hat tapped him on the shoulder.

"Congratulations on a good season," said Paul Brown, extending his hand.

"We came up a little short," said Gregg, shaking Brown's hand.

"You had a fine season," said Brown, with a thin smile, "a fine season."

VIII

LEGENDS
ACROSS
THE AGES

RED GRANGE:
THE GHOST GALLOPED INTO HISTORY

January 30, 1991

"ALL GRANGE CAN DO is run," Fielding Yost, the football coach of Michigan, was quoted as saying.

"All Galli-Curci can do is sing," said Bob Zuppke, the football coach of Illinois.

Harold "Red" Grange, that marvelous man and the subject of that long-ago exchange, died Monday morning in Lake Wales, Florida, at the age of 87. It was the morning after the Giants had beaten the Bills in the Super Bowl in Tampa, some 75 miles west of where Red Grange died.

In an indirect but significant way, Red Grange helped invent the Super Bowl, something he would have taken no credit for. First, because he was genuinely self-effacing, and secondly because, as he once told me, he had little interest in football anymore. "I've played and seen so much football," he said, "that I've been footballed up to my eyeballs."

There is an old, grainy black-and-white film clip I have of Red Grange running. It was shot on a rainy, miserable, muddy Saturday in October of 1925 when Grange ran for Illinois against Penn, one of the nation's best teams then. Wearing a helmet without bars, the haberdashery in those days, Red Grange is running in the thickness and ooze. But he runs with extraordinary grace and swiftness and change of pace and power.

He runs as if the other players are playing in the rain and mud, and he, except for the mud dripping from his uniform and the mud flying from his cleats, is running on a dry field.

In that game at Franklin Field in Philadelphia, Grange scored three touchdowns and gained 363 yards as Illinois won, 24–2. He did stuff like that a lot, and, in that age of the blooming of ballyhoo, earned the label, The Galloping Ghost.

One of the sportswriters at that Penn game was Damon Runyon. "This man Red Grange of Illinois," wrote Runyon in his newspaper account, "is three or four men and a horse rolled into one for football purposes.

"He is Jack Dempsey, Babe Ruth, Al Jolson, Paavo Nurmi, and Man o' War."

Grange's fame endured. He was one of the sports heroes of the Roaring '20s that included people like Ruth and Dempsey and Bobby Jones and Bill Tilden and Johnny Weissmuller. And Red Grange was the last of them.

Grange left college to turn pro when pro football was so little regarded in comparison to the wildly popular college game that its crowds were small and the stories of the games were often buried in the sports sections.

One man changed all that, Red Grange. He signed with the Chicago Bears for $100,000 in 1925—an incredible sum then—and people flocked to the stadiums to see him run. A Red Grange industry emerged. There were Red Grange caps and T-shirts, and people bought radios because they couldn't wait until the next day to read what Grange did. He went to Hollywood and made films, including serial cliff-hangers and a feature, *The Galloping Ghost*, starring the Ghost himself.

"We were through with World War I and all the boys were back and radio was just coming in and there was prosperity and the country and writers were looking to make big names of people," Grange recalled. "They needed someone in football and I guess I was the one they picked. I was happy that I was, too."

A number of years ago I asked him how he liked the modern players. "Some are wonderful," he said. He mentioned Larry Csonka and Dick Butkus, in particular. "But Bronko Nagurski was the best football player I ever saw," he said. "He played both ways like all of us did—and he played linebacker as good as Butkus and fullback as good as Csonka."

Grange retired from football in 1935, was a charter member of the Pro Football Hall of Fame, lost most of his money during the Depression, got back on his feet by selling insurance—"I'm very proud of that because I did it alone," he said. "In football you have 10 guys blocking for you"— and later was a sports broadcaster.

The old great runner lived the latter years of his life in a comfortable home in Indian Lake, Florida, with his wife, Margaret, and their two dachshunds. The Galloping Ghost was still broad-chested, still had that gentle smile that I remembered from pictures, and still had his hair, though the red had turned white.

His trophies and scrapbooks were closeted somewhere, or given away. He said his neighbors knew he played football "a long time ago for some Midwestern college, and I let it go at that." He seemed more excited by the pair of sand-hill cranes that had alighted on his front lawn. "They're panhandlers," said Grange. "They like to come around here because they know we'll feed them."

About his football days, Grange said: "I never knew how I ran; I just ran. They built my accomplishments way out of proportion. There are a lot of doctors and teachers and engineers who could do their thing better than I could."

I asked him whether his wife called him Harold or Red. "Neither," he said. "She calls me honey."

BRONKO NAGURSKI APPEARS!

January 21, 1984

TAMPA, FLORIDA—"IF BRONKO NAGURSKI shows up," said Sid Hartman, sports columnist for *The Minneapolis Tribune*, "it'll be a miracle."

Hartman said that over the years a number of feature writers had traveled to Rainy Lake, Minnesota, four miles from International Falls at the Canadian border, where Nagurski lives, to interview the old football player. "But they all come back without a story," said Hartman. "He's refused to see anyone."

Last Thursday afternoon, Hartman and about 70 other journalists gathered in a room in a downtown hotel here, waiting for Nagurski.

Bronislau "Bronko" Nagurski was scheduled to appear at a news conference for him at 2:30 PM, called by the National Football League. He was supposed to have been flown in from his home to be the honorary coin-flipper at the Super Bowl tomorrow.

Nagurski is famous as one of the best, if not the best, football players ever. His strength and prowess as a fullback, end, tackle, and linebacker in the 1920s, '30s, and '40s, for the University of Minnesota and the Chicago Bears, has created an aura about him that rivals that of another from his region, Paul Bunyan.

"They used to say that Bronko was the only man who could run interference for himself," said one reporter. Someone else mentioned that Grantland Rice wrote, "Eleven Bronko Nagurskis could beat 11 Red Granges or 11 Jim Thorpes."

Another remembered the legend that he was recruited by Minnesota when the football coach, Doc Spears, saw Nagurski lift a farm plow.

Nagurski did not show up for the news conference at 2:30. At 2:45, no Nagurski. People checked their watches.

At about a little after 3:00, the double doors opened and an elderly man, accompanied by a few others, entered the room. The man walked with an aluminum cane and a steel elbow brace. He wore very thick glasses and the cane seemed to have a dual purpose, to aid his balance and to help him feel where he was walking. He was rather hunched and his legs were broadly bowed.

"Hello, Bronk," someone said.

Nagurski, who is 75 years old, craned his neck and looked at the seated reporters. "What am I in here for?" he asked with a smile. It drew a nice laugh from the journalists.

Nagurski moved slowly to a desk on a little platform in a corner of the large room and sat down. His gray hair had receded on his forehead, and his face was lined, but his cleft jaw was still prominent and looked firm. He wore a white knit shirt with a brown unbuttoned sweater over it, patterned gray slacks, white socks, and brown corrective shoes, size 13.

He seemed surprised that there might still be such interest in him, and he appeared a little shy.

By today's football standards, he would not seem particularly big, but in his time he was a huge player at 6'2" and 235 pounds.

"I'm still about the same weight," he said in a husky voice. But he stands only about 6'0" now. "I've shrunk some," he said. "From the arthritis. I've got arthritis in about every joint, in my shoulders, legs, ankles. They're from the football injuries and the wrestling."

Nagurski took up wrestling in 1938, after eight seasons as a pro football player, when the Bears' owner, George Halas, refused to pay him a requested $6,000 for the season.

"People told me I could get into wrestling and make millions," said Nagurski. He wrestled many of the standouts at the time, like Jim Londos and Strangler Lewis. "I did it for about 12, 13, 14 years. It was tough work, and I didn't make millions."

In 1943 the Bears asked him to return, and at age 35—after having been out of the game for five years—he helped them win a championship. Then he quit again. "I had other interests," he said.

He would eventually open a filling station, and for many years pump gas in International Falls. "It's a great tourist country, and that was good," he said.

For the last several years, however, he said he has spent most of his time sitting at home because moving about is too painful.

Later, he would say why he hasn't seen many people. "I wanted people to remember me the way I was," he said, "and not the way I am. I became sort of a recluse. But I come out on special occasions."

In his house there is at a reminder of the old days: photographs of him in his Bears uniform, wearing No. 3, hang on a wall.

"Is it true, Bronko, that you hit a wall in Wrigley Field so hard you cracked it?" someone asked.

"I hit a wall right behind the goal line because I couldn't put the brakes on in time after scoring a touchdown. I don't know if I cracked the wall. I have a feeling it was cracked before, but I did hit it pretty hard."

"Did you really lift up a plow?"

"If I did," he said, "it would have to have been a small one."

He said that he thought the teams of old were more "close-knit" than they are now. "We had 18 players on a team and then 22," he said. They have 49 today.

Nagurski also said that in his day players didn't jump up and down after scoring a touchdown as they do now. "We were too tired," he said, "we used to play on offense and defense."

He does watch some football on television.

"I'm very impressed with, oh, what's his name, the great back with the Redskins—I'm a little slow on names," he said.

"Riggins?" someone suggested.

"Who?"

Louder, respectfully: "Riggins."

"Yes, Riggins," he said.

From the audience, Augie Lio introduced himself. Lio, a onetime football player, is a reporter for *The Herald-News* in Passaic, New Jersey.

"Bronko, I played against you in New Jersey, when I was with the Lions," said Lio. "I was a guard on the right side and you were on the right side on defense. When I saw the size of your neck, I was glad I was on the opposite side of you."

When the news conference ended, some of the reporters gathered around Nagurski.

"Hello, Bronko, I'm Sid Hartman," said Hartman.

Nagurski looked at him. "You're not Sid Hartman; I've known Sid Hartman a long time," said Nagurski.

"No, I'm Sid Hartman."

Nagurski looked closer. His glasses glinted from the lights in the room.

"You are Sid Hartman!" Nagurski threw his arm around him. "Good to see you, Sid, good to see you! It's been years."

WHEN JOHNNY BLOOD RODE

July 11, 1982

JOHN BLOOD McNALLY, HEARING the news about the current drug scandals in professional football, recalls his own use of stimulants. He does not claim to be the first football player ever to take drugs. But he says he never heard of anyone taking them before him.

He remembers popping Benzedrine pills, "uppers," as far back as 1935. "In the early days of football, with the light padding and the glove-sized helmets, as they were called, a player needed strong fortification to attain an ethereal frame of mind," the 78-year-old Hall of Famer said recently from his home in Palm Springs, California.

Fortification also took the form of alcohol. "That's a drug, too, you know," he said. "Yes, some guys took a drink before a game to raise the spirits."

Known as Johnny Blood, he made the first all-pro National Football League team in 1931, played halfback from 1925 through 1939 for the Milwaukee Badgers, Duluth Eskimos, Pottsville Maroons, Green Bay Packers, Pittsburgh Pirates, and Pittsburgh Steelers. He coached the Steelers from 1937 through 1939, when he was dismissed for missing a team train because of a hangover.

Art Rooney, the owner of the Steelers, said: "On most teams the coach worries about where the players are at night. Our players worried about the coach."

Blood was not simply a high liver, he was also one of pro football's intellectuals. He earned a master's degree in economics and taught for a period at St. John's University in Minnesota.

A few years ago, he headed a group of old pro football players attempting to get pension money from the NFL. He called those old pros "The Naked Alumni, because we weren't covered."

He stays current on football because he has friends who are still associated with the game. "Drugs are a problem, certainly," he said, "but I think they're exaggerated in football. I don't think pro football is any worse than anyplace else. Today, doctors and lawyers and just about everyone is carrying on."

Blood said that he first became aware of drugs when he was a sailor on a ship to China. It was in China where he experimented with a stimulant.

"I smoked opium, something they had been doing in China for hundreds, maybe thousands, of years. But I quit fast," he said, "I thought it was too risky for my health."

Blood first experimented with uppers when, as a feed salesman in Wisconsin in the off-seasons, he would take long drives at night across the state.

"I remember reading in *Time* magazine about a drug that helped keep you awake—and made you feel good, too," he said. "I thought, well, if it's good enough for driving, maybe it's good enough for football, too. So I tried it. I don't think the pill had any effect on my play, but it sure did give a lift. I told some of the other players about it. In those days, nobody talked about drugs, nobody really took notice of them. Not like today. They were nonprescription drugs, available to anybody."

It was the drug of alcohol, however, with which Blood had his biggest problem. "I guess I could drink with any man. I had the reputation, and sometimes I'd drink the night before a game. I was the manic type." Blood recalled one of his most imposing imbibing feats. In January 1932, the Packers had traveled to Honolulu to play two postseason games against the local all-stars.

The Packers won the first game, and Blood was magnificent. So the Honolulu team got it into their heads to capitalize on Blood's reputation, in hopes of diluting his skills.

"They invited me to a luau before the second game," said Blood. "That's their big bash. And they put me up against their toughest drinker, a big tackle for their team.

"We drank their national drink, okolehau, and we drank into the night and morning. I got about an hour's sleep, but I showed up at the game.

Their big tackle didn't. I remember I was not feeling too terrific as the game started. Then a shower burst through the sun. And I got my refresher, and then went on to score a couple of touchdowns.

"I don't know how I did it, but I know I paid for it. Games like that took a few years off my career." Blood quit drinking seven years ago. "I thought I saw King Arthur's Court, and walked through a plate glass window to get there," he said. "I decided then, either King Arthur had to go, or I was going."

"Some people," he added, "can handle drugs better than others. But in the end, no matter how well you handle it, it winds up handling you."

JIM THORPE AND THE "SCOOP"

February 21, 1973

IT WAS NOT WIDELY know that Roy Ruggles Johnson wrote what often is considered the greatest sports "scoop" of the first half of the 20th century. But the impact was worldwide and tragic and is still in the news.

Obituaries across the country carried the fact that Johnson, who died at age 89, wrote the story disclosing Jim Thorpe's professionalism.

Johnson was the county editor of the *Worcester (Massachusetts) Telegram*, when he wrote the copyrighted story that broke on January 22, 1913. He was tipped off that a man visiting relatives nearby was bragging that he managed Jim Thorpe on the Rocky Mount, North Carolina, baseball team in the Piedmont League. Johnson found the manager, who told him that Thorpe, an outfielder, had been paid $15 a week. Johnson returned to his office, flipped through his Reach Baseball Guide, and saw Thorpe posing with a smile in the Rocky Mount team picture.

The story resulted in the Amateur Athletic Union stripping Thorpe of medals and trophies he had won in the 1912 Stockholm Olympics (where he had won, incredibly, both the decathlon and the pentathlon).

Thorpe tried to explain: "I did not play for the money. I was not very wise to the ways of the world and did not realize this was wrong. I hope I will be partly excused by the fact I was simply an Indian schoolboy and did not know I was doing wrong, because I was doing what many other college men had done, except they did not use their own names."

His medals were never returned and his name has not been restored in the Olympic record book despite various efforts through the years. Today, a group headed by former Yankees pitcher Allie Reynolds, also an Oklahoma Indian, plans to petition the president to plead the case to the International Olympic Committee. Don Johnson, son of Roy Ruggles Johnson, says that his father supported the idea that Thorpe's name and medals be restored.

"My father felt that the AAU was too strict," said Don Johnson, now an executive with the *Worcester Telegram*. "There were other athletes playing for money under assumed names in those days, and Thorpe was simply guileless to that."

Did Roy Ruggles Johnson ever regret writing that story?

"I'm sure he didn't." said Johnson. "The old gent—that's what my brother and I called my father—was a man of rectitude and high moral principle. He felt it was his job as a newspaperman to write the story.

"He never boasted about the scoop. He rarely talked about it. In fact, I didn't know he had written it until I was in college.

"And he never exploited it. He never wrote magazine stories about it. A year after the story broke he did get a job with the *Boston Globe*, but he didn't even get a writing job. He got a desk job, and I'm sure it had nothing to do with the Thorpe story."

It was the lone scoop in Johnson's life. He went on to write some 3,000 columns for the *Globe* on Yankees folklore. Meanwhile, he followed Thorpe's career, which went from pro football and major league baseball to drunkenness, destitution, three marriages, and, finally, death in an obscure trailer at age 64.

Johnson, himself a teetotaler, continued to believe in the sanctity of the free press, according to his son.

"It was the classic example of a dedicated newspaperman doing his job," said Don Johnson. "It takes a lot of integrity to tell the truth when the truth is unpalatable, as it so often is.

"I was always glad about one thing for my father. That was what happened when he met Thorpe in 1952, forty years after the Stockholm Olympics. The *Boston Globe* sponsored a Sportsmen's Show. Thorpe came, since he was a great fly caster. Someone got the idea to bring him up to the office to meet my father. They had never been face-to-face before.

"My father said, 'Jim, I'm proud to shake your hand. I always thought you were the greatest athlete that ever lived.' Thorpe bore no rancor to my father. 'You were only doing your job,' said Thorpe."

Thorpe died one year later.

In Washington, Grace Thorpe, a daughter of Jim's, said, "No, I don't think the loss of the medals or the fact that his name was taken off the record books made much difference to Dad. He felt that his achievements were proof enough of his abilities.

"But I would like to get the medals back to put in the Indian Hall of Fame in Kansas. And I'd like Dad's name restored in the official books. It would be for Indian kids, something for them to try to emulate."

SID LUCKMAN: "I REMEMBER IT
ALL AS IF IT WERE YESTERDAY"

December 2, 1994

THE QUARTERBACK OF THE Erasmus Hall High School football team in Brooklyn, a 17-year-old named Adrian Bailey, came to watch a ceremony yesterday honoring a predecessor of his, an Erasmus quarterback who played 60 years before him.

"Had you ever heard of Sid Luckman before this?" Bailey was asked.

"No," he said. "But I was curious."

On a sunny but chilly afternoon, Bailey would learn about Luckman while among the audience at the small, renovated football field on McDonald Avenue where Erasmus plays its home games, the place where Sid Luckman played and Adrian Bailey played, the place that was dedicated to Luckman yesterday and named for him.

The differences in the worlds of Bailey and Luckman are vast. When Luckman went to Erasmus, one didn't have to go through a metal detector to enter the building on a school morning. The student population was mostly Jewish and Irish. Today it is primarily black.

But there are similarities. The Jews and Irish were of immigrant backgrounds, as are many of the Haitian, other Caribbean, Indian, and Pakistani students today. "You feel a lot of school spirit," said Dr. Elaine Dawes, the acting principal, "as I'm sure was the case in Mr. Luckman's time."

And when the players ran onto the field for a game this year during a 3–4–1 season, they still ran out in the blue school colors, seeking to win one for "the Dutchmen," the nickname derived from their Dutch philosopher namesake.

Bailey, sitting in the stands and wearing a modest Rastafarian hairstyle with head band and a windbreaker, would learn how Luckman led Erasmus to the city championship as a junior in the mid-1930s; how he went on to become an All-American at Columbia University; how he went to the Chicago Bears in 1939 and won honors as the first great T-formation quarterback; how he guided the Bears to four National Football League titles in a seven-season span; and how he was later inducted into the college and pro football halls of fame.

In some ways, Bailey could identify with Luckman. After all, besides playing the same position, they are about the same height and weight, 5'11", 185 pounds.

"I think it's great that they're doing this," said Bailey, "to have all these people come out for it—the students, the coaches, all those old people."

One of those old people was Luckman himself, who is 78. He sat in the first of two rows of wooden chairs along a sideline. He wore tinted glasses, an overcoat with a carnation, and looked trim, if a little tired.

He said he had "been ill in the hospital for 16 days" and had battled a serious illness for 13 weeks, and while the doctors had suggested he not make this trip from his home in Chicago, he said that nothing could have prevented him from appearing for this honor.

"I'm gratified and thrilled," he said. "I feel wonderful."

One reason for the field's dedication, as Dawes said, was the hope of "galvanizing" students to know their local history "and reach for the stars."

The dedication was the idea of Dr. Ira Warheit, a New York dentist, who believes that not enough is made of the great fund of people who have become national and international successes from Brooklyn. Erasmus has produced such star-studded alumni as Barbra Streisand, Beverly Sills, Bobby Fischer, Eli Wallach, Al Davis, Billy Cunningham, and Barbara McClintock, a Nobel Prize winner in medicine, as well as Bob Tisch, co-owner of the football Giants, who was on hand yesterday.

Marty Glickman, the former track star and sports announcer, played high school football for Madison High and twice played against Luckman's team for the city title, winning one game and losing another.

"He was the best all-round football player that New York City ever developed," Glickman said. In one game, Glickman intercepted a Luckman pass and ran it back for a 75-yard touchdown, racing past the last Erasmus player, the quarterback.

Luckman never forgot it. He recently called Glickman by phone and said, "This is the guy who chased you all over the field and couldn't catch you in 1934."

Allie Sherman, another Brooklyn native and former pro quarterback, as well as a former Giants head coach, recalled studying films of Luckman passing, the way he threw arcing balls to his wide receivers—he set and still shares the NFL record of seven touchdown passes in one game—how he could "brilliantly" learn 150 plays with numerous formations.

"And he was supposed to be able to see what everyone on the field was doing," said Sherman. "When I went behind the center for the snap, I could see only about two people."

"I remember it all as if it were yesterday, how I first came on the field as a freshman, in 1931," Luckman said now standing in front of the microphone. "I can hear the cheers of the crowd. I remember the field being rocky, and patchy grass like a vacant lot and a locker room like you wouldn't believe."

The field behind him now was a smooth green artificial turf. He was about to speak again when the F train rumbled past right alongside the field.

"I—I never in my wildest imagination all those years ago thought this would ever happen to me," said Luckman, appearing genuinely touched, and looking around at old friends and numerous family members. "This is one of the most thrilling days in my life."

Adrian Bailey, like the others, applauded the old Erasmus quarterback. Bailey will be heading for Lock Haven (Pennsylvania) University on a football scholarship. What about his future?

"I have my dreams," he said. "Like I'll bet Mr. Luckman did."

MARSHALL GOLDBERG LED TWO TEAMS TO FOOTBALL TITLES

April 7, 2006

MARSHALL GOLDBERG, AN ALL-AMERICAN running back who led the University of Pittsburgh team to the consensus national championship in 1937 and who later became a six-time All-Pro defensive back for the Chicago Cardinals, helping them win the NFL championship in 1947, died on Monday in Chicago. He was 88.

Marshall Goldberg was twice an All-American, in 1937 and 1938.

His wife, Rita Goldberg, said he died in a nursing home, where he had been suffering in recent years from the effects of brain injuries caused by 14 or 15 concussions he received as a football player.

Though he made his mark as an offensive star in college, Goldberg became best known in the pros as a defensive standout. After a knee injury limited his abilities on offense in 1947, he became a one-way player, believed to be the first in the National Football League to play defense exclusively. In the 1947 title game, he made an interception that was instrumental in the Cardinals' 28–21 victory over the Philadelphia Eagles at Comiskey Park in Chicago. It was the franchise's only championship won in a title game. (The 1925 Cardinals were awarded the championship for having the best record.)

The Cardinals had a chance to repeat the following season in Philadelphia but lost, 7–0, in a game played in a blizzard. It was Goldberg's last game. He retired from football at age 31. (It was also the last appearance in a title game by the Cardinals, who later moved to St. Louis and then to Arizona.)

Goldberg was born on October 24, 1917, in Elkins, West Virginia. His father owned the local movie theater. Goldberg was captain of his high school football, basketball, and track teams, winning all-state honors in football. He was recruited by numerous colleges, including Notre Dame.

"In those days, a Goldberg at Notre Dame would have been a big thing," he once said in an interview, alluding to his being Jewish and the university's being Roman Catholic. He chose Pittsburgh.

At 5'11", 190 pounds, Goldberg was an explosive runner. As a sophomore, he was part of the 1936 team that beat Washington in the Rose Bowl, 21–0. In one game that season, against mighty Notre Dame, he ran for 131 yards. He also made first-team All-American at halfback in 1937.

In 1938, when the team was shorthanded at fullback, Goldberg volunteered to play the position. He went on to win All-American honors again, surprising even his coach, the legendary Jock Sutherland, and was runner-up for the Heisman Trophy.

In all, he rushed for 1,957 yards at Pittsburgh, a program record that stood until 1974, when Tony Dorsett broke it.

Goldberg was drafted by the struggling Cardinals in 1939. The Cardinals hardly gave their runners much protection, and in his first season, Goldberg played with a broken foot. The team finished 1–10. By 1941, however, he had developed into one of the league's better players. Playing both offense and defense, he led the league in interceptions and was third in rushing yardage, third in punt returns, and first in kickoff returns. But the Cardinals finished 3–7–1.

"In those years," he once said, "the Bears, Giants, Packers, and Redskins controlled the league. The rest of the league was just cannon fodder for them. We never had any depth. One year we finished with 17 players. The rest were released. They didn't want to pay a guy $150 a game if they weren't going to use him."

Goldberg joined the Navy in 1943, spending two years in the South Pacific during World War II and earning the rank of lieutenant. After football, he owned his own tool machinery company.

In addition to his wife, he is survived by a son, Marshall Gavin; a daughter, Ellen Tullos; two grandchildren, and four great-grandchildren.

Goldberg was voted into the National College Football Hall of Fame in 1958. But he had not been elected to the National Football League Hall of Fame. He was asked if that bothered him.

"I haven't thought much about it," he said. "I know a lot of great football players who aren't in there. I don't worry about that. There's an old Italian proverb that says 'Life begins tomorrow.' I can't worry about those things. I worry more about the stock market than I do about getting into the Hall of Fame."

IX.

AT ISSUE

O.J. SIMPSON AND THE WORSHIP
OF FALSE SPORTS GODS

June 25, 1994

I WAS STRUCK WITH a statement in a column in another newspaper the other day about O.J. Simpson, which said that "it had taken courage for him to run against men who were twice his size."

The writer went on to say that "it took no courage at all to murder the mother of two children and her companion, if in fact he was the one who did it. And it took no courage to repeatedly beat and terrorize the same woman, which we know for a certainty that he did."

It took no courage, however, for him to play football games, other than those required in summoning up his particular skills in that game, which is nothing more than a game, regardless of how society has often painted such games.

O.J. Simpson was blessed with immense athletic skills. He was strong, he was fast, he was shifty. He was one of the most talented running backs ever, combining the swivel hips of a Gale Sayers with the torpedo-like thrusts of Jim Brown. Simpson, in full football armor, also had blockers blocking for him. When he was with the Buffalo Bills, Simpson called his offensive linemen "the Electric Company," because "they turn the Juice loose."

But it is not uncommon to equate athletic talent with courage. It is done all the time by those in the game to perpetuate their economic base or aggrandize themselves, by the fans as a form of hero worship, and by the press, wittingly or not. Even one of the best sportswriters ever, Red

Smith, once looked back and said he, too, at times, had been guilty of "godding up the players."

Sometimes we are so entranced with skill that we ascribe larger elements to those fortunate enough to have been born with them. We seek to make icons of them. "Like a young god, Hercules—something like that," said Willy Loman, about his son, Biff, a high school football player, in *Death of a Salesman*. "And the sun, the sun all around him. Remember how he waved to me? ...and the cheers, when they came out—Loman! Loman! Loman! God Almighty... A star like that, magnificent, can never really fade away." But Biff did, disastrously.

When Charles Barkley appeared in a television commercial and said that he didn't want to be looked upon as a role model, for people really didn't know him, he received criticism from some quarters. How dare he! And yet all we know of Barkley, and all we knew of Simpson, is that they were sports stars.

But what and who are sports heroes? Was Mickey Mantle, who hit home runs but didn't look after himself or his family, a hero? Was Lawrence Taylor, who said he lusted to slam rivals so hard that their snot flew?

David Cone once told me that what he did wasn't courageous but a father or mother who gets up every morning to go to work to put food on the table for his family is courageous.

People who risk their lives in battle are courageous. During World War II, players like Hank Greenberg and Bob Feller enlisted in the military, and some, like the little-known Red Sox pitcher Earl "Lefty" Johnson, were awarded a Bronze Star for bravery in European action.

People who risk their lives on a ballfield are courageous, as was Jackie Robinson, who braved death threats from those who were against his breaking the color barrier in the majors. Or Pee Wee Reese, who befriended him.

People who overcome great handicaps, who refuse to allow the world to tell them something is impossible, are courageous, like Jim Abbott, the one-handed pitcher of the Yankees.

Courage can come in the little moments, such as the time Jesse Barfield saw a female reporter maligned in the clubhouse and, risking a kind of ostracism, befriended her in a casual but powerful manner.

Mainly, we must look to qualities beyond the playing field. And athletes can be as worthy of respect here as anyone else. Like Roberto Clemente flying off on a mercy mission to bring food and clothing to people in Central America who had suffered an earthquake. Or Dave Bing, who has developed a business and has hired numerous minority-group workers, far exceeding any accomplishment he produced in his Hall of Fame basketball career.

If O.J. Simpson were to be admired for a special characteristic, it might have been his rise from ghetto gang leader to a heretofore contributing member of society.

"I remember that at first I hated O.J.," his first wife, Marguerite, told me in 1968, when they were first married and he was at U.S.C. "He was a tough, always wanting to fight. Once I was at a party, and he and his friends were not allowed in. So they broke windows and came in. It broke up a nice party."

But he changed. Or so we imagined.

Dr. King and the Super Bowl

November 10, 1990

Five states in the United States combine Martin Luther King Day with Robert E. Lee Day. It is ironic that the man who fought for greater freedom for blacks in America is so paired with the man who commanded the Confederate army to, in effect, retain the slave system in this land.

Alabama, Arkansas, Louisiana, Mississippi, and South Carolina annually set aside the third Monday of January to honor King and Lee. Another state, Virginia, honors three on the same day: Dr. King, Lee, and Stonewall Jackson who, like Lee, was a Rebel general and a native son of Virginia.

Since their January birthdays are coincidentally so close together, the men are lumped into one honor day. Many states likewise combine the birthdays of Washington and Lincoln to form Presidents Day, famous now for white sales in department stores.

Sometimes honorary days are little more than an excuse either for an extended weekend, or to sell pillow cases, explode firecrackers, or throw a parade.

Sometimes they may be more meaningful but in the end, hollow or otherwise, such days are symbolic gestures.

Why all this matters now to football fans and others is that the site of a Super Bowl, America's most overwrought extravaganza, is uncertain.

Last March, Phoenix, the home of the National Football League Cardinals, and its adjacent town, Tempe, were selected by the NFL to be host to the Super Bowl in January 1993. But with a condition: Phoenix (Tempe is where the football stadium is located) would get the big game if the citizens of Arizona voted to make Martin Luther King Day a state holiday. Arizona is one of only three states (Montana and New Hampshire are the others) that does not have an official King Day.

In elections last Tuesday, Arizona voters rejected the proposal, and, swiftly, Paul Tagliabue, the commissioner of the NFL, issued this statement: "I do not believe playing Super Bowl XXVII in Arizona is in the best interest of the National Football League. I will recommend to the NFL clubs that this Super Bowl be played elsewhere. I am confident that they will endorse my recommendation."

The football league, a private enterprise, can generally do what it wishes. And Tagliabue's personal motives and intentions may surely be honorable and sincerely felt. But all of it seems heavy-handed, not unusual for an NFL undertakinIn the best of all possible worlds, people everywhere would wish to take a day to genuinely honor and reflect upon all men or women who have made a significant, positive impact on our lives, and emulate them.

It is one thing, however, to enact laws and ordinances to insure equality in jobs, in housing, in education, in where to sit on a bus and in seating at luncheon counters. It is yet another to make an attempt, however well intentioned, to twist the arm of an electorate to pay homage by dint of a symbol. A more effective way for the NFL would have been to declare from the beginning that it would not hold a Super Bowl in any state that does not observe King Day; if the voters want it, then that's up to them.

More perplexing, the cities of Phoenix and Tempe both already observe King Day. It appears unseemly that those municipalities should be penalized because of others in the state.

And why, in fact, should the stipulation for a King Day in Arizona be so crucial to the NFL anyway?

Primarily, it seems, because 56 percent of the players in the league are black, and many of them, as well as a number of white players, according to Joe Browne, a spokesman for the league, are sensitive toward the issue. Thus, the league deemed it important.

Also, perhaps, the NFL Players Association in general is a consideration. It is headed by Gene Upshaw, a black man. Tagliabue seems eager to heal old wounds with the union and work out a collective bargaining agreement, a document absent since the strike of 1987.

The league, receiving assurances from Arizona politicians, was confident the King proposal would pass. A majority of voters, apparently, thought this was a case not of bigotry, but of a kind of blackmail, and voted, by a narrow margin, "No." The guess here is that Arizona has about the same percentage of bigots and nonbigots per square foot as most other states.

The matter of the Super Bowl there, however, isn't concluded. After all, state and private businesses stand to gain an estimated $100 million from Super Bowl week. Beyond that, the bad publicity might also affect their attracting other businesses and conventions, even the Fiesta Bowl, played there.

So another vote by the Arizona legislature is expected in coming weeks, and the NFL believes that an attempt will be made to combine a King Day with another of the state's 10 legal holidays.

Virtue, as the saying goes, has its own rewards.

AT THE SUPER BOWL:
GAS MASKS AND FACE MASKS

January 28, 1991

"ARMS UP, SIR," SAID the man in the yellow security jacket who was standing outside of Gate 1 at Tampa Stadium yesterday afternoon.

In the warm sun, a man wearing a cap with a miniature buffalo head dutifully raised his arms as instructed. The man in the security jacket then patted the man down with a black metal detector that looked like a fraternity paddle.

"Turn around," the security man said. The black paddle made a buzzing sound, as if there were bees inside it, as it roamed over the man's body.

"What's that in your pocket?" the security man asked.

"Just keys," said the man wearing the buffalo head, who also had on a Buffalo Bills jacket.

"Gonna have to see them," security said.

The Bills fan dug them out.

Overhead, there was the whir of helicopters. Behind those people being searched at the gate was a long line of fans also waiting to get into the stadium. Nearby were the concrete barriers and the chain-link fences that had been erected especially for this event. Mounted police officers patrolled those areas. On top of the stadium were men in camouflage uniforms, part of a SWAT team. They held machine guns.

Everyone and everything was searched as thoroughly as possible before the football game, or was supposed to be. Every car that drove into the stadium area was stopped. Every hood was raised. Every trunk was scrutinized.

There had never been a Super Bowl like this Super Bowl. And the Super Bowl hadn't even started yet.

If there were fears that the Super Bowl was a dangerous place because it posed an irresistible temptation for terrorists, those fears appeared to be subsumed for many fans by the excitement of seeing a football game. The constables, of course, had a different perspective.

Suddenly, however, it seemed indecent that there were bombs exploding and gas masks at the ready and troops facing a terrible ground war and countries besieged in the Persian Gulf, and that there was this football game over here—a sports bacchanal, and people pressing in to cheer it all on.

But then one recalled that reports from the front showed great interest there in the game, and that soldiers eagerly planned to watch and listen to it. Unless, of course, as one said, there was an attack.

All of this—celebrations at home while a war is being fought elsewhere—has happened before, and the republic has survived. And rather nicely. So maybe there is indeed something to be said for going on with this Bills-Giants championship game.

At Tampa Stadium it was a literally isolated world. There were no radios and no portable television sets allowed into the game. So people couldn't keep up with any late-breaking developments in the war.

Inside the stadium, before the game, fans waved small flags and viewed scenes on the huge television screens behind each end zone depicting American soldiers on the home front with their children, or with compatriots in the battle zone. At halftime, and in between plays by Jim Kelly and Jeff Hostetler and Thurman Thomas and Ottis Anderson and Bruce Smith and Lawrence Taylor, there were more shots of soldiers, more flag waving.

Next on the screen, President Bush and Barbara Bush spoke about the war effort and the bravery of the troops. Immediately afterward on the field, huge Mickey Mouse and Minnie Mouse and Goofy floats were inflated. All of it lent an air of unreality.

In a nation that was built on the strength of diversity, this was diversity at its maddest edge. Our attention shifted from Saudi Arabia to the White House to the football field to Disneyland. What was the game? What was the marketing (another word for propagandizing)? What was the message? All of it seemed to blur, into colors of red, white, and blue.

"I'm thrilled that they're doing this," said Bill Robertson, from Sayville, Long Island, before the game, as he was being searched. "I feel safer. But nothing would keep me from this game. I'm a Giants fan all the way."

"We've been overlooking a lot of little things today," said Ken Jackson, of the Pasco County sheriff's office. "Like some of the drunks that we'd normally haul into jail. We just tell their friends to get 'em outta here."

Somewhere else, a man began to scream: "My wallet's gone! Someone just took my wallet! Help! Oh, all my credit cards are gone! All my money! I've had my pocket picked!"

War or no war, Super Bowl or no Super Bowl, security or no security, for many it was still business as usual.

WHAT IS SHE DOING IN HERE?

October 7, 1990

ZEKE MOWATT MAY NOT remember or may never have known that there was a time only a relatively short while ago when he would not have been allowed into a professional football locker room, except, of course, as an attendant to pick up soiled jockstraps, or to shine someone's football shoes.

Zeke Mowatt happens to be a black man. He is 29 years old. The National Football League Fact Book lists him as a tight end with the New England Patriots, in his ninth year in the league, who attended Florida State University.

It may be news to Mowatt, but there was a color barrier in the NFL until 1946, when Woody Strode and Kenny Washington broke through. There were color bars in other sports as well, but they have since been knocked down. And right-minded people cheered.

Three weeks ago, Mowatt made it very uncomfortable, if not impossible, for another person in a locker room to do the job assigned. Lisa Olson, a reporter from *The Boston Herald*, says he and a handful of other players with the New England Patriots sexually harassed her. Her crime was that she had been born a woman.

When the owner of the team, Victor Kiam, heard about the incident in the locker room, he said it was a "fly speck in the ocean," and reportedly said that, well, Olson was a "classic bitch." He has since denied the quote, saying he never uses a cliché like "classic."

And then last week after a loss, the coach of the Cincinnati Bengals, Sam Wyche, tossed out of the locker room a reporter from *USA Today* named Denise Tom.

There is a certain history in America that some people know, whether they have, like Mowatt and Wyche and Kiam, attended college, or have not. And that is: there has been, and continues to be discrimination in this country in regard to race, religion, ethnic background, and sex. Some people fight it; some remain slaves to it. National Football League policy, as well as court rulings that go back to the late 1970s, declare that such discrimination regarding women in the locker room is unacceptable behavior, as well as unlawful.

In fact, in every standard contract signed by, and every playbook issued to, an NFL player or coach, there is clearly stated a provision that the league "recognizes that each member of the media has a job to perform," and such individuals should be treated with "courtesy." If courtesy is too much, then at least professional respect.

The locker room is part of the work area for players; it happens to be part of the work area for the news media, as well. It is the way the business has evolved. The professional leagues have understood that publicity generated from locker room stories—the lengthy quotes, the emotion after victories or losses, the humor or the various little dramas played out there that could never be duplicated in relatively buttoned-up interview rooms— is often translated into dollars not just for the owners and league officials, but for the players and coaches as well. Dolts can't figure this out yet. And since women in this land of the free and home of the brave, if our anthem is to be believed, are allowed to compete for jobs—just as, now, blacks and Jews and Irish and Eskimos, among others, are supposed to—then women like Olson and Tom must be able to receive the same access that men get. And if that entails such hardships on the players in the clubhouse as learning to knot a towel around their waists or climb into robes (as most do now), then said players must suffer this vexation, or find another job.

An NFL spokesman said he did not know the ethnic heritage of Wyche and Kiam. And when Bob Sales, the sports editor of *The Boston Herald*, was asked about Kiam's background, he said: "I don't know specifically. But he's American. We're all from somewhere."

Some thought Wyche was a German name, or Irish, possibly; and Kiam Lebanese, or Jewish, maybe. It doesn't matter. In each instance there was someone at some time calling their mothers and fathers, or grandmothers or grandfathers, "damn furriners." If women are denied access to a locker room, then they are being denied a chance to compete equally with men.

And a sports editor would be nuts to hire one under such circumstances. Thus he would in effect be hanging out a sign like those of old: "No Irish need apply," and "No Jews or dogs allowed." Of course, there are chivalrous males who believe that women should simply stay home baking cookies, and wonder what happened to those good old antebellum days. But who are these citizens to tell other citizens how they should or should not be allowed to earn a living? Perhaps they would also deny women the vote, and fire them from the police force and stand in the doorway of the operating room and prevent them from performing surgery.

In the end, the only proper response to this issue was given by Red Holzman, former coach of the New York Knicks. About 15 years ago, a hireling with the Knicks came running into Holzman's office. "Red," shouted the man, "there's a woman in the locker room!" Holzman looked at him. "Does she have proper credentials?" he asked. "Uh, yeah," said the man. "So?" said Holzman.

A "TOUCHDOWN"
TEACHES A LESSON FOR LIFE

October 29, 2003

ON A RECENT SATURDAY morning, on the home football field of the Somers Middle School here, in this quiet town about an hour's drive north of New York City, the coach of the Somers team of primarily seventh graders called a play to begin the second quarter. He had alerted the opponents, John Jay Middle School, as well.

It was hardly something that Vince Lombardi or Bill Parcells might do. But when Bud Von Heyn, the Somers coach, met before the game with Jeff Tepper, the John Jay coach, to go over the ground rules, Von Heyn said: "I need a favor from you." Tepper listened, and agreed.

"Okay, guys, line up," Von Heyn told his young players, in their red jerseys and white pants and silver helmets, on the sideline. "We're going to run the E.J. Shuffle."

Then Von Heyn shouted across the field to the John Jay coach. "Here we go, Jeff."

And Tepper, who had explained the plan to his team before the game on October 18, passed the word to his team.

The play, which would start on the John Jay 35-yard line, was going to be run for E.J. (Eugene Joseph) Greczylo, a 15-year-old eighth grader who had come into the game for the first time—it would be the only time—and was instructed where to position himself in the backfield.

"Remember," Von Heyn told E.J., "follow the fullback. He'll do your blocking."

And so on this lovely fall day, with the flush of brightly colored trees as background, and a modest, but enthusiastic, crowd of parents and friends looking on in the bleachers, the ball was snapped to the quarterback, who then handed it off to E.J.

E.J., the husky lad with the gentle face and an intense but slightly wobbly running style, tucked the ball beside his belly, made his way toward the sideline, and then turned upfield toward the goal line.

"Go, E.J., go!" came shouts from the Somers side of the field—and the players who stood along the John Jay bench.

E.J.'s blocking teammates barely touched their opponents, but the opposing players, giving chase, seemed to fall or trip or lunge and, with arms outstretched as though they were about to embrace a long-lost friend, repeatedly missed the ballcarrier by wide margins.

"The John Jay kids were really into it, maybe even overacting a little," Von Heyn said with a smile. "And when I talked to Jeff after the game, he told me that, yes, he thought his players should get Academy Awards."

Behind all this was the effort to make one kid feel good, to make him feel a part of things. And that kid was E.J. Greczylo, who has Down syndrome, but who had desperately wanted to be on the football team, who had not played in the team's first game the week before and was disappointed.

"When he told me he wanted to play football," said Katie Greczylo, E.J.'s mother, "I thought it wasn't a good idea." Her other child, her son, 12-year-old Alex, was in the kitchen at that moment, and her husband, George, was at work. "Alex said to me: 'Mom, you're always telling us to follow our dreams. Well, football is E.J.'s passion—this is his dream.'"

"'But Alex,' I said, 'What if someone hurts him?'"

She said Alex responded: "E.J.'s a big boy. He could hurt someone, too. I know, I'm his little brother."

Katy Faivre, who teaches the eight children—five of whom have Down syndrome—in a class for disadvantaged seventh and eighth graders at Somers, and who has been E.J.'s teacher since the second grade, said: "In this school, we try to treat the disadvantaged kids as though they are like everyone else. For the most part, they do what the others in the general education do. E.J.'s been in two school plays, he's in the marching band—plays the bass drum. The kid thinks he's a kid."

She added: "As long as you explain to the other kids that the disadvantaged students have certain disabilities, they listen. We make it comfortable for them to ask about it, and the stigma disappears."

In the school corridors, other students hail E.J. as they do any of their other classmates. "Hey, E.J." "What's up, E.J.?" And in his somewhat muffled articulation, E.J., with short blond hair and his book bag strapped on his back, responds in kind, as he heads for football practice.

Down syndrome, a genetic condition that affects an estimated one in 1,000 births in the United States, includes varying degrees of mental retardation.

"The way we feel about E.J.," said Matt Corning, a teammate, "is that he's one of us, part of the team. It feels no different than anyone else. And the E.J. Shuffle? We practice it. So everyone is cool with it."

Von Heyn said: "What amazed me is that when we do something like the Shuffle for E.J., you don't hear the normal grumbling from the other players that you might expect. It's like they look forward to it."

The collaboration that allowed E.J. to score a touchdown was not unique. An article in *Sports Illustrated* a year ago depicted a similar effort in Ohio involving a handicapped member of the high school football team. That youngster was 17 at the time, two years older than E.J.

Katy Greczylo said that when E.J. was born, "We never could have dreamed that all this would happen for him. He's exceeded all our expectations, with the help of this incredible school, and the Special Olympics, which also gave him confidence in the sports he participated in. And this football thing—when you think of all the troubles with sports and football that you read about like the hazing, the overemphasis, this brings you back to what it ought to be about. And the kids that were involved, they'll never forget this. It changes all our lives."

And when E.J. crossed the goal line, he was greeted with congratulatory slaps on the helmet and endearing bumps and high-fives from his teammates. The John Jay players, Von Heyn recalled, some still on the ground from their futile tackles, observed all this with broad smiles.

"My kids are still talking about it," Tepper said. "On the bus back after the game, they were asking me, 'What's Down syndrome?' It was a great learning experience."

The touchdown didn't count, though E.J. wasn't aware of that, and John Jay won, 16–12.

"But E.J. was so pumped with the touchdown," his mother recalled. "And he tried to find me in the bleachers: 'Mom, Mom!' And he put his thumbs up. It blew me away. He looked like just a regular, typical kid out there. And when he came home, he said: 'Dad, I made a touchdown! I made a touchdown!'"

And what did her husband say?

"You mean," she said, "after he wiped away the tears?"

JERRY SMITH:
THE COURAGE OF THE GENTLE

August 31, 1986

THE RECENT NEWS THAT Jerry Smith has been suffering from AIDS for eight months was met with what, on the surface, might seem an unusual reaction from his former Redskins football teammates.

Smith, who has discussed his illness but not his lifestyle, played tight end for the Redskins for 13 seasons, from 1965 to 1977. He caught so many passes, and in such clutch situations, that George Allen, who coached him for more than half his pro career, called him Home Run Smith.

Smith, who is 43 years old, is seriously ill in Holy Cross Hospital in Silver Spring, Maryland. He has dropped from 210 pounds to 150.

"Certainly I'm not going to judge someone else's life style as it affected them," Calvin Hill, the former all-pro running back, told *The Washington Post*. "In terms of how Jerry affected me, both on and off the field, it was very positive. He was an effervescent, helpful guy who was concerned when other guys were down."

"I liked him then and I like him now, AIDS or no AIDS," said Dave Butz, a Redskins defensive tackle.

"If you love a guy," said Bobby Mitchell, a National Football League Hall of Fame receiver and now assistant general manager of the Redskins, "you love him. That's all there is to it. Jerry G. has been a very dear friend almost 20 years."

Those reactions might have come from some less brawny community. But football players? Hard-nosed tough guys? The image of American masculinity?

One of the players who was asked his reaction to Smith's illness, the former free safety Mark Murphy, said: "What Jerry has done, coming out and talking, takes a lot of courage. I think he's right. It will heighten the public's awareness about the disease."

But courage was demonstrated by those who were football friends and teammates of Jerry Smith's. It's a courage greater than plunging for a first down, or chasing down a breakaway runner. It's the courage of character, the courage not to accept stereotypes. It's the courage of true virility. Perhaps it is true, as Leo Rosten wrote in *Captain Newman, M.D.*, that "it is the weak who are cruel, and that gentleness is to be expected only from the strong."

A spokesman at Holy Cross Hospital said that every third phone call there has been for Jerry Smith. There were "lots of Redskins, ex-Redskins, and friends" calling, he said. "It's been phenomenal."

Smith never said he was a homosexual, but it could have been easy for friends to reject what they readily believed to be a lifestyle that may not have been consistent with their own, and not consistent with the image that they have fostered, or had thrust upon them.

And there will surely be some who in fact will now shy away from an association with Jerry Smith. The concern was expressed by his mother, Laverne, at his hospital bedside. Smith is scheduled to be inducted into the Washington Hall of Stars at R.F.K. Stadium this fall. "Do you think when they find out," she asked, "they'll change their minds?" No, her son whispered. The hall committee has confirmed that there will be no change in plans.

The awareness grows that AIDS, which primarily afflicts homosexual men, can reach into the world of the arts, of law and law enforcement and industry and international business and politics and garbage collecting and sports, even football.

Will there be increased research from increased awareness of the disease, due in part to Smith's public acknowledgement?

Possibly, and it might begin in the most unexpected of places, the NFL Charities, which in the last 10 years has committed $7 million to numerous causes, but none to AIDS research. Commissioner Pete Rozelle says it's now a possibility.

Beyond that, there is another important aspect to the Smith case. And Sam Huff, a former star linebacker, said it clearly: "I think it's time that people view football players as people. Because you can play football, what makes you a celebrity? Because you can block and tackle and run? We're people. Sometimes I think people forget that."

And there is a variety of people born with athletic talent. Nowhere is it written that only heterosexuals are allowed to be coordinated.

Dr. Bruce Oglivie, a retired professor of psychology at San Jose State, is a consultant to three National Basketball Association teams, the Portland Trail Blazers, the Milwaukee Bucks, and the Golden State Warriors, and has been a consultant to half a dozen NFL teams over the last 20 years. "Incidents of homosexuality—or, at least bisexuality—have been known, of course, in athletics," he said. "But that shouldn't be surprising. About 6 percent of the male population in America is homosexual. I think it's safe to say that that same percentage of incidence would appear in any field you could name."

He said that some players have asked him about "coming out of the closet." He advised them that it was hazardous, given the potentially negative reaction by teams, the community, and religious leaders. "You cannot anticipate how others would respond," he said. "The possibility is great that they would treat it as a threat to their idealized concept of masculinity, and what sports represents to them—the essence of manhood. It would fly in the face of the projected needs of the public, their fantasy of what a man should be."

Dr. Oglivie had recommended that they retain a private lifestyle. Those few athletes—such as the former NFL running back Dave Kopay and the former Dodgers outfielder Glenn Burke—who did acknowledge their homosexuality, did so after their playing career was over.

Dr. Oglivie said that he was heartened by the response of Smith's teammates.

"It indicated how much we've grown as people, and are willing to accept a diversion from ourselves," he said. "And that we don't measure the acceptability of a human being on the basis of a single dimension such as sexual orientation, one tiny, tiny segment of the totality of the human being.

"I think the response of these football players to Jerry Smith is a beautiful thing."

IT'S TIME FOR "REDSKINS" TO EXIT

November 15, 1996

SPORTS TEAMS IN AMERICA, and environs, insist on nicknames, for some reason. This has been going on for a hundred years. Most of the nicknames are so dumb they are beyond the pale of rational discussion. Why, for example, anyone would want to go around calling himself a Raptor, or a Net, or a Heat—or, for that matter, a Blue Devil or a White Sock or, in the case of the Scottsdale (Arizona) Community College athletes, an Artichoke—ought to be fodder only for a psychiatrist's couch.

But some nicknames have taken on a different hue in modern times, and have come to offend people, and not just those who have a soft spot in their heart for a Raptor, et al. They are the nicknames associated with American Indians.

I received in the mail the other day a "Message to Miamians," from the president of Miami University in Oxford, Ohio. President James C. Garland wrote a letter to alumni, of which I am one, saying that the Miami Board of Trustees had agreed to seek a new nickname for its sports teams, that the name, the Redskins, was inappropriate for use by an institution of higher learning.

This has been years in coming, since many people associated with the university were dead set against change. Some said it was part of school tradition to retain that name, others said the university had more pressing issues to deal with. Others added that Redskins was a name that held in high esteem the Miami Indian tribe that once lived in the region, for which the university was named. The Miami tribe, which now lives in Oklahoma, sent a formal letter to the university seeking the change, and the university, to its credit, is honoring it.

But other schools with tribal references have already changed. Stanford, for one, went from the Indians to the Cardinal, and Marquette from the Warriors to the Golden Eagles.

Professional teams like the Washington Redskins, the Atlanta Braves, the Kansas City Chiefs, and the Cleveland Indians have resisted name alterations, even though there have been numerous protests by various groups over the years. The political and economic clout of these tribes has been underwhelming, and the fans still come to the game in feathers and war paint, carrying rubber tomahawks, with their mindless chopping and chanting, much to the delight of the owners of these organizations.

A few years ago, St. John's University changed the nickname of its athletic teams from the Redmen to the Red Storm.

"Sure, some people hated the change, but some people hate any kind of change," said Lou Carnesecca, the former St. John's basketball coach. "But it wasn't our posture to offend anybody, even if it's one person. And I know we did.

"I once got a call from an athletic director of an Oregon high school which was on an Indian reservation. He told me, 'Coach, I love to see your team play, but it makes me very uncomfortable to see the mascots go around scalping people, and that kind of thing.'

"And I thought, 'What kind of message are we sending, and this being a university?' Few people seem to care anymore that the name has been changed."

Miami is now seeking suggestions for a new athletic nickname. Some of the several hundred entries by alumni that have been sent to Dr. Phillip R. Shriver, head of this search committee, have sought to maintain the "red" and the "skin" appellations. Thus the Red Bricks, the Red-Skinned Potatoes, and, inevitably, the Sun Burns. Someone suggested Feather Heads, which seems unbookish, while Climbing Ivies seems unsportsy.

One that probably stands little chance of acceptance is Miami Vice.

Most school and professional nicknames reflect the animal kingdom, from Horned Frogs and Mighty Ducks to Tigers, Lions, and even Anteaters (California-Irvine), but where are those college names with learning aspirations, such as the Intellectuals or the Literati or the Bibliophiles?

Nor do current nicknames reflect what these sporting groups are supposed to be all about. Badgers, Hoosiers, Avalanche. They make absolutely no sense. I considered sending this entry to Dr. Shriver: the Miami

Nothings. But some feelings in Oxford might be hurt. So I've settled on a name simple but resonant, a name strong with purpose and studious vigor, a name unique in the annals of sports nicknames. I propose: the Miami Team.

A BEVY OF BRUISES

December 24, 1983

A THIGH. A NECK. A leg. Is it an anatomy class? A butcher's inventory? It's the National Football League's injury report!

Each week readers of many newspapers across the country are treated to a long list of the limp and halt among the 28 teams. On the report for any given weekend, there may be more than 300 players, catalogued with more than 400 injuries.

To some fans, it's a way of finding out to which of their favorite players they should send chicken soup. To other readers, it's indispensable information for betting games. (In part because it is seen as simply a gambling tool, some newspapers don't print the information.) To yet others, the list reads like an accident report from an emergency ward.

The roster of the ailing mentions the team, the player and his position, his disability, and his status: "Probable" means likely to play, "questionable" means it's 50-50 whether he'll play, and "doubtful" means he'll most likely not play.

For example, a random look at the wounded for the two first-round playoff games, today and Monday, included: "Broncos S Mike Harden (ankle), probable."

"He's got an ankle," said Mike O'Brien, an assistant in the Broncos' public relations department, using the parlance of football in describing the injury. "He's actually got two ankles, but only one is sore."

Some time ago, Rick Upchurch, a wide receiver for Denver, had a pinched nerve on the left side of his neck, and it was listed as "left neck."

"We got some calls from people wondering how his right neck was," said O'Brien.

Some guys are hurting in more than one place. For Monday's game, Vince Ferragamo, the Rams quarterback, is listed with "right hand/flu," though "probable."

"Our record for one person with the most listed hurts," said Merrill Swanson, the Vikings' public relations director, "is our cornerback, Rufus Bess, this season. We put him down for ribs, ankle, shoulder, and wrist."

But Tony Dorsett of the Cowboys may be the all-time leader for multiple injuries. We'll never know. At one point this season, he was listed with "general all-body soreness."

Sometimes the ailments aren't related to football. Ed Croke, the Giants' P.R. man, mentioned that Chris Foote, a center, recently had "a stomach"—food poisoning.

Croke was asked about the rest of the player: "Does Foote have a foot?"

"I'm sure he does," said Croke.

Croke recalled that there was a player named Arms with the Cardinals years ago.

Anyone else in the NFL with an anatomical name? Croke thought a moment. "Leonard Tose, but he's an owner," Croke said.

One may read of players suffering from "tibia" and "fibula" and "Achilles" and "clavicle," but the reports by the NFL try to keep things simple.

"A stretched left brachial plexus," said Greg Aiello of the Cowboys public relations department, "comes out 'neck.'"

There is also a covey of concussions dotting the injury-laden landscape. "It's the most common injury," said Joe Gordon, publicity director for the Steelers, "with knees second."

In the NFL, a player is considered to have a concussion when he has taken a hard blow to the head—and the head remains on his shoulders, even though, to the player, it may not always seem that way.

Steve Dils, the Vikings quarterback, was banged in the head during one game and suffered a memory loss. "He couldn't even remember where his locker was," recalled Merrill Swanson. "We listed him as questionable, but he played the next game."

Sometimes players will play when one would think they couldn't get out of bed.

In January 1975, the Steelers' Dwight White, with viral pneumonia, tackled the Vikings quarterback Fran Tarkenton for the first safety in

Super Bowl history. Jack Youngblood played for the Rams in the 1980 Super Bowl with a broken leg, and a specially fitted cast. Keena Turner, the 49ers linebacker, played in the 1982 Super Bowl with chicken pox.

These are players who will go through walls to play football—hospital walls.

The phenomenon of injury lists in newspapers is a relatively new thing, no more than six or seven years old. Its primary function, it seems, is to be fair to gamblers.

"Before the reports were in the papers, you'd have to scramble around to try to get inside information on injuries," said Rocco Landesman, Broadway producer, financial consultant, and regular sports bettor. "There were guys making money by selling the information that they somehow obtained. Now the NFL provides it as a service.

"The betting line follows the injury reports. If there's an injury to a key player, the whole complexion of a game might change."

Landesman cited the San Diego–Denver game of October 23. "San Diego was a two-point favorite until it was reported that Dan Fouts, the Chargers quarterback, was injured and wouldn't play," said Landesman. "Upon publication of the information, the betting line changed, and Denver became a 2.5-to-3-point favorite.

"The NFL doesn't like it if some gamblers have an advantage over others. So they give us all an equal shot. It's kind of them."

According to Jim Heffernan, director of public relations for the NFL, "the injury list insures the integrity of the game."

There is an argument. Some people believe that it insures the integrity of the bet.

Why should one team tell its rival about injuries? It doesn't tell the other team about game plans, does it? Injuries are none of the other team's business. But NFL officials seem to understand that gambling is a reason for the tremendous interest in their sport, and they are wise enough to make the games sporting for gamblers. Meanwhile, the injury lists tumble along—with their array of ankles and legs, hamstrings and sternums, arms and fingers, and hips and heads.

It's a game that requires, on one level, a speculator's spirit, and, on another, good health insurance.

FOR THE BIG GAME,
INSPIRATION BEFORE PERSPIRATION

January 25, 1992

MINNEAPOLIS—A FAMILIAR SOUND IN the Buffalo Bills locker room before a game is the thump, thump of Leonard Smith's head against a metal door, or a cement wall, whichever he happens to locate first.

"He bangs his head like that all the time," said Jeff Wright, the team nose tackle, regarding the singular activity of Smith, the strong safety. "It's his way of pumping himself up for the game."

Does Smith wear a helmet when he's attacking the building?

"Oh, no," said Wright. "No helmet. He hits his head on the wall and then he shakes the head around a little, and he's ready to go. Personally, I think it's a little crazy. But to each his own."

Wright himself says he paces a lot, like a lion in a cage, and may periodically mumble to himself, but otherwise he does nothing he might be apprehended for on a city street.

Football players have often found uncommon ways to raise their emotions so that they come out of the locker room as though shot from a cannon. Certainly nothing will change before the Super Bowl Sunday.

"You want everything perfect before the game, you want no distractions," said Gary Clark, the Redskins wide receiver. "Like if a shoelace breaks, or the equipment manager hasn't put your towel exactly where you want it, or your tape is feeling a little tight, well, you may go off a little. You're all gigged up for the game. So you kind of explode. I know I can't stand still. You try to hold back the horses to game time, but it's hard."

"Dexter Manley was one of the most highly charged I've ever seen. No blackboard was safe in the locker room when he was around. He'd run around screaming and foaming at the mouth and then you'd hear a blackboard being smashed and disintegrating. As for myself, well, I'll punch a locker or a helmet. But I've never broken a hand. Just jammed a few fingers is all."

A seemingly gentle soul like Steve Tasker, the special teams ace of the Bills, can get excitable over little things. "Like when there's no Juicy Fruit in the gum box," he said. "Gets me wild."

Matt Millen of the Redskins takes another tack. He says he sits in front of his locker and tries to relax before a game. He closes his eyes, listens to music on his headset, goes over his game plans, even prays some. "I don't want to waste energy," he said. "I want to be alone. And I don't want anyone messin' with me. I get real sore if they do."

Once upon a time, he said, he and others in the National Football League got ready for a game in a somewhat different manner. "You took whatever bennies you had," he said, referring to a drug of choice. Now, he said, the players will drink coffee or Coke to get the high they had sought before. What changed the drug-taking? "Drug testing," he said.

Meanwhile, Glenn Parker, an offensive tackle for Buffalo, sits in front of his locker and listens to music that inspires. "One I like is the theme song from *The Lion in Winter*," he said. "I like to think I'm going into a medieval battle, with charging horses and damsels in distress, that sort of thing."

Bruce Smith, the Bills linebacker, says he listens to rap: "I want something up-tempo." So does his teammate and fellow linebacker, Carlton Bailey. One of the things Bailey also does before a game is watch out for Leonard Smith: "Leonard goes high-fivin' after everybody. He tries to break your hand, basically. You try to avoid him, but he finds you."

It is almost certain Leonard Smith, who has an infection in his knee, won't play Sunday, but he is expected to be in the locker room. "So they tell me," said Bailey, absently flexing his fingers.

Jim Kelly, the Bills quarterback, said he doesn't hit anything or scream before a game. "I stay calm," he said, "because once I take the field I know it's all in my hands."

For the most part, Tim Johnson, a Redskins defensive tackle, remains cool before a game, too, though "once every blue moon," he said, "I may vent some emotion."

"In high school I was more the other way, very excitable," said Johnson. He remembers a game that his team in Florida, Sarasota High School, was going to play against an archrival, Lakeland. "In the locker room, I was talking, I was shouting, and I banged my head against a locker, hoping to get my team stoked up for the game."

Did they win or lose? "You know, I can't remember," he said.

Did he think he might have remembered if he didn't bang his head against the locker?

"Maybe," he said.

X

A TRIO OF U.S. PRESIDENTS AND SHOULDER PADS

THE GIANTS MEET THE GIPPER

February 14, 1987

THE COMMODIOUS EAST ROOM of the White House became very crowded suddenly when the Giants football team trooped in.

They arrived yesterday afternoon on a field trip and, like many such groups, brought cameras and tape recorders and wide eyes. They also brought a hefty helping of thick shoulders.

Some 300 spectators and guests had been invited to view them on this excursion—the highlight of which was to meet The Gipper, or the man who played George Gipp many seasons ago in *Knute Rockne, All-American*.

Many in the crowd looked to see which of the Giants had signed on.

"Is George here?" someone asked, craning his neck. "I don't see him."

"He's right there," someone else replied, pointing to the full-length portrait on the wall.

"Not George Washington, Dumbo, I mean George Young."

Young, the Giants general manager, was indeed there, as would be expected. Field trips are nothing new to Young, who once served his apprenticeship as a high school history teacher in Baltimore.

Normally when they're in town, these weighty citizens end up at R.F.K. Stadium, where they spend Sunday afternoons crashing into an assemblage of local denizens. But not this afternoon. In the handouts that read, "Schedule of the President" for Friday the 13th, President Reagan would meet with the vice president and Donald Regan at 10:00 AM, receive his national security briefing from Frank Carlucci at 10:30, meet with welfare-reform experts at 11:00, lunch with Veep Bush at noon, meet with

Secretary Shultz at 1:00 and then at 2:30: "The President Greets the New York Giants, Super Bowl Champions."

The president has recently had his hands full, what with matters of state as well as matters of the diamond: he greeted the Mets after their World Series triumph; more matters of the gridiron—he welcomed Joe Paterno and the Nittany Lions after their ranking as the top college football team in the country after their victory over Miami in the Fiesta Bowl. And matters of the sea—he was there with congratulations when Dennis Conner and his America's Cup deck hands showed up on the White House doorstep.

Thirty-two members of the team were there now. Of the most prominent players, only Joe Morris was unable to attend. Coach Bill Parcells was also conspicuous by his absence. Neither Morris nor Parcells, apparently, was playing partisan politics. Each reportedly had family obligations that took precedence.

"Ladies and Gentlemen, the President of the United States!"

Those seated stood and applauded, and the players smiled and applauded.

President Reagan wore a brown striped suit, brown tie and brown shoes, and moved among the players, smiling and pumping hands.

Someone seeing him close up for the first time is struck with how hardy he looks at 76, yet the streaks of gray in his black hair are more apparent than on television, and a hearing aid is in place in his right ear.

He also appeared slightly shorter than his official playing height of 5'11", but that certainly could be because of the crowd he was hanging out with at this moment—guys like Brad Benson, at 6'3" and 270 pounds, and Leonard Marshall, 6'3" and 285, and Lawrence Taylor, 6'3" and 243.

When he finished shaking hands, he said into the microphone, "They're gonna be big when they get as old as I am." The president, though, apparently understands hugeness in football players. He once played guard for Eureka College, and when George Martin later presented him with a gift, a replica of the Super Bowl ring that looked as big as a bowl, he said, "I once played against a guy who could have worn that."

He had said that he had suggested inviting the Giants to his birthday party on February 11, but, he said, referring to his wife, Nancy, "She thought that wearing Gatorade was not very presidential."

This was in reference to the Giants' unusual predilection at the end of winning games for dumping a bucket of Gatorade over the head of their coach.

The president was all upbeat and talked about the spirit of the Giants and how they loved to have fun but loved winning more, and told a couple of football anecdotes—he mentioned a Notre Dame coach, but quickly said, "No, not the one you're thinking of, but Frank Leahy. We'd be here all day with Rockne stories."

Then he referred to the Giants' supporters as "our fans." He quickly corrected himself. "Your fans, I should say, I don't have many fans anymore," he said, with a little smile.

He dropped the subject of popularity polls and said a few more kind words about these beefy gentleman who surrounded him, and then departed.

He was on his way to Camp David for a weekend of relaxation from Iran, from the economy, from, presumably, football.

He had invited the Giants to see him off on the South Lawn, and they assembled there, as he went upstairs to change.

When he came down, he did so from the stairs leading from the second floor, and surprising the Giants. And he surprised them again by taking a familiar-looking orange bucket and dumping the contents over the head of the team captain, Harry Carson, who is the culprit who gets Parcells.

The bucket was filled with popcorn. Carson took the rest of the contents and dunked the president with it.

Everyone laughed, and the president climbed into his helicopter and took off, smiling and waving at the Giants, and the Giants smiling and waving back at him.

RICHARD NIXON'S FOOTBALL ORIGINS

April 26, 1994

RICHARD NIXON SAID THAT if he had his life to live over, he would like to have ended as a sportswriter. When he was the president he was known as the No. 1 sports fan. When I met him for the first time and we chatted, on opening day at Yankee Stadium 10 years ago, on a walk between the press box and George Steinbrenner's box, he said, "I'm sure you lead a very interesting life." I replied, "Not as interesting as yours, Mr. President."

He smiled and shrugged. "Oh, well," he said. A man approached and politely asked Mr. Nixon if he would sign three baseballs. Mr. Nixon obliged, and took the baseballs and the man's pen. With the baseballs signed, the man left and disappeared into the crowd.

As we started talking again, Mr. Nixon suddenly turned to the Secret Service agent at his side. "Would you give this to that man?" he said. "I don't want to steal his pen."

Mr. Nixon didn't laugh at what I silently took to be a kind of irony. It was 10 years since he had been forced to resign as president and, sometime before that, he had said, "I am not a crook."

But when I met him he was already in a comeback mode, seeking to climb from a disgraced president to a respected elder statesman. While I had rarely shared his politics, I had to admire certain traits. As one aide said, Mr. Nixon always kept bobbing back up, like a cork.

The drive to win, or to stay on top, has its negative side, as well, and Mr. Nixon's intensity to trample his foes contributed to his being toppled, as I saw it. Like holding in football, or scuffing a baseball, Mr. Nixon considered the deceptive elements just part of the game. But the former third-string tackle and end at Whittier College, who took a "terrific lick-ing" in practices, according to his coach, Chief Newman, was able to get back on his feet again and again. "Dick liked the battle, though," said Newman, "and the smell of sweat."

So when Richard Nixon, this most fascinating and contradictory of public figures, invited me to his office downtown to continue our conver-sation, I took him up on it.

He wore a gray-blue wool suit and blue print tie and black shoes. He sat in an arm chair in the corner of the room. The mid-morning light streamed in through the high windows but he sat under a turned-on lamp, creating shadows on his face and making his famous ski nose look more sloping.

The chair I sat in was placed just beyond normal conversation distance. He also sat with his suit coat buttoned and he put his feet up on the foot stool. All of it a little formal, a little awkward. But he was friendly and his interest in sports and their broader lessons was genuine.

He brought up Tommy John, the Yankees pitcher, who was back on the mound after undergoing arm surgery. "He's amazing, to come back with that arm," the former president said. "Comebacks are an important element in politics. Churchill suffered a defeat with the Dardanelles in 1914 and was in disgrace. He wasn't brought back to lead the government until he was 66 or 67 years old. And came back again at 80. Adenauer was under house arrest and returned as an old man. De Gaulle was in the wilderness for a long time before he made it back.

"But never be afraid of losing, because losing only has to be a tempo-rary condition. Politics is like sports, in that we're very competitive and want to win. And you learn that if you lose one race, there can always be another."

He said that President Carter was correct in not allowing the United States Olympic team to go to Russia in 1980. "I would have done the same thing," he said. "How can you jump hurdles with the Russians when they're raping their neighbor, Afghanistan?" He said: "I felt sorry for the athletes, but politics shouldn't be held hostage to sports. And even though I'm an avid sports fan, it has to take a secondary place to national concerns."

He recalled the 1984 opener and sitting with delight next to Roger Maris who told him that he could never have hit 61 homers in 1961 with-out a strong supporting cast. Mr. Nixon remembered, "I didn't want to ask him about his condition"—Maris had cancer—"it might have embar-rassed him."

After my visit, we ran into each other on occasion and shared a mod-est correspondence. At lunch once with some people in the Yankees press room, I mentioned the incident of Mr. Nixon and the man with the pen. "That was me!" said Barry Halper, a Yankees limited partner. I had just met Halper and hadn't recognized him from that moment years earlier. "You know," he mused, "I never did get my pen back."

Was Mr. Nixon's heart, after all, in the right place, despite his profound and clumsy faults? For now, just days after his death, the thought gives some pause.

GERALD FORD:
A LINEMAN'S DREAM COME TRUE

September 11, 1974

NEW YORK—"PRESIDENT FORD IS getting to enjoy a lineman's dream—he has a chance to handle the ball and score all the touchdowns he wants," said Merlin Olsen, defensive tackle for the Los Angeles Rams.

"All linemen dream about that. We all want to be the quarterback. I think the reason is that when you enjoy the game, you want to have as much impact on it as you can."

As has been noted in periodicals from the *Grand Rapids Press* to *Pravda*, President Gerald Ford was an offensive center and linebacker for the University of Michigan from 1932 through 1934. Ford was captain and most valuable player on his team his senior year, and was a capable enough bruiser to make the College All-Star game in Chicago. He turned down professional offers from the Green Bay Packers and the Detroit Lions.

Ford, however, has absorbed much ridicule for his football days. In a now celebrated quote, then President Johnson once criticized then Congressman Ford (who was fighting a Johnson proposal) for "playing one too many football games without a helmet."

The stigma of the bewildered, snaggle-toothed lineman crept up in the 1972 campaign, when Democratic vice presidential candidate Sargent Shriver made a speech blasting President Nixon's economic advisers as "a bunch of big, slow, dull-witted linemen protecting the quarterback."

That statement so irritated Merlin Olsen that he wrote Shriver a letter. Olsen, who then supported Nixon's economics, wrote, "I'd be glad to debate the subject with you anytime you choose—that is, if you don't mind sitting down with one of those big, slow, dull-witted linemen."

The 6'4", 250 pound Olsen is more than a mere pea-brained mastodon. He holds a master's degree in economics from Utah State University and his thesis, on the effects of the Cuban revolution on the world sugar market, was called, "An Economic Evaluation of the Product Sugar with Special Emphasis on the Abnormal Sugar Market of 1963-4."

"I'm sure Shriver is now sorry he made that slur on linemen," said Olsen, "but I never did get a reply from him."

"Some of the best thinkers in football are the linemen," said Olsen. "Guys like Alan Page ad Bob Lilly and Reggie McKenzie. Anyone familiar with the game knows that linemen cannot be dumb and be good. There is too much to know, too much to respond to. There are a thousand assignments and combinations we must be ready to read and react to in a split second. We have to know as much as the quarterback."

Recently, linemen have been getting some of their due, particularly with the Buffalo Bills. Star running back O.J. Simpson has given much credit to his line. And Reggie McKenzie has said of himself and his fellow blockers for Simpson: "We're the Electric Company—because we cut the juice loose."

Merlin Olsen said that Ford's ascension to the presidency "pleases me: it is a tremendous triumph, and I'm sure he has the vote of confidence of all the linemen in the country."

"Usually," continued Olsen, "linemen do the work and get little glory. And Ford for the past 25 years or so has done yeomen service as a congressman, but kept a low profile. In other words, doing work in the lineman's tradition.

"What I like about Ford so far is that he has a quiet, relaxed confidence about himself. It reminds me of something Bill Russell, the former Celtic said: 'In order to be effective, you have be in touch with yourself.' You know, you have to understand your role and be content and happy with it.

"I think Ford has demonstrated so far that he can handle himself in a critical situation, without overstatement and without overdramatics. It may be that he learned those qualities early being a lineman. But to say that he is where he is because of football would be bull.

"I think too often in this country we overemphasize sports, and so-called sports heroes. We attach superhuman qualities to athletes on the field. And that's doing a disservice to young people.

"Athletes are just people. And not necessarily superior people. Just because they have particular skills, are performance-oriented and very competitive, doesn't mean that they lead exemplary lives, or that one should pattern his life after them.

"President Ford spent much more time in the classroom and in Congress than he did on the football field, and I'm sure that those two experiences had a greater impact on him than football did.

"Like any experience, you only get out of it what you put into it. And a man and his character are made by his total environment.

"Remember, Richard Nixon was a college lineman, too, though he wasn't the outstanding athlete Ford was. Still, he shared some common experiences but, obviously, was a very different kind of man.

"But we won't go into Nixon. There are enough Monday morning quarterbacks doing that right now, including, I imagine, Nixon himself."

XI

PRIOR TO
THE PROS

WHEN BEAR BRYANT
CONSULTED ANN LANDERS

June 24, 2002

IT BEGAN FOR ME 20 years ago this year, when I learned that Bear Bryant had written to Ann Landers for advice. I wrote a column about it, thinking that if there ever was an odd couple, this was it. Bryant, the tough, old, iconic Alabama football coach, and—excuse my repeating myself two decades later—Ann Landers, "America's equivalent of the Oracle of Delphi."

Bryant wrote her about her columns more than once, and when I asked him about it, he said he had read "jillions of 'em."

Landers became a fan of Bryant's, especially after he wrote requesting an article of hers titled "Dead at 17," regarding the tale of a boy who takes the family car, drives carelessly, has a wreck, and then sees himself declared dead and buried.

"It's a story that really gets to ya," Bryant said. He wanted to read it to his players. She reran the column for him. "I'll take advice from anyone if it's good," he said.

She said: "I can't hack football. I keep looking for the ball while everyone else is cheering." But she liked the Bear. "He must be a very sensitive, warm person to care so much about the kids who pass through his life," she said.

After I wrote the column, I got a letter from her commenting that she "loved running into her name" in a sports column, of all things, and it began a friendship between us that lasted until Saturday morning, when she died of cancer at 83.

Esther Lederer—Eppie to her friends, and Ann Landers to her legion of fans and readers around the world (at her peak, in the 1970s, she was said to be read by as many as 90 million people daily)—knew little about sports but a lot about people, and people in sports interested her as much as Desperate in Denver or Upset in Upper Sandusky.

She was a small, impeccably dressed and coiffed woman with a great laugh and a sense of dignity and humanity and candor. She was born in Sioux City, Iowa, but lived virtually her entire adult life in Chicago, in a large apartment on East Lake Shore Drive. She didn't play sports that I was aware of, but she said every day she put on her "gym shoes," the Chicago equivalent of New York "sneakers," and ran around her apartment.

I said, "You run around your apartment?"

"Sure," she said, "it's a big apartment." But sometimes the elevator operator and doormen of her apartment building—for whom she brought back cookies after a dinner at a restaurant—were aware that she was running up and down the back stairs of the residence.

She liked Bill Bradley's politics but told me that when she met him she said, "You just have to learn to speak more forcefully."

When I wrote a column criticizing Michael Jordan for not supporting the senate candidacy of Harvey Gantt, a black liberal, in his home state, North Carolina, and found Jesse Helms winning by a narrow margin, she wrote me: "I too wondered why he was silent when a simple gesture of support for Gantt could have beat the"—here she used a Yiddish word that is an expression of, at best, contempt—"of all times, but didn't give it." She grew up using Yiddish and it was part of her everyday vocabulary.

While she disapproved of Jordan's evasiveness on a significant issue, she was a big fan of his mother, whom she met at a fund-raising event. "Mrs. Jordan," she said, "has class. I wish Michael would have displayed more of it."

She thought John Rocker's remarks about New Yorkers, subway riders, people of color, among others, were detestable. I wrote a column about Rocker that she thought didn't go far enough in condemnation. "Your column on John Rocker was okay, but no Pulitzer," she said. "You were much too easy on the jerk. Yes, you nailed him, but the nailing was too subtle."

On yet—surprisingly—another football topic: "If you've done anything on the Mike Ditka story I haven't seen it," she wrote about Ditka, the Chicago Bears coach. "In my opinion the Chicago papers have been very rough on McCaskey"—Mike McCaskey was president of the Bears. "I guess the blue collar and the blue blood just don't mix."

She used an item in a column two years ago that was meant to show that even great people fail at times: "Babe Ruth struck out 1,330 times—a major league record." She received a letter from a man in Honolulu saying that Reggie Jackson, not Ruth, was the leader in strikeouts.

She scripted a note to me on the margin of that letter: "Is this true? I haven't had any other mail about it. Help. R.S.V.P. Eppie."

Alas, it was true. Reggie, I replied, whiffed 2,597 times. She ran a correction.

When I learned of Eppie's death, I called her daughter, Margo Howard, her only child, in Boston. I expressed my sympathy and asked about the funeral.

"My mother made it emphatic that she did not want a funeral," Margo said. "She said she didn't want to have people bothered by flying across the country for it."

For one of the few times, Eppie was wrong. It would not have been a bother to fly anywhere for Eppie, for any reason. I, and some 90 million others, will miss her greatly.

John Gagliardi: An Unconventional Tradition of Success

November 6, 2003

THE TINTINNABULATIONS OF THE Abbey Church tower bells mixed with voices as the only sounds heard on the football practice field. It was on a recent gray late afternoon, and the St. John's College team was running plays in this relatively isolated area in the central part of the state, located amid a forest with the trees nearly bare of leaves.

There were no whistles.

"I don't like to have someone raise his voice to me, and I believe it's the same for the players," the head coach has said. "A whistle is like raising your voice. The players can get my drift with normal tones."

For a long time in football, it was considered a resolution of toughness for coaches to withhold water from players, even on very hot days. But water was readily available here, and the coach said he has never withheld it from his players.

"I grew up in a coal-mining region in Colorado, and I remember the mules sweating like crazy when they came out of the mines," the coach said. "They were given water and it surely didn't hurt them. When the miners came out, they got water. It only helped. So I figured, how couldn't it be good for my football players, too?"

And there is no tackling in practice. Never has been. "Why risk injury in practice and not have the player ready for the game?" the coach said. "Most teams protect the quarterback in practice. We protect all the players. We assume they'll get to do enough tackling in the game."

And here the gentle coach shows another side. "And if we don't," one of his players said, "well, John tells us he'll just have to get someone in our place who does."

That's another thing. The coach insists on being called by his first name. Not the traditional "Coach." "They know I'm the coach," he said. "I don't find it necessary to keep reminding them."

When considering Vince Lombardi or Bill Parcells or even Amos Alonzo Stagg, this unconventional approach would seem to be effective maybe for a sandlot team in touch football, but for a college football team, even a Division III team, like St. John's?

But, at this school run by Benedictine monks, it works, at least for John Gagliardi. And "winning with No," as he calls it—there are about 100 such "no's"—works so well that Gagliardi, at 77, stands to have the most coaching victories in the history of college football.

On Saturday, at home in Clemens Stadium, the red-and-white-clad Johnnies (8–0), take on Bethel, another unbeaten team in their Minnesota Intercollegiate Athletic Conference. If St. John's wins, it will be the 409th college victory for Gagliardi, in his 55th season as a head football coach. It would move Gagliardi one victory past the record he holds with Eddie Robinson, the retired Grambling coach. Gagliardi (408–114–11) is 68 victories ahead of Florida State's Bobby Bowden and 70 ahead of Penn State's Joe Paterno, both of whom follow him in the victories column. Gagliardi has also won three NCAA Division III championships and has a record of 20–9 in NCAA playoff games. (Robinson's record was 408–165–15.)

"Bethel is tough," he said. "They make me nervous."

Gagliardi (pronounced guh-LAHR-dee) never underestimates an opponent, which is part of the secret of success. And sometimes he is right to be concerned. Before last Saturday's game, on the road against St. Thomas, he said he was terrified that the game might be played in the mud—rain was forecast—and that St. Thomas, a longtime rival, would be up for the game. This despite St. Thomas' being 3–5, riddled with injuries and a young squad, as opposed to the St. John's team, which has three All-American players: wide receiver Blake Elliott, quarterback Ryan Keating, and linebacker Cameron McCambridge, all seniors.

It turned out that Gagliardi had reason for alarm. The Johnnies, before an overflow crowd of some 7,300 fans, fell behind in the second half for the first time this season, and they were losing, 12–7, with eight minutes to go in the game. It hadn't rained, but it was cold, and on the sideline Gagliardi pulled his maroon parka hood over the red baseball cap that covered the sparse gray hair on his head. He stood in ankle-high winter boots with his hands behind his back, watching a play through his wire-rim spectacles, seeming as calm as someone waiting for a light to change at a street corner.

When the play would end he would take a short stroll, sometimes dipping into his pocket to check the 15 or so note cards that he keeps his plays on—his team has no playbooks—and perhaps say something to one of his assistants. And then Gagliardi would stop to watch the next play, hands again folded behind his back.

"He looks so casual, so stoic out there," said Pat Reusse, a reporter for *The Minneapolis Star Tribune* who covers the team regularly, "but no one takes losing harder than John. He's churning up inside."

In fact, when Gagliardi was asked recently how long he thought he would stay as a coach, he replied: "As long as my health holds out, or if we start losing. And if we start losing, my health will surely not hold out."

Well, the Johnnies cut their deficit to 12–9 with a safety, and then Brandon Keller, a 5'7" junior place-kicker, booted a 20-yard field goal to tie the score with 3 minutes 16 seconds left. After another march downfield, Keller kicked a 35-yard field-goal with eight seconds remaining to give Gagliardi his 408th career victory, 15–12—on his 77th birthday, no less.

The large St. John's contingent in the stands warbled "Happy Birthday" to him; he allowed himself a smile after the winning field goal, and gave a congratulatory pat on the back to the kicker and a little wave of appreciation to the fans. "I don't go in for celebrations," he said afterward. "I'm too old for celebrations."

Although it is not often apparent, he does derive great satisfaction from his achievements, like winning another football game. And he enjoys the attention, such as the profile on him that College Sports Television is airing throughout this month.

"I've never thought about goals, or how many games my teams can win," he said. "Really, it's the old cliché—I play them one game at a time."

Elliott, the wide receiver, said the players "wanted to get it done for John."

"We moved it up another level in the fourth quarter," Elliott said at a news conference after the game.

Elliott also praised Gagliardi's ability to adapt to different generations and to find a variety of ways to achieve victories, "from the '50s and '60s and '70s and on to today."

Gagliardi interjected: "I'm not stupid. When I have a receiver like him I'm going to throw the ball."

Keller, the place-kicker, said he simply did what he was taught to do, that those kicks were what he practiced every day, with positive rather than negative reinforcement.

"John expects us to get the job done," he said. "Like he says, 'Just do it.'"

The players hear regularly the coach's mantra: "It's ordinary people doing ordinary things in an extraordinary way."

And if Keller didn't "just do it"?

"What he probably doesn't know," said Gagliardi, seated beside Keller at a table in the St. Thomas gymnasium, "is that we would have strung him up back at the bell towers on campus if he would have missed."

It is Gagliardi's sense of humor as well as his perspective, his assiduous preparation, and his candor laced with charm that is behind much of his success. He began coaching when he was 16. As a junior in high school in 1943, he was quarterback and captain of the Trinidad (Colorado) Catholic team when all the coaches were called up for service in World War II.

"The school officials asked me to coach the team, or they were considering eliminating football," Gagliardi said. "So I took on the job. And I treated the players the way I wanted to be treated—since I was a player, too."

The team won the championship. Rather than work in his father's body shop—as several of his brothers did—Gagliardi went to a junior college and then was hired by Carroll College in Helena, Montana, to coach football. His teams won (24–6–1). In 1953, at age 26, he was offered the job at St. John's and accepted.

He has had offers to move on, including one with the Minnesota Vikings, as an assistant coach. What he has accomplished has been without scholarships (there are none in Division III), with recruiting primarily in-state, and no recruiting beyond phone calls and visits to the campus.

"I came here because of John," said Damien Dumonceaux, who is a sophomore defensive lineman and one of 18 St. John's players whose fathers had played for Gagliardi. "Because he wins and he makes football fun, the way it's supposed to be."

The Rev. Timothy Backous, the monk who is athletic director at St. John's, said: "John is simply a football genius. He knows how to make a difficult situation come out right."

No greater example was when he was courting Peg Daugherty, a student nurse at St. John's nearly 50 years ago. She was 20; he was 28. Gagliardi's mother, who came from the Calabria region of Italy, was, he said, "a great cook, especially of spaghetti." Daugherty was not Italian, but she wanted to please Gagliardi, and so she made a spaghetti dinner for him at her apartment.

"I used tomato soup for the sauce," she said. "I didn't know any better."

Gagliardi had a dilemma. "Should I tell her the truth, or not," he said. "If I didn't, she'd make it again and again for me. I couldn't stand that. And if I was straightforward, would she ever see me again?"

He decided that honesty with what gentleness he could muster was the best policy. "He said, 'I know you tried hard to get this spaghetti great,'" she said, "'and I don't want to hurt your feelings. But this spaghetti is terrible.'"

And what happened? "She learned to make the spaghetti right," Gagliardi said. "I love her."

FOOTBALL AS FIRST FIDDLE

January 2, 1990

"THE TROUBLE IS," THE college president says, cracking open a bag of walnuts with the telephone, "we're neglecting football for education."

"Exactly, the professor is right," reply the two toadying academics in his office.

"Where would this college be without football?" continues the president. "Have we got a stadium?" "Yes." "Have we got a college?" "Yes." "Well, we can't support both. Tomorrow we start tearing down the college."

The president is the man with the funny mustache and unmistakable lope, Groucho Marx, in the 1932 movie *Horse Feathers*. Groucho plays Professor Quincy Adams Wagstaff, a man hired by Huxley University to bring a winning football team to the campus.

Education as second fiddle to football has also been the stuff of real life. Some 20 years after *Horse Feathers*, the president of the University of Oklahoma, Dr. George L. Cross, seeking funds from the state legislature, was asked by one senator about the prospects of the school football team. "We want to build a university our football team can be proud of," he replied.

Dr. Cross meant this as a cynical remark—as cynical as Dr. Wagstaff's— though it was taken by some, including, presumably, that senator, as a totally apt undertaking.

Now, another president of a school in that same conference— Oklahoma's, not Huxley's—E. Gordon Gee of the University of Colorado, a member of the Big Eight, writes that "colleges and universities must stand first for academic values."

He declared this startling concept in an Op-Ed page piece in *The New York Times* yesterday, on the day, as he said, of the "glut of bowl games."

He affirmed that there were enough postseason college football games and that the "growing pressure" to have a College Super Bowl would be the "ultimate sellout."

"Ultimate" might be the key word. For "sellout" by the colleges in regard to sports has abounded for quite some time, if sellout means that colleges have too often neglected education for football, or basketball, its sibling in regard to "revenue producing student-athletes," the adopted euphemism of college officials.

Over the summer, Dexter Manley, then a defensive end for the Washington Redskins, admitted that he went through four years at Oklahoma State University despite being functionally illiterate. Dr. John Campbell, the O.S.U. president, expressed embarrassment. But, he said, "there would be those who would argue that Dexter Manley got exactly what he wanted out of O.S.U. He was able to develop his athletic skills and ability, he was noticed by the pros, he got a pro contract. He would not have had that opportunity had he not gone to Oklahoma State or some other university that had a decent, recognized athletic program. So maybe we did him a favor by letting him go through the system."

From recent reports, we learn that Dexter Manley and Oklahoma State—which, it happens, is also in the Big Eight—are hardly exceptions in receiving and dispensing such favors. Schools are delighted to have outstanding football players, regardless of their academic proclivities. In fact, the more time the athlete spends in the weight room and the less in Physics 101 or even Advanced Bowling, a course Devon Mitchell took when he was a defensive end at Iowa, the happier coaches are.

Overall, college officials are delighted because outstanding football teams can make a lot of money for the university. For its participation in the Orange Bowl last night, Colorado earned a shade over $4 million. Of course, it would have to divide it with the seven other schools in the conference, but it will come away with at least half a million, and perhaps closer to a million. Last year, Notre Dame made off with $3 million from the Fiesta Bowl, and, as an independent, kept it all.

It is difficult to imagine how much more teams could earn if they went to a Super Bowl. But when dealing with commercialism on this level, it is just a matter of splitting hairs, or television and gate receipts. In fact, it seems only a matter of time before the institutions of higher learning will comprehend the educational benefits of a College Super Bowl and agree to it. Just as they've done with the NCAA basketball tournament.

"A national playoff game," concludes Gee, "would have nothing to do with the tradition of collegiate athletics or the academic enterprise."

In fact, it would have much to do with collegiate athletics, at least on a big-time basis, and as they have been applied in much of this century.

Deion Sanders understood it. Rick Telander, author of *The Hundred Yard Lie*, asked Sanders, then a defensive back for Florida State University, what college football was all about.

"Money," Sanders said.

HERSCHEL WALKER'S RIGHTS

March 6, 1982

AN AMERICAN CITIZEN NAMED Herschel Junior Walker is being deprived of his right to earn a living—and by people who say, essentially, that they're doing him a favor.

Herschel Walker is a sophomore at the University of Georgia and an extraordinary college football player. He might like to seek his fortune as a professional football player. But he cannot unless he successfully sues the National Football League, which has a monopoly on professional football in this country. Walker says he is considering the suit.

The league has a rule against allowing any player whose college class has not graduated to attempt to enter its hallowed ranks. Walker, then, would have to stay on campus two more years before he would be eligible to be drafted by an NFL team.

Pete Rozelle, the league's commissioner, has said that "the NFL adheres to its rules because we've been urged to do so by those who would be hurt most without them." He means the colleges. "We also believe our rules work to the ultimate benefit of the players themselves," Rozelle says.

On the surface, it seems that Pete Rozelle is the greatest benefactor of the student-athlete since Cecil Rhodes. This is not the case, and the Herschel Walker situation illuminates the sanctimonious, self-serving, and hypocritical position of the NFL. Not only is the stance un-American, it's un-football.

"Our society," wrote Justice William O. Douglas, "is built upon the premise that it exists only to aid the fullest individual achievement of which each of its members is capable."

And sport, we are often told by its spokesmen, is supposed to mirror this.

In his two years at Georgia, Walker, the swift, muscular 6'2", 220-pound running back, has gained 3,741 yards, scored 37 touchdowns, and led his team—not a particularly remarkable one without him—to two postseason bowl games and, two seasons ago, a ranking of No.1 in the nation. He has been a first-team consensus All-American twice. In fact, he has been an All-American as a track sprinter, too, the only collegian to earn All-America honors in two sports in his freshman year.

Pro football scouts and coaches have described his play as "awesome" and "unbelievable." "Herschel Walker and Earl Campbell are the only two backs I've ever seen who could have gone directly from high school into the pros," said Gil Brandt, the head of personnel development for the Dallas Cowboys.

Walker, who, it is generally agreed, would stand to earn literally millions of dollars, has said it is "unfair" to restrain a man "from making a living when he sees fit, not when somebody else decides he's old enough."

"I think I'm mature enough to play in the NFL right now," he says, "but I don't have the option." This is why he doesn't: The league has a sweet relationship with the colleges. The colleges provide a minor league system for the pros. This saves the pros costly player-development expenses. In baseball, by contrast, each major league team spends a minimum of $1.5 million a year on developing players.

In return for these savings, the NFL keeps its hands off the collegians until their eligibility runs out. This is of great benefit to the colleges, who reap a tremendous amount of money from their football programs. It includes bowl game revenues, television contracts, and alumni donations. It is historical fact that alumni become more generous to the school when there is a good football team than when there is a good chemistry department.

So Georgia revels in Herschel Walker. And so does the Southeastern Conference, which gains because of the fame—and the television revenue—that its teams share with Walker playing against them.

The argument by coach Vince Dooley of Georgia as to why Walker should stay in school is that, if the pro eligibility rule were changed, "very, very few underclassmen would make it in the NFL, and if you consider the number who would throw away their educations to try, you'd realize it would be bad for most."

The eligibility rules of the National Basketball Association were challenged—and defeated—by Spencer Haywood in a landmark case in 1971. And there has been anything but a vast influx of college students trying out for the NBA before their college eligibility is up. The players are aware of how stiff the competition is.

It is reasonable to assume that the same would be true of football players. But the rule is not designed for the individual athletes, anyway. If the NFL is so concerned about athletes' getting a college education, why does it allow them to play without first attaining degrees?

A survey taken of entering NFL players from 1960 through 1980 found that nearly 65 percent had left college without a degree. The reason is that a significant number had been majoring in eligibility maintenance. That is, they had taken just enough easy classes in just enough hours to keep up their so-called academic standing in order to stay on the football team but not enough to graduate. (Walker, a B student majoring in criminology, is apparently not in that category.)

College officials also contend that, if football players were allowed to turn pro before their college eligibility was up, then agents would descend like vermin on these poor, callow, beefy souls and sell them on glorious tales of professional football. This is very similar, in fact, to how the hordes of college recruiters scramble after choice high school seniors.

If Herschel Walker does not wish to stay in college—surely as much a personal decision as going to college—why shouldn't he be allowed to leave and go on to earn a living in the profession at which he is so eminently qualified? If he were a lawyer and had equal credentials, he'd be sitting on the Supreme Court.

If Herschel Walker decides to challenge the eligibility rule, he will be running into formidable opposition. The college establishment is against him, the professional football establishment is against him, and the NFL Players Association, which presumably would look to preserve jobs for its current membership, might be against him.

In fact, if Herschel Walker decides to seek his civil liberties as a citizen and as a football player, perhaps all that he'll have going for him is the Constitution of the United States.

XII.

STRICTLY PERSONAL

Going to the Root of the Super Bowl

January 29, 1983

LOS ANGELES—MORE THAN 100,000 fans will be packed into the Rose Bowl in Pasadena tomorrow to watch Super Bowl XVII, more than 100 million people will view it on television, and an estimated $600 million will be bet on whether the Miami team or Washington can push a football across a stripe of white paint with greater frequency.

The event is of such magnitude that only Roman numerals and not your garden-variety Arabic digits are used to describe it. Football, clearly, has strayed from its roots. I can recall what they are, at least for me. It is the early 1950s. Springfield Avenue on the West Side of Chicago. It was a neighborhood street that, with cars parked on either side, was just wide enough for two-way traffic to squeeze through.

Primarily, though, it was a football field for two-hand touch, with normally three or four kids on a side. The goal lines were two sewers, one adjacent to where Mr. Massarelli lived with his vicious bulldog, and the other alongside Cutler's grocery store.

It was serious football, to be sure, and cars that traversed the black field during games were deeply resented. Certain moments come to mind. "Hey, what is this, anyway, a boulevard?" John Browne once called to a driver when a play he was diagramming in the huddle was interrupted.

"Stick it, kid," came the reply. Not everyone was a football fan in those days. The plays were the thing. They were drawn on the street with a stone. It was not an uncommon trick for the other team, waiting for the offense, to play catch with the ball—and throw it toward the huddle and have one player try to sneak a glimpse of the play.

It rarely worked since the offense, crafty beyond its years, hunkered down to hide it. Besides, even the players with the ball had trouble following it.

"Henry," John Browne the quarterback whispered, "you go 10 steps and banana peel right between the green Ford and the yellow Chevy. Pinhead, you go long. Start slow and then put on the steam. I'll hit you around the fireplug." On every play one receiver always went long and one went short. "Hey," shouted John Browne the quarterback, back to pass, "come back, I didn't tell both of you to go long!" Pinhead came running back. So did Henry. "Go back!" cried John Browne. "Go back!"

Pinhead had ducked between two parked cars, not the designated ones, but he was shouting and waving, "I'm clear! I'm clear!" Henry was racing back out, hollering, "Hit me!" Two cars behind each goal line were honking to get through. Mr. Massarelli's dog was barking. Old Man Witcoff had been out late the night before and he opened his apartment window and stuck his blowzy head out and hollered for everyone to shut up.

John Browne, dodging the player coming in, finally threw long and the ball slammed into the branches of an overhanging tree, and then, as in a pinball machine, it eventually came through and dropped onto a red Studebaker, denting the hood, as Henry crashed valiantly into the car, denting the door.

The games always seemed to be interrupted for one reason or another, besides passing cars. Harry Jaffe, in his twenties, thought he was a star. He'd come by and always want to get in the game for a few plays. One guy would have to sit out, and no one liked to.

"Aw, c'mon, Harry." "Couple plays, that's all." Of course, he always made himself the quarterback. He'd throw a few stupid passes, blame his receivers, and then leave. People liked when Harry Jaffe left.

Mrs. Padilla once was sweeping the sidewalk in front of her home when a coffin-corner kick hit her in the head. She shook it off, picked up the ball, and marched into her house. I don't remember how the ball was retrieved.

But it took even more guts to get the ball back when it bounced into Mr. Massarelli's yard.

M r. Massarelli was short with a thick neck and hanging belly and eyes that burned with hatred for football. His dog looked just like him.

Now and then, just for spite, during a game Harry Jaffe would decide to wash his beat-up Dodge parked on the street. Harry Jaffe thought he was the life of the party. But the games went on. One that remains clear in memory was tied at four touchdowns each and the team that scored next would win the game. Pinhead's team was threatening, and was closing in on the goal near Cutler's grocery store. Just then the Wonder Bread truck drove up and double-parked right beside the sewer. Screams of protest from the players. "Be right out," said Al the Wonder Bread driver, grabbing his basket stuffed with bread and hustling from the open door of the truck into the store.

Pinhead was struck by a brainstorm. He called a huddle. His team clapped in unison and came to the line of scrimmage. "Let's go," he said. The other team was delighted. The truck cut off a good portion of the field—simplifying defense. "24-76-99-38-65-49 Hut!" The ball was snapped to the quarterback. Pinhead streaked right for the truck, and scaled it. He scrambled to his feet on the roof and the quarterback threw and the ball sailed softly into Pinhead's arms.

"Yeeeooowww!!" Pinhead screeched. "Touchdown!!!" Suddenly Al the bread driver hurried out of Cutler's, jumped into his truck and began to drive off. Pinhead, panic in his eyes, flung himself flat on the roof.

"No touchdown," called John Browne, who was on defense. "Whaddya mean?" said Henry, Pinhead's teammate. "He caught the ball over the goal line." "But he didn't touch ground," said John Browne. "He doesn't have to." "Sure he does." The argument raged—and continues to this day. And Pinhead? Well, what about him?

HARRY GILMER:
A GIFT THAT I KEPT ON KICKING

December, 2012

TRYING TO MIND MY own business—but as a reporter is wont, minding others' as well—I was having coffee in the press room before a Giants-Cardinals football game in St. Louis when my ears perked up. It was December 9, 1984, a time when the holidays and gift-giving are in the air, or on the credit card. I was there to write a Sports of the Times column and, as it happened, I soon found myself in conversation with two other sportswriters and a third man. The third man wore a cowboy hat and a genial manner, and was introduced to me. "Like you to meet Harry Gilmer," said one of the sportswriters. I didn't have to ask "Who?"

Harry Gilmer was then a scout for the Cardinals, but that wasn't the "Who" I knew. I hesitated for a moment or so. But when one of the sportswriters mentioned something about growing up with two sisters, I said: "Well, I grew up with a Harry Gilmer football. I got it as a present for the holidays when I was nine years old."

Now, Gilmer, who had played primarily as a backup quarterback for nine seasons in the National Football League in the 1940s and 1950s, and I had never met. Gilmer smiled at me and said, "Did the football make you ill?"

"Uh, no," I replied, "why?"

"Because it made the manufacturer ill."

The football didn't do much for Bobby Drain's health either. Bobby lived across Springfield Avenue from me on the west side of Chicago. On that quiet, crisp holiday morning in 1949 (probably Hanukkah, but

I'd sometimes get a bonus at Christmas—perhaps in honor of a song my father enjoyed, "White Christmas," written by the Jewish Irving Berlin), I took the football into the snowy street and began to kick it. The thump of foot meeting ball and the boom of ball bouncing off parked cars roused Bobby from his sleep. It was early and Bobby, then in his twenties, had probably been out celebrating late the night before. He didn't look so good as he hung out the window he had opened and hollered, "Get that damn football outta here!"

Calendar pages had fallen away, and it was odd but enjoyable now to run into the man who autographed the sports present I received 35 years before. And what pleasure it had given me. I kicked it and kicked it, played touch football with friends in nearby Independence Park and on the street. At some point, the hide began to tear and the bladder to peep through, and it was soon curtains for my beloved Harry Gilmer football.

When Gilmer came out of the University of Alabama as an All-America quarterback and a Rose Bowl MVP and the first-round draft choice of the Washington Redskins in 1948, George Marshall, the owner of the team, made a deal with Dubow, a sports equipment company based in Chicago, for a line of football paraphernalia with Gilmer's signature.

"The idea was," said Gilmer, "that if I would make it big, we'd make a lot of money." He smiled, and added: "It never quite panned out. I think the stuff was on the market for one season."

Gilmer was supposed to have replaced the great Sammy Baugh at quarterback. "But," said Gilmer, "Sammy played five more years."

Meanwhile, Gilmer played some on the defensive backfield, and in 1952, when Charlie "Choo Choo" Justice broke his arm Gilmer was used at running back and led the Redskins in number of rushes. He made the Pro Bowl team that year, but for his entire pro career he never played first-string quarterback.

In 1955, he was traded to the Detroit Lions, for whom he was the backup for, yes, the great Bobby Layne. This lasted for two years, before Gilmer decided to retire. He went on to become an assistant coach in the pros and head coach at Detroit.

I asked Gilmer, then 58, 6'0" and looking as trim as in his 170-pound playing days, if he had ever received a football for Christmas. He said no, that his family, living in Birmingham, Alabama, during the Depression, had been too poor. But he recalled that once he did receive a pair of old shoulder pads. They were given to him by an assistant coach at Alabama, when Gilmer was a freshman there in 1944.

"The two of us had gone down into a storage room under the athletic building to get something," recalled Gilmer, "and I saw these old little bitty pads in a corner of a dirt floor under a pile of rubbish. I never saw pads so small. They interested me.

"A quarterback always wants light pads in order to throw better. I brought them into the light. The only inscription on the pads was the name HERKEY MOSLEY. Herkey had played for Alabama about 10 years before. His brother, Monk Mosley, played with me there. Anyway, who knows how old those shoulder pads were before Herkey put his name on them?

"I asked the assistant coach if I could have them. He said, 'Sure, but I don't know what you're gonna do with 'em.' There was a leather flap missing on the right side, and I asked the equipment manager if he'd sew on a new flap.

"I used those pads for all four years at Alabama and for all nine years in the pros. And every year I had an equipment manager repair them and renovate them. Guys were shocked at how small they were, and were always joking about throwing them in the garbage, but I loved them." Near the end of Gilmer's playing career, a Detroit defensive back named Jack Christiansen broke his arm, and coach Buddy Parker said to Gilmer: "I want you to play in Jack's place against the 49ers. But you can't wear those old pads."

Gilmer reluctantly put on new pads, and it happened that Carroll Hardy, a 49ers receiver, got behind him and caught a touchdown pass. "Parker yanked me," said Gilmer, "and brought in Christiansen, broken arm and all."

When I mentioned to Gilmer that maybe the new pads had been too heavy for him to lift his arms to block the pass, he smiled and said, "Gee, hadn't thought of that excuse."

"I was never much of a saver, but I did save those old pads," Gilmer continued. "Now, I had made many moves after my playing days, but I always took those pads wherever I went. One day I got a call from Dick McCann, who was then with the Pro Football Hall of Fame in Canton—Dick was an executive with the Redskins when I played there—and he asked if he could get those pads for the Hall of Fame.

"I was never the kind of player to be elected to the Hall of Fame. But my shoulder pads were—I thought that was great. I told Dick, 'Sure, I'll look for them.' But I couldn't find them. I guess they had gotten lost in one of my moves."

Perhaps somewhere in this favored land, in the bottom of some pile, lie old shoulder pads with one flap off and the name HERKEY MOSLEY on them, and nestled alongside an old football with the bladder showing signed HARRY GILMER.

.   .   .

Harry Gilmer was inducted into the College Football Hall of Fame in 1993, and now lives in O'Fallon, Missouri, a suburb west of St. Louis. He has four children, eight grandchildren, and 10 great grandchildren. He is 88 years old and "is doing fine," said his daughter, Connie, by telephone.

THE HAWK LIVES

January 11, 1986

CHICAGO—WEATHER IN CHICAGO IS generally an idiosyncratic factor. And both the Los Angeles Rams and the Chicago Bears have naturally addressed it in relation to their National Football Conference Championship Game at Soldier Field tomorrow morning. (Morning is correct, since the game, for the benefit of television markets, will begin at 11:30 AM, Chicago time.) The Rams left the warm and gentle breezes of California and landed in Chicago Thursday night. "My own personal experience is, the first time you walk out to extreme weather, you think you're going to die within six minutes," said their coach, John Robinson. "There is a mental adjustment that takes place."

The Bears' coach, Mike Ditka, playing his little mind game, said with a tight smile that he hopes it's as warm for the Rams game as it was for the Giants game.

Last Sunday, when the Giants played the Bears there, the wind-chill factor fell to 13 degrees below zero. Meteorologists, working night and day, have determined that tomorrow's game might be played in relatively balmy weather—around 40 degrees. But more than once, a meteorologist has been found to have a flaw in his weathercock.

Beyond that, the wind—known endearingly in Chicago as The Hawk—that comes flapping in off Lake Michigan can work strange wonders.

Last week, for example, Sean Landeta, the punter for the Giants, had a near-whiff on a kick. He contends that as he dropped the ball to boot it, a gust virtually snatched the ball and took it away, like—well, like a hawk making off with a barnyard chick.

On Michigan Avenue, not far from Soldier Field, the wind has been known to howl so fiercely that people have been blown down and blown across streets. Once, these very eyes saw a small woman hanging onto the pole of a No Parking sign at Michigan and Erie. Her coat was billowing and it appeared that her feet were actually off the ground. She looked like a flag fluttering at half-staff.

When it's cold in Chicago, it's cold like almost nowhere else in the world, and that includes Siberia—it has to include Siberia, though your intrepid reporter has never been there. The closest he's gotten has been to the frozen tundra of Fargo, North Dakota, in December, which has to be just like Siberia, except for the malls. No matter how heavily sealed one is against the cold of Chicago, though, no matter how well wrapped one is in furs and scarves and hats and ear muffs and coats and galoshes and leggings and woolen underthings, the cold comes in across the flatlands with the sound of nasty laughter and digs inside the garments and works through the body with malevolence and icy daggers. It claws at the cheeks, and it also has quite an appetite, preferring such delicacies as noses and toes.

It is a weird coincidence that the most famous football player in the world today is a Chicago Bear called The Refrigerator.

One year a hardy soul named Ian Levin, a longtime Chicagoan who has fought off the weather with, among other weapons, an unrivaled hat with woolen bill that partly covers the eyes and woolen ear flaps that cover the cheeks and a chin strap of great esthetic and practical value, one year this Ian Levin said, "It's official. I have not survived the winter."

It happens that your intrepid reporter has had some experience with the vicissitudes and viciousness of weather in this city.

As a young yout', as the term is used by some football coaches and aldermen in town, he recalls walking seven blocks to Bryant grammar school backward against the wind. He wasn't the only one. Everyone walked that way. The teachers drove to school that way. It's a wonder we didn't learn to read from right to left. (Oh, wait, some did!) The weather in Chicago changes drastically, something of which the people on the field, as well as those surrounded by barometers and barographs, must be cognizant and cautious.

Your intrepid reporter recalls an afternoon when the weather was something like 50 degrees. Not bad at all. He went to a cobbler to have a shoe cobbled and several minutes later emerged to find that the temperature had plummeted 20 degrees, and the wind was blowing like crazy. These things happen in Chicago even, or especially, when there's a football game about to break out. The Rams know it. So do the Bears. So does your intrepid reporter, who has played touch football games in Grant Park, right near Soldier Field. He has experienced that wind and that cold on that lakefront.

There was actually a touch football tournament championship game in which he was involved. It was about two or three years before the Giants-Bears National Football League title game in 1963 was played in near-zero weather.

The weather for this touch football game was such that when people spoke, their breath would remain in the air looking clear and solid. It was as though the words were floating out of your mouth in large ice cubes.

Intrepid reporter was the punter on this team, so he has particular sympathy for Mr. Landeta.

To begin with, intrepid reporter didn't want to play the game. It was so cold that the lake had frozen over, and so had the field. The game could have been played on Lake Michigan. Maybe it was. Anyway, he wore the Hudson Bay coat that was once owned by Uncle Leo but was given to the reporter by Aunt Rose when Uncle Leo died. It is a great coat, actually made out of blankets and, like Joseph's, a coat of many colors. It's not exactly a coat designed for football, but if you had to play football that day, and you had that coat, you'd have worn it, too.

Well, it was a forgettable day. And one punt—Were there more? Who knows?—is recalled. The foot was so cold and the ball so heavy and the wind so wicked that the mind didn't want to kick. And so the shin did the work, and the ball traveled about as far as Landeta's: about a foot, sideways.

Clearly recalled, however, is intrepid reporter back home. His body is quite stiff and he is lying in bed under several covers. He is contemplating. He is thinking that maybe later, maybe tomorrow, maybe then, he'll take off the coat.

JOE CRISCO AND JOE TUNA

January 30, 1971

THIS IS A TALE about two tourists named Joe who found fame, if not fortune, in Miami Beach.

These two working-stiff Joes had come all the way from Chicago to help close Tropical Park, to help open Hialeah, to cheer on Dallas in the Super Bowl, and on the last night of their four-day stay, to go to Tony's Fish Market for some pompano. They never made it to Tony's.

Their collision with fame began on the Sunday night after the Super Bowl when, on their way to Tony's, a Mercedes-Benz banged into their rented car. The Joe driving (known to his pal as "Charley Tuna" because he is such a fish on the golf course) climbed out to check the damage.

There wasn't much, except for the busted radiator in the Mercedes. As both parties exchanged licenses and waited for the cops, the other driver said he was Carroll Rosenbloom and he was owner of the Baltimore Colts.

"I do not care who you are," said Joe Tuna, "but if you are, then you cost us a lot of money. We took Dallas. Besides that, we paid 40 bucks apiece for 15-buck tickets."

"Gee," said Rosenbloom, "I'm sorry. You should have got in touch with me before the game."

"We did not know you before the game," recalled Joe Tuna.

The other Joe, Joe Crisco (he's called that because he is fat in the can), suggested they get a quick beer across the street while they waited. Rosenbloom had a better idea. He and his passenger, Gino Marchetti, were headed to this country club for the Colts' victory party, and the Joes were invited. Everyone thought that a fine idea. Rosenbloom then mentioned that these two Joes in open-collared flowered shirts might repair to their hotel and put on ties.

But the Joes said that to go back to the hotel, then way out to the party would take too much time because they were leaving for Chicago on the 4:00 AM plane.

"Well, then come over now," said Rosenbloom. And since his automobile was on the bum, he and Marchetti piled into Joe's car.

"We thought we would drop in for a little swally," Joe Tuna said later.

But they stayed longer. They had steak dinner in an elegant dining room with candlelights at the table. They sat at the same table with several Colts, including Gino and Johnny Unitas, and they looked around a lot and always had a pitcher of beer in front of them.

They also had a Super Bowl program and Joe Crisco, who is not the retiring type, would call out, "Hey Bubba. Bubba, how 'bout an autograph?"

Joe Tuna said he called home to talk to his 18-year-old boy who is a Colts fan and who would not believe this. "He was not home so I talked to my 90-year-old ma," said Joe Tuna.

"'Ma,' I say, 'Guess where I am.'

"'Jail,' she says.

"'No, ma,' I say, 'I am at the Baltimore Colts' victory party.'

"And she says, 'But Joe, I thought you bet on Dallas.'"

No sooner had he hung up than another unexpected guest popped in. It was Muhammad Ali. Joe Crisco waned to clobber him. "But my pal here held me back," said Joe Crisco. "I do not have anything against Clay except I wanted to show him my left. That's my best punch."

"If Clay had started something I would of let Joe hit him," said Joe Tuna. "But I did not want Joe starting it."

After supper the others at the table left to mingle. The two Joes sat alone, the candlelight throwing shadows on their faces. They drank their beer and more and more looked into their steins and now and then glanced at their watches. Joe Tuna and Joe Crisco would soon have to excuse themselves from the victory party because they had a plane to catch.

HENRY THOREAU: FOOTBALL TO
THE BEAT OF A DIFFERENT DRUM

December 18, 1982

WITH PROFESSIONAL FOOTBALL BACK in reasonably normal stride, we decided to visit Walden Pond to discuss recent developments with its famous resident and sage, Henry David Thoreau.

In 1845, he left his hometown of Concord, Massachusetts, to live alone in the nearby woods. He did so, he said, "to front only the essential facts of life." He wrote of the experience in *Walden*, from which came the stuff of the following interview:

Q. Mr. Thoreau, have you been reading in the newspapers about the end of the players' strike and the return of the games?

I am sure that I never read any memorable news in a newspaper. If you read of one man robbed, or one house burned, or one vessel wrecked, or one steamboat blown up, or one lot of grasshoppers in the winter—we never need read of another.

Q. All right, reading is out. But what about television? Monday night football, for example, has become a national institution of sorts. People go wild for it. How do you feel about Monday nights?

This is a delicious evening, when the whole body is one sense, and imbibes delight through every pore.... The bullfrogs trump to usher in the night, and the note of the whip-poor-will is borne on the rippling wind from the water....yet, like the lake, my serenity is rippled but not ruffled.

Q. So you stay in the woods and aren't glued to the tube like millions of Americans. But on Sundays, you must be aware of people going to the games. Some must even pass by the pond.

The cars never pause to look at it; yet I fancy that the engineers and firemen and brakemen, and those passengers who have a season ticket and see it often, are better men for the sight.

Q. Well, what do you think of the game of football itself?

The savage in man is never quite eradicated.

Q. But football is highly developed; there are large, detailed playbooks the players must learn and even the coaches don't know what happened until they watch the game films—and sometimes not even then.

Our life is frittered away by detail. An honest man has hardly need to count more than his 10 fingers, or in extreme cases, he may add his 10 toes, and lump the rest. Simplicity, simplicity, simplicity.

Q. Isn't there much to be learned from the experience of football? Coaches tell us it builds character.

If you are acquainted with the principle, what do you care for the myriad instances and applications.

Q. What do you think of football players?

It is not necessary that a man should earn his living by the sweat of his brow, unless he sweats easier than I do.

Q. What are your thoughts on ticket prices?

I am convinced, that if all men were to live as simply as I…thieving and robbery would be unknown.

Q. Do you think that management should be forced to hire marching bands at halftime that are able to keep in step?

If a man does not keep pace with his companions, perhaps it is because he hears a different drummer. Let him step to the music which he hears, however measured or far away.

Q. Yes, to go on. The Jets and Giants have had poor teams for a number of years, and now they are contenders again. Isn't that good for relieving the average fan of frustration?

The mass of men lead lives of quiet desperation…. A stereotyped but unconscious despair is concealed even under what are called the games and amusements of mankind.

Q. At any rate, the New York fans, particularly Jet fans, seem jubilant over their team. How do you interpret this?

When we are unhurried and wise…we perceive that petty pleasures are but the shadow of the reality.

Q. But you must admit, this is exhilarating.

This is always exhilarating.... By consenting to be deceived by shows, men establish and confirm their daily life of routine and habit everywhere, which still is built on purely illusory foundations.

Q. Do you see any social value in the recent successes of the New York football teams?

If one advances confidently in the direction of his dreams, and endeavors to live the life which he has imagined, he will meet with a success unexpected in coming hours.

Q. Don't you miss the excitement of being a part of a crowd?

I never found the companion that was so companionable as solitude.... We live thick and are in each other's way.

Q. How do you feel about the characteristic of some fans to boo?

Nothing can rightly compel a simple and brave man to a vulgar sadness.

Q. Do you think there is too much emphasis on winning?

Not till we are lost, in other words not till we have lost the world, do we begin to find ourselves, and realize where we are and the infinite extent of our relations.

Q. Well, Mr. Thoreau, it seems your views of football and attending football games are quite clear, so there is no need to ask your thoughts on the Super Bowl. But what about the World Series?

In October I went a-graping in the river meadows.

ON SPORTS IN OCTOBER

October 8, 1970

OCTOBER IS AN ODD month, combining the sober reality of a crisp afternoon one day with an illusory Indian summer the next.

It combines, early on, crack of bat against ball with the dreamed-up "Fall Classic"; and ends thus: the factual smack of shoulder-padded people with a complex playbook mystique.

October is the simplest month in sport. Summer sports are gone. Water is employed to carry a fallen golden leaf instead of a crew in a canoe. In November, the water will be swabbed with ice for skating.

In the North, golf courses begin to shudder with a ghostly gust. Flags atop pin placements flutter and snap. Only the most crusty, ruddy fellow, nose and eyes a-drip, fingers rigid, crunches along the fairway now.

With a bright sun that defies the breeze and belies the coming onslaught of snow, tennis players in shimmering white rush to embrace the fading glimpse of sun.

Overhead wild geese, mysteriously released, arrow southward. Perhaps they will elude the blunderbuss in the blinds below.

On a day that crackles with the brittleness of a twig, a World Series crowd sits collared and scarved and sends up smoke signals with a cheer.

But on a day that was misplaced in May, a football crowd sits amid the smell of burning leaves, sits in shirt sleeves, and squints at the game from under the shade of a palm.

On such a day, a flask may contain the tang of apple cider instead of something conventionally harder.

The sky can be bright blue or mellow yellow or soft gray with a sharp relief of charcoal clouds. No matter the hue or whim of the October day, there is a purity that joins air and soul. On such October days the world must stand still and let the hypocrisy in sport, the racism in sport, the authoritarianism in sport pass.

Permit for a suspended moment a nation caught up, eyes raised, mouths agape at the overwhelming importance of a high fly, and whether when it decides to topple off a cloud it will thump into the hardening ground on the other side of the fence, or into a fielder's yawning glove.

Permit for a suspended moment the short flight of a halfback, dangling on a concealed string at the goal line, as a mass of men, waiting for him to descend, crouch with arms wide like the jaws of crocodiles.

Soon winter will be here with a different sense, a different chill, different sport, different thrill.

October ends. A month of reality and myth. It ends with eerie gaps in a Jack O'Lantern's grin.

ABOUT THE AUTHOR

IRA BERKOW, A SPORTS columnist and feature writer for *The New York Times* for 26 years, shared the Pulitzer Prize for national reporting in 2001 and was a finalist for the Pulitzer for commentary in 1988. He also was a reporter for the *Minneapolis Tribune* and a columnist for Newspaper Enterprise Association. He is the author of 23 books, including the bestsellers *Red: A Biography of Red Smith* and *Maxwell Street: Survival in a Bazaar,* and, most recently, *Counterpunch: Ali, Tyson, the Brown Bomber, and Other Stories of the Boxing Ring.* His  work has frequently been cited in the prestigious anthology series, Best American Sports Writing, as well as the 1999 anthology Best American Sports Writing of the Century. He holds a bachelor's degree from Miami University (Ohio) and a master's degree from Northwestern University's Medill School of Journalism, and has been honored with distinguished professional achievement awards from both schools. In 2009 he was inducted into the International Jewish Sports Hall of Fame and also received an Honorary Doctorate of Humane Letters from Roosevelt University in Chicago. Mr. Berkow lives in New York City.